The Rise of the Arabic Book

THE RISE OF THE ARABIC BOOK

Beatrice Gruendler

Harvard University Press
CAMBRIDGE, MASSACHUSETTS
LONDON, ENGLAND
2020

Printed in the United States of America

First printing

Library of Congress Cataloging-in-Publication Data

Names: Gruendler, Beatrice, 1964– author.
Title: The rise of the Arabic book / Beatrice Gruendler.
Description: Cambridge, Massachusetts : Harvard University Press, 2020. | Includes bibliographical references and index.
Identifiers: LCCN 2020010113 | ISBN 9780674987814 (cloth)
Subjects: LCSH: Books—Islamic Empire—History—400–1450. | Books and reading—Islamic Empire. | Book collecting—Islamic Empire. | Arabic literature—Islamic Empire. | Bibliographical literature—Islamic Empire. | Islamic Empire—Intellectual life.
Classification: LCC Z8.I79 G78 2020 | DDC 002.0917/67—dc23
LC record available at https://lccn.loc.gov/2020010113

To my family

ALICE, INES, JENS, LILO, MATTHIAS,

NAUSIKAA, NIKE, *and* NORMAND

in gratitude for their love and support

and

to the loving memory of my father

WILFRIED GRÜNDLER

June 12, 1927–December 1, 2019

CONTENTS

The Rise of the Arabic Book

INTRODUCTION

The first cave paintings, tens of thousands of years ago, already showed the human urge to communicate, even if their images remain silent to us. The beginning of communication through language is equally difficult to grasp, as it left no traces other than our evolved neurological hardwiring that enables us to acquire language.[1] It is only the written remnants of language from several millennia later that we can investigate. Here, our species' ability to code objects into shapes and develop these into systems of notation has triggered an endless inventiveness in ever-new ways of sharing information, recorded on stone, clay, metal, wood, papyrus, cloth, and animal skin.[2] Since then, our ways to communicate have never ceased to evolve, though the pace has been uneven, and there are certain moments in history when several factors came together to accelerate innovation to a dizzying degree. Our experience over the last three decades since the inception of the internet has taught us how quickly new technologies can change in fundamental ways how we keep in touch with our fellow humans in public and private life, business and leisure. The internet has become a universe of options, ranging from contact with friends and family through social channels to complex commercial transactions and business ventures. The fast and vast acceptance of the latest installments of the ongoing "information age," including social media and smartphones, has made details about the most personal matters so universally accessible that to be forgotten has recently been claimed as an individual right. It has changed our everyday language: *friend* has become a verb, *like* a noun, and one's best friend has received a double with the "best internet friend." This deep and rapid transformation, which also has created new divides between generations and parts of the globe, has attuned us to other such moments of change in the history of media, to contrast and compare and learn how preceding generations of fellow humans coped.

Well known among the turning points of human communication is the impact of movable type in the fifteenth century and the concomitant growth of readerships in vernacular languages. Likewise, we know much about the invention of complex writing systems in Egypt and Mesopotamia in the third millennium B.C.E., and around 2,000 years later the invention of the phonetic alphabet, which allowed for a utilitarian way of writing with less than thirty characters. The alphabet did away with cumbersome hieroglyphic and cuneiform systems and broke down small elites' control over writing and, therewith, knowledge. Movable type and the internet are products of the West (though movable type emerged independently in several places across the globe, including Korea); the earliest scripts and the alphabet we owe to the Near East, and the alphabet is still with us as an unsurpassed system of notation and ordering.

One turning point, however, has been overlooked among the grand moments of media history—the book revolution in the Arabic-Islamic Near East.[3] It is blank space on our mental map, although its "writing space" was filled by a cultural efflorescence unleashing a veritable flood of books. Its surviving codices from the thirteen centuries before the adoption of printing have been estimated at about three million by the World Survey of Islamic Manuscripts, and the original figure must have been many times higher.[4] In the thirteenth century, when the largest library in Europe, Paris University, counted fewer than 2,000 volumes, five libraries in Baghdad alone numbered between 200,000 and 1,000,000 volumes each, including multiple copies of standard works to ensure many readers' simultaneous access. Exact estimates are of course difficult, but surviving book and library catalogues and later copies of lost originals give ample evidence.

THE ARABIC CODEX

The manuscript book, or codex (folded and gathered sheets inscribed with a continuous text), per se, was not a new invention when it entered the Arab world in the outgoing eighth and beginning of the ninth century, corresponding to the late second and early third century in the Islamic calendar.[5] It was known by the Romans from the time of Cicero and had already in pagan times won out against the papyrus scroll. At the end of the third century C.E., the book form had already been adopted for three-quarters of all texts, and it achieved its true predominance during the fourth century in Christian Byzantium.[6] Arabic civilization knew of the book format since its earliest stages. With its proximity to, and contacts with, the adjacent cultural giants of Byzantium and Persia under the Sasanian dynasty, the idea that knowledge came in the form of books (even if not in one's own language) was familiar. Closer to home, the Christian communities throughout the Near East produced books on parchment in Greek, Coptic, and Syriac, a late Aramaic language and script.

Soon, the Arabs had with the Qur'ān their own foundational book, which exerted an impact far beyond religion; it led to a spread of the Arabic language and the refinement of the writing system, and it spurred multiple fields of scholarship, from recitation and exegesis to the study of the Arabic language in all its aspects. In fact, the second Arabic "book" (*kitāb*) after the Qur'ān was a systematic grammar of what had become classical Arabic (*ʿarabiyya*), written by the Persian Sībawayhi (d. 793) at the end of the eighth century. Though it was the first grammar, it has remained foundational ever since. A younger contemporary declared that Sībawayhi "produced [*ʿamala*] his book which was unprecedented, and unmatched thereafter" and added, "Anyone who wants to create a compendium [*kitāb kabīr*] on grammar after Sībawayhi should be ashamed of himself."[7] Although books on grammar would abound thereafter, Sībawayhi's comprehensive concept and systematic presentation was unique, and all subsequent grammatical writing built on it.[8] Grammar was not the only discipline that started with a bang; in numerous fields books were composed beginning in the eighth century and en masse in the ninth century.

Books on paper could spread so rapidly in the ninth century because the book format was already in use. The rise of the book can be measured, for instance, by the steep increase in the stationers' trade (see Chapter 3) but also by the *Catalogue* (*Fihrist,* a Persian word, adopted in Arabic), compiled in the late tenth century by Ibn al-Nadīm (d. 990), the most famous representative of this craft and our most valuable source.[9] Organized by discipline, his *Catalogue* listed biographies of authors and the titles of all their books "available in manuscript," which he either had in hand or learned about from a reliable source.[10] The number of authors he listed is estimated variously at 3,500 or 3,700.[11] A vast proportion of these were active at the end of the eighth and during the entire ninth century, and their works, if lost in the original, either survive in complete copies or were excerpted and cited by later authors, since compilations on all sorts of topics were a major book genre in Arabic literature. Extant works are indicated in the new edition of the *Catalogue* by Aḥmad Fu'ād Sayyid, and an example of a reconstructed book is the modern edition of *The Pre-Islamic Battles* (*Ayyām al-ʿarab*) of Abū ʿUbayda (d. c. 822–828).[12] This most famous authority on the subject was much cited in classical Arabic sources and these citations have been compiled into a book by ʿĀdil Jāsim al-Bayātī. Even if this procedure is questionable—and one might call it ahistorical, for some material may have been transmitted orally and never written down by the author himself—it shows the reuse and preservation of much early scholarship in the written transmission.

In the *Catalogue,* the writings of the biographer of the Prophet, Ibn Isḥāq (d. 767), the genealogist Hishām b. al-Kalbī (d. 819), the historians al-Wāqidī (d. 823) and al-Madā'inī (d. 843), and the philologist Muḥammad b. Ḥabīb (d. 860) each take up many pages crammed with book titles. We ignore the full range of sizes and formats of their books, as there are only a few surviving codices or fragments of these before the ninth century, and Stefan Leder has cautioned that not every single title should be counted as an independent book.[13] Since then, many of these writings, such as those of Abū ʿUbayda, have been folded into later compilations and lost their original shape. Neither do we know a lot about their physical makeup or the organization of their contents, which was still emerging (on which, more in the next section), and the individual size of some books may have been modest. For larger works, the *Catalogue* often supplies lists of chapter headings, and for books Ibn al-Nadīm could inspect, he supplies the numbers of folios in increments of ten. But in any case, large numbers of books and notebooks of loose or sewn-together folded sheets of parchment and papyrus existed already when paper came into use and accelerated book production. While paper was quickly adapted, it did not displace immediately the older writing materials, parchment and papyrus. Qur'āns and Bibles continued to be written on the more durable parchment; the earliest paper Qur'ān dates to the tenth century.

COMMON LANGUAGE, ORAL LITERATURE, AND PAPER

How did this happen? Why did the Arabic paper codex gain acceptance so rapidly? How and by whom were books used and produced? What did the new medium mean to those who read and wrote, rewrote and excerpted, collected and compiled, or bought and sold books? These are the questions to which the present book attempts to give answers. Regarding the codex's swift acceptance, as in all complex cultural processes, no single factor can suffice as an explanation; rather, a number of factors coincided to produce this effect. The following is a list of the most important ones.

To begin with, a production of books requires a common language and topics of shared and immediate concern for their writers and readers. Indeed, the thriving of the codex format went hand in hand with the newly codified classical Arabic language, which rapidly became an integral part of daily life.[14] In 697 and 700 Arabic was declared the state language in Iraq and Syria under the aegis of the Umayyad caliph ʿAbdalmalik (r. 785–705), the builder of the Dome of the Rock, and his Iraqi governor al-Ḥajjāj (d. 714). Arabic effectively supplanted the previously used Middle Persian and Greek in the administration.[15] This event foreshadowed the general availability of the *ʿarabiyya* for other purposes. Since the Umayyads, Arabic was used for everything from inscriptions and coinage to private letters.

A particular feature of this classical Arabic is that no one grew up with it. It was a formal idiom to be acquired through study. The subsequent Abbasid dynasty (750–1258) had come to power by fostering a cultural cosmopolitanism whose participants came from a number of linguistic backgrounds: they spoke Aramaic, Persian, Greek, or Romance. The linguistic situation of Arabic was complex too, being a case of multiglossia constituted by many dialects in addition to the *ʿarabiyya*. The city-dwelling Arabs spoke a dialect referred to as hybrid (*muwallad*) that was deemed not fit for writing. Rather, the written Arabic language had been created from the prestigious pre-Islamic poetry (as practiced by Bedouin tribes, mainly in the eastern deserts of the Arabian Peninsula) and the Qur'ān. This linguistic material was considered exemplary and had been collected, systematized, and laid down in handbooks, grammars, and dictionaries for study. The high prestige of the written Arabic language and the fact that every person, Arab or not, had to learn it, was key: it gave members of all ethnic and religious groups access to acquire it, and its mastery afforded employment in the state administration, including social advancement and high salaries, and thus offered ample incentive to make the effort. The empire needed a vast number of administrative scribes (*kuttāb,* literally "writers"), and several families of high officials of Aramean and Persian background even established veritable dynasties. Scholars and poets travelled from faraway Cordoba (modern Spain) in the west or Herat (modern Afghanistan) in the east to study or find patrons in Baghdad, which became the caliphate's cultural center, where sponsorship was lavish and reputations were made.[16] A side effect of the avalanche of books was the phenomenon of the autodidact who could make a living as an independent author, as Hugh Kennedy describes it: "Abbasid Baghdad was probably the first place in the world where an author could make a living, not by being independently wealthy or having a wealthy patron, or even being part of an institution like a monastery that subsidized his activities, but by writing books to be sold in the market to a literate public."[17] Book copying provided also an easy source of income for educated individuals who had fallen on hard times, such as the poet Bakr b. Khārija al-Warrāq (alive at the end of the eighth century).[18] This meant that books could be written on any subject without the aid of patronage. The leveling effect of the *ʿarabiyya* created a diversity of authors and a reading public that extended beyond the educated ruling class to a new urban sub-elite.[19] The early book authors were mostly men, as women's education required the support of their families, and learned women more often chose a teaching career. Earlier poetesses such as al-Khansā' (d. after 644), however, had their oeuvre collected and edited, and verses of lesser-known or anonymous female poets found entry into anthologies solely devoted to women, such as *Women's Eloquence* (*Balāghat al-nisā'*) by Ibn Abī Ṭāhir (d. 893), or Abū Tammām's (d. 845 or 846) poetic anthology *On Bravery* (*al-Ḥamāsa*), of which (mostly anonymous) women make up a substantial portion.

Beyond the presence of a common language, a second factor that propelled book usage was the large amount of oral literature already in circulation, kept intact through professionalized transmission; it simply needed to be turned out onto the page. This oral heritage was constituted by both an older extant corpus and newly composed works. Preserving the former was a matter of urgency. The copious and prestigious oral poetry was at risk of disappearing, because many poets had perished in the Islamic conquests and the conventional method of using an apprentice poet to keep one's works in circulation had changed with the advent of a new style of poetry, the so-called modern poetry (*badīʿ*). This came into vogue in the ninth century, and was composed more often in writing. However, only the older corpus was deemed to be the linguistically impeccable and irreplaceable prime material, apt to serve as a model for codifying grammar and lexicon and in particular as a tool to interpret the obscure passages of the Qur'ān. Fieldworking grammarians armed with ink flasks turned out editions of collected poems of any poet (gleaned from his surviving transmitter). At the same time, new branches of scholarship emerged: the collection of the Prophet's deeds and sayings (Ḥadīth) gave rise to theology and law; the collection of pre-Islamic tribal battles and Islamic conquest narratives spurred historiography.[20] Ḥadīth in particular showed interesting fault lines, as its codification was not immediately regarded as an advantage. Serving as a foundation for law and doctrine, Ḥadīth was an authoritative source in many spheres of scholarship and daily life, and it was easier for scholars to keep it under control and adjust it to changing circumstance if it was kept unwritten, which is why Ḥadīth experts were most vocal in protesting the turn to writing in the eighth century.[21] Yet, resistance to the book—an attitude more often adopted for show than a reflection of reality—was surprisingly short-lived, disappearing in the first quarter of the ninth century. In the face of flourishing book production, it had become a moot point. All this occurred extraordinarily quickly. To compare, the Chinese elites took two centuries (eleventh to twelfth centuries C.E.) to "relax their hostility to the new technology" of block print.[22]

Writing, however, did not do away with orality, not even gradually; instead, the two modes merged with each other in a variety of ways. One might say that Arabic book culture embraced and celebrated oral practices. Books show manifold traces of this, depending on the book's topic. Poetry, for instance, the first major form of Arabic literature, relied on human memory as its medium: poets composed it orally and transmitters (*ruwāt,* often apprentice poets themselves) performed it, preserved it, and handed it down.

This poetry was kept stable by its internal structure of meter and rhyme, a semantic web of topoi, and the trained memories of its professionals. Poems thus survived (with the variations intrinsic to an oral tradition) up to two centuries before being fixed in writing.[23] For the poet, his transmitter (*rāwī),* and his public (and in odes of praise, for the named recipient), writing things down became a new option that broadened and facilitated access to the verses and helped preserve them. It also encouraged scholarly and critical treatment of poetry. The first order of business of the emerging philologist guild was to go to the outskirts of towns or into the desert and write down the tribal lore from Bedouin poets or their transmitters.[24]

Poets appreciated the new convenience of having their work in writing, to protect its integrity from transmitters wont to "improve" it (e.g., in the case of the poet Dhū l-Rumma, d. c. 735) or to aid failing memory (e.g., in the case ʿUmāra b. ʿAqīl, d. between 847–861).[25] Before the middle of the ninth century, poets such as Kulthūm b. ʿAmr al-ʿAttābī (d. 823 or 835) and Abū Tammām had also begun to consult the works of their predecessors in the form of written collections (*dawāwīn*) as inspirations for their own compositions.[26] The codex was a complementary medium and its use was a choice that bolstered an ongoing oral tradition that was deeply entrenched in private and public life.

On the other end of the spectrum were the translations of foreign works. These too had their beginning in the second half of the eighth century in the cosmopolitan society of the Abbasid dynasty, and they were produced with the support of the government and the expertise and prompting of non-Arab secretaries.[27] Greek science and Persian statecraft as well as popular lore were translated among others by early government scribes such as Sālim Abū l-ʿAlāʾ (d. after 743) and Ibn al-Muqaffaʿ (d. 757), who were non-Arab converts (*mawālī*), a class that would be instrumental in the Abbasid cultural mosaic.[28] To Sālim we owe the *Epistles of Aristotle to Alexander,* crafted from translated Byzantine pieces.[29] To Ibn al-Muqaffaʿ we owe the mirror of princes *Kalīla and Dimna,* masquerading as animal fables, framed by a didactic dialogue between a Brahmin-turned-philosopher and his king, first compiled in a (lost) Middle Persian version based on Indian sources.[30] Those books came as a treasured cultural import to a civilization whose representatives aspired to live up to their western Asian dynastic predecessors. The translations—themselves a creative feat, expanding the Arabic language in the translation process with novel styles and new terminologies—were reworked in the process of cultural appropriation, received prefaces and insertions, and underwent adaptation. The Arabic language blossomed through this ingestion and integration of foreign elements.

Between the translation of foreign books and local poetic traditions lay the vast and growing disciplines of Qur'ānic studies, prophetic tradition (Ḥadīth), philology, and history.[31] These are at times difficult to separate from each other, because many scholars were simultaneously engaged in several of them, particularly because the Qur'ān, together with poetry, served as the prime material for hammering out the classical Arabic language. For instance, early scholars from Kufa (later labeled the "Kufan school," though they created no method like their Basran counterpart) were often both professional reciters of the Qur'ān and lexicographers.[32] The four named areas of scholarship gave rise to more varied and nuanced attitudes toward the book.

The text of the Qur'ān itself was soon turned into a written document (specimens in the Ḥijāzī script from the seventh century survive).[33] The Qur'ān conceives of itself as a book (*kitāb*), especially in the later chapters (*sūras*); to thus reproduce it followed logically, and its bound form (mostly on parchment) became the earliest object of scribal art.[34] The first copyist known to sell Qur'āns was the renunciant Mālik b. Dīnār (d. 748).[35]

The written scripture existed side by side with its oral recitation, carried out by professional reciters *(qurrā')*, whose knowledge in cases of dispute was trusted more than written versions of the text.[36] This had to do in part with the nature of Arabic writing, which contained many similar-looking letters (homographs) and did not denote short vowels. In the middle of a word, the letters *b, t, th, n,* and *y* all looked the same (as is still visible in seventh-century Qur'ān specimens). Since its inception, the script offered the option to distinguish those homographs by dots or strokes. By the end of the eighth century, additional vowel signs had been developed, but usage was not regular until the following century and then only in certain texts. For Qur'ān reciters and other scholars this was less serious, as the codex was not meant to provide a phonetic transcript in the sense of a written version of an audiotape—the discipline of recitation (*qirā'a*) fulfilled that purpose—but rather to serve as a memory aid (beyond its symbolic function as a sacred object). What is more, the partially elliptic script permitted slight variations of the phonetic realization to coexist; they would later be brought into a system of accepted canonical readings. Imprecision had the advantage of being inclusive for a geographically widespread religious community constituted of speakers of Arabic (in various colloquial forms), Persian, Aramaic, Greek, and Romance.[37]

Prophetic tradition was the subject that generated most debate about its codification. This is surprising, at first, in a culture where the book had been so rapidly embraced in some quarters, and it must therefore be viewed from a broader ideological perspective. The transmitters of prophetic lore, or traditionists (*muḥaddithūn*), marshaled a body of texts that provided (together with the Qur'ān) the basis for the formulation of Muslim ritual, faith, and law, and their activity carried religious authority. Their expertise was imparted on an oral and interpersonal basis, and if writing was used (*ṣaḥīfa*s, or loose sheets containing prophetic traditions, survive among the earliest papyri), it was not shared outside the circle of one's colleagues and students.[38] The reluctance to make Ḥadīth available in codex format stemmed less from a backwardness in media usage and more from a desire not to part with the intellectual control over this corpus and to retain the flexibility to adapt it to changing circumstances. Only with pressure from the government, which desired independent access to Ḥadīth, which served as a foundation of the law, were the first books of them composed.[39] Conversely, the nonusage of books became a topos illustrating the excellent memories of those scholars who imparted their knowledge orally. Nonetheless, many who were praised for their feats of memory and for "never touching or consulting a book" did use notes in the privacy of their homes.[40]

Once the book had become a sine qua non, the orality of Ḥadīth was retained in the convention of transcribing, at the beginning of each single tradition, name by name the individuals through which it had been handed down (the so-called *isnād,* literally "backing up"), and binding the texts into an oral transmission process. Ḥadīth tried desperately to remain oral, and one might argue that this way of transcribing strengthened orality.[41] Purely written access to Ḥadīth was frowned on and the teaching from it not regarded as licit, and at times, copied traditions not authorized through personal contact with a scholar were even destroyed, such as those of the stationer-traditionist Abū Bakr Muḥammad b. al-Ḥusayn Ibn al-Khaffāf (d. 1027).[42]

The field of philology comprised lexicography, grammar, and a knowledge of Arabic lore and genealogy, which was taken from, and authenticated by, the poetry. Though philology did not have the status of Ḥadīth, it was bound into the same interpersonal teaching process. Notebooks were used but shared only within the teaching circuit. Kufan philologists once tried to shut down a weekly dictation session by the grammarian al-Farrāʾ (d. 822) by boycotting it. They had asked him to dictate a book on syntactically difficult verses (*abyāt al-naḥw*), but they realized after the third meeting that "if this continues, children will be taught syntax," and so they boycotted the class to shut it down. Al-Farrāʾ, however, angrily vowed to persist even if only two people attended, and continued to dictate it for sixteen years.[43]

Philologists supplied learned entertainment for rulers and high dignitaries, such as the mutual recitation of poetry (*tadhākur*) or accounts of historical lore (*ahkbār,* literally "reports," or *ayyām,* literally "days"). It was not unsual for a sleepless or traveling official to send for a scholar to help him pass the hours of the night with educated conversation. Rulers, too, made this the focus of regular gatherings (*majālis,* literally "sessions") and employed philologists as their courtiers or as tutors of their sons, or remunerated them with stipends and periodic gifts. Such oral performances at gatherings were often recorded in books afterward without any change of format or organization of the contents. Other early books were conceived according to an overall plan (as opposed to being simple transcripts of the conversations in literary or scholarly gatherings) as a result of the order of a caliph or vizier or the inspiration of a secretary in government service.[44] Examples of commissioned books are the poetry collection *al-Mufaḍḍaliyyāt,* named after its creator al-Mufaḍḍal al-Ḍabbī (d. after 780), and a comprehensive history of Islam by Ibn Isḥāq, which survives only in a later redaction by Ibn Hishām (d. 834).[45] Philologists were thus an essential part of literary life. They helped place books at society's disposal as they transmitted, explained, and edited poetry, a text corpus that was older, larger, and more diverse than the Qurʾān, and together with it supplied the linguistic material for formulating the rules of classical Arabic.

Historians worked with the same primary materials as philologists—oral records taken down in writing—but it took a while for them to be recognized as a distinct branch of scholars. First, they were referred to simply as *akhbārīs* and differed from other compilers only in their more or less chronological arrangement of gathered accounts. Gradually, however, historians took as their focus the identity and message of the newly forged Islamic empire, and they reshaped earlier narratives according to their own vision of it.[46]

The two essential ingredients, a common written language and a rich body of literature, were thus in place when the third ingredient, rag paper, became available in Baghdad at the end of the eighth century. This abundant and affordable writing material was introduced from China via Central Asia within a decade of the grammarian Sībawayhi's death. In 794 to 795, his brief governorship of Khurasan (northeastern Iran) acquainted the Barmakid al-Faḍl b. Yaḥyā (d. 808) with Samarqand paper, and he introduced it in the capital Baghdad. Initially made of the bast fibers of the mulberry tree in China, Arabic paper was produced from discarded rags, textile waste, and ropes made from cotton, flax, or hemp. Although it was a factor in paper's subsequent spread, the unlimited producibility of paper, which was essentially recycled trash, seems not to have been the main reason for its initial adoption.[47] Rather, the government in Baghdad had become concerned that its dependence on the previous writing material (papyrus), produced in only one of the provinces (Egypt), was making the administration vulnerable. This had led Caliph al-Manṣūr (r. 754–775), when contemplating a storehouse full of papyrus scrolls, to declare, "We need to write on something for which we do not pay governors," and to instruct his secretary to "leave the papyri and find a remedy against the state of [dependence on] them [*istiẓhāran ʿalā ḥālihā*]."[48] Furthermore, paper was safer for recording documents because the ink seeped into its fibers, as opposed to parchment and papyrus, where it remained on the surface and could be washed off or scratched off. Once paper was available, its use in the Abbasid bureaucracy very soon made it a widespread and common writing material.[49]

Previously, the high cost of parchment and the geographically limited and labor-intensive production of papyrus had placed limits on the output of books. Paper changed this, and it also provided employment to numerous stationers (*warraqūn,* literally "folio-makers"), whose number increased tenfold between 767 and 1010 C.E. This quantitative assessment relies on the largest extant Arabic biographical dictionary, comprising circa 30,000 entries (see Chapter 3).[50] While paper was not indispensable for book production, which had preceded it, it greatly accelerated it. With all other factors in place—the book format, the *ʿarabiyya,* the emerging disciplines and their scholarly practices—paper became the catalyst for the Arabic book revolution to gain its momentum.

DEARTH OF ARTIFACTS

In taking a closer look at the Abbasid book revolution, it may appear that the most obvious source would be the extant remains of books from the time. Unfortunately, although we know of multitudes of authors and titles that survive in later copies or figure in the abovementioned *Catalogue,* actual specimens from the ninth century are sparse. The dearth of artifacts from the period is a puzzle in the history of the Abbasid book revolution. Only about forty reliably datable Arab Muslim and Christian texts survive, and many of them are incomplete. The following is a survey of titles based on the list of François Déroche, classified here by subject (the numbers refer to Déroche's scripts charts, divided into Muslim and Christian texts; see figs. 1a and 1b):[51]

QUR'ĀNS (14 items):

(fragments, nos. 1, 3, 5, 9, 13–14, 16–17, 22, 36–40)

PROPHETIC TRADITION, ISLAMIC THEOLOGY, AND LAW (11 items):

Wahb b. Munabbih, *Vita and Campaigns of the Prophet* (*Maghāzī al-rasūl*) and *The Story of David* (*Ḥadīth Dāwūd*) (fragment, no. 2 and figs. 3a and 3b)[52]
ʿAbdallāh b. Wahb, *Comprehensive Collection of Ḥadīth* (*al-Jāmiʿ fī l-ḥadīth*) (two specimens, nos. 23, 33)[53]
al-Shāfiʿī, *The Epistle* (*al-Risāla*) (no. 11 and figs. 8a and 8b)[54]
Yaḥyā b. ʿUmar, *Argument in Response to al-Shāfiʿī* (*al-Ḥujja fī l-radd ʿalā l-Shāfiʿī*) (no. 18)
Ibn Ḥanbal, *Questions* (*Masāʾil*) (no. 12)
Ashhab b. ʿAbd al-ʿAzīz, *The Book of Pilgrimage* (*Kitāb al-Ḥajj*)[55] (no. 24)
Mālik b. Anas, *The Well-Trodden* (*al-Muwaṭṭaʾ*), a canonical Ḥadīth collection (no. 30)
Abū Zayd ʿAbdarraḥmān b. Abī l-Ghamr, *The Gatherings [on Islamic law]* (*al-Majālis [fī l-fiqh]*)[56] (no. 19)
Asad b. al-Furāt, *The Asadiyya* (*al-Asadiyya,* a legal compendium) (fragment)[57] (no. 25)
Abū Isḥāq al-Fazārī, *The Vitae* (*al-Siyar*)[58] (no. 15)

LINGUISTIC SCIENCES (3 items):

Abū ʿUbayd, *Rare Vocabulary of Ḥadīth* (*Gharīb al-ḥadīth*) (no. 6 and fig. 6)[59]
Ibn Qutayba, *Rare Vocabulary of Ḥadīth* (*Gharīb al-ḥadīth*) (no. 26)
Abū l-ʿAmaythal, *Transmitted Homonymous Polysemous Words* (*al-Maʾthūr fīmā ttafaqa lafẓuhū wa-khtalafa maʿnāhu*) (no. 28 and fig. 4)[60]

NEW TESTAMENT (6 items):

Collections of Gospels, Pauline Letters, and Acts of the Apostles (4 specimens, nos. 4, 7, 29, 32)[61]
Paul, *Epistle* to the Jews (no. 27)
Paul, *Epistles* to Timotheus and to Philemon (fragment, no. 35)

CHRISTIAN RELIGIOUS TEXTS (6 items):

Christian legends (no. 20)
Vitae of saints (no. 21)
Vita of St. Stephen of Mār Sāba (no. 34)
Vitae of martyrs (no. 8)
A monastic anthology (no. 31)
Theodore Abū Qurra, Treatise on Theology (no. 10)

The small sample does not allow for a representative analysis, yet from what survives, besides the obvious frequency of the Muslim Scripture, works on Prophetic tradition and Islamic theology and law dominate. Another, smaller group of specimens belong to the linguistic sciences. There is no work of history preserved. Christian texts, both from the New Testament and religious literature, comprise about one third of the specimens. Codices of the New Testament contain mostly the Gospels, the Acts of the Apostles, and the letters of Paul, translated from Greek or Syriac or a combination of both. To these one can add further undated specimens such as Codex Vaticanus Arabicus 13, perhaps the earliest Christian Arabic text and the earliest collection of biblical chapters in Arabic (see figs. 2a and 2b).[62] Their strong numeric presence is part of a surge of Christian translations observed in the ninth century, which Sarah Schulthess attributes to a "progressive Arabization of Christian communities, following the arrival of Islam and Arabic."[63] They arose probably in the Melkite milieu in Syro-Palestine, where Greek predominated, and the switch to Arabic occurred sooner than in areas such as Alexandria, where indigenous liturgical languages like Coptic or Syriac held sway.

The materials of these early codices vary. Islamic and Christian scriptures were written mostly on parchment. As to the scholarly books, the *Story of David* and the Prophet's biography by Wahb b. Munabbih (d. 728 or 732), dated 844, and the Ḥadīth collection of Ibn Wahb (d. 813) dated 889, are written on papyrus; Abū l-ʿAmaythal's (d. 854) *Transmitted Homonymous*

Polysemous Words, dated 893, uses parchment; and Abū ʿUbayd's (d. 838) *Rare Vocabulary of Ḥadīth,* dated 866, is the earliest Arabic codex on paper. Regarding the script, Déroche, who presents script charts of the dated specimens, notes the variety of the early Arabic scripts, which was greater in Muslim codices than in Christian ones (see, figs. 1a and 1b, Déroche's script charts; and figs. 2a and 2b, Cod. Vat. 13, displaying the different hands of scribe a and scribe b). Nonetheless, the shapes of single letters in the scripts of this period show common traits. For example, the *alif* in initial position has its foot bent toward the right and the *alif*'s downstroke in final position crosses beneath the baseline; the *dāl* has two possible shapes—a steep-angled version and another with parallel strokes; the *ṭāʾ* often has an oblique shaft; the tail of the *lām* is bent at an angle rather than curved; the tail of the *mīm* is short and oblique; and the tail of the *nūn* is limited to a quarter circle, to mention just the most salient traits.[64] However, the general ductus of the script varies between a slightly inclined and dense arrangement, such as in al-Shāfiʿī's *Epistle* (figs. 8a and 8b, see Chapter 3), and a vertical arrangement with the letters more spaced apart, such as in Abū ʿUbayd's lexicon (fig. 6, see Chapter 1).

Considering the newness of the medium, the variety of the mise-en-page of the early Arabic codices is striking. The *Story of David* and the Prophet's biography by Wahb b. Munabbih already demonstrate the feature of extending rhyme words of poems at the baseline to produce a justified left border of the text, characteristic of later Arabic manuscripts. The first page shown (PB 10) contains the prophet's miraculous protection by a spider that wove its web over the entrance to the cave in which the Prophet sought refuge on his flight from Mecca. The first poem is by his persecutor Abū Usāma, expressing his realization of the Prophet's divine protection, and the second, by a learned man named ʿAbdallāh, describes his recognition of the prophetic seal on Muḥammad's shoulder. The other page shown (PB 13) contains poems by the Prophet's poet al-Ḥassān b. Thābit (d. before 661) and the Companion (and later caliph) Abū Bakr (r. 632–634) about Muḥammad's true prophethood and the miraculous holding up of Surāqa, another persecutor, whose horse's legs were swallowed by the earth. The papyrus also includes marginal corrections written within a curved line (see figs. 3a and 3b).

Within the *Story of David* there is an intriguing single sheet whose text is framed. It contains the scene in which two angels appear before David in the guise of two men asking him to judge between them: one, the owner of

I
N° 2 (229) GD PB
N° 6 (252)
N° 11 (av. 265)
N° 12 (266)
N° 23 (av. 276) "1" "3"
N° 25 (av. 278)
N° 26 (279)
N° 28 (280)
EAA, BII (IIIè s.)
alif
ğīm
dāl
ṭā’
‘ayn
lām
mīm
nūn
hā’
lām-alif

(*a*)

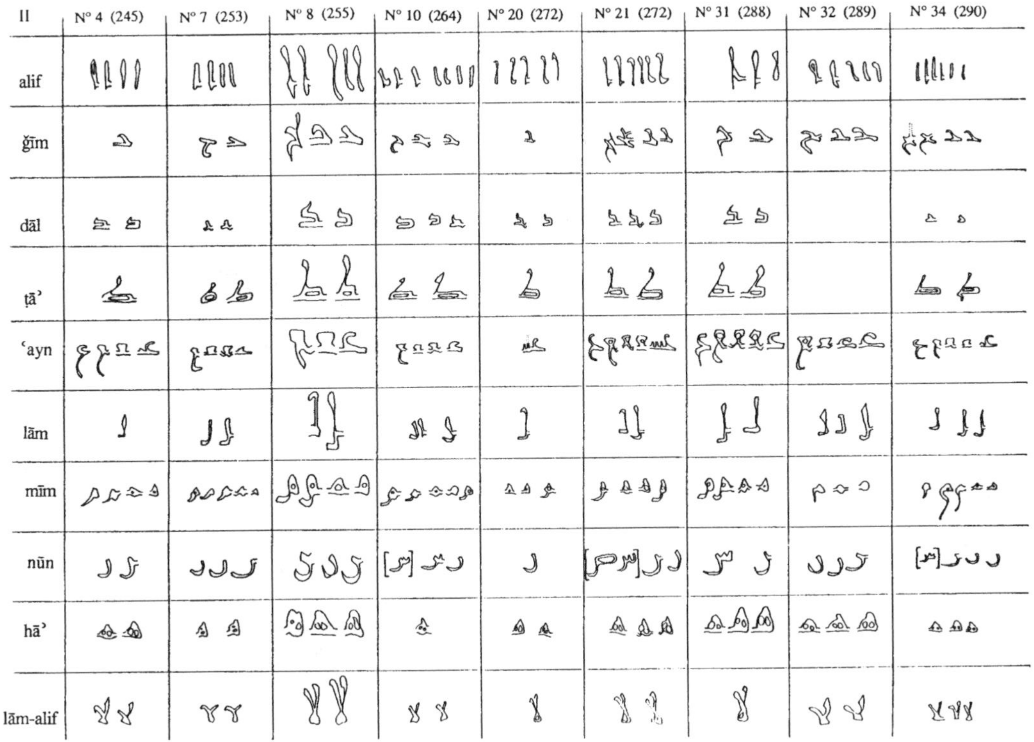

(*b*)

FIGS. 1A AND 1B. Script charts of dated Arabic codices of the third/ninth century. Fig. 1a shows Islamic codices; fig. 1b shows Christian codices. (Reproduced from François Déroche, "Les manuscrits arabes datés du IIIe/IXe siècle," *REI* 55–57 (1987–1989): 378–379.)

(*a*)

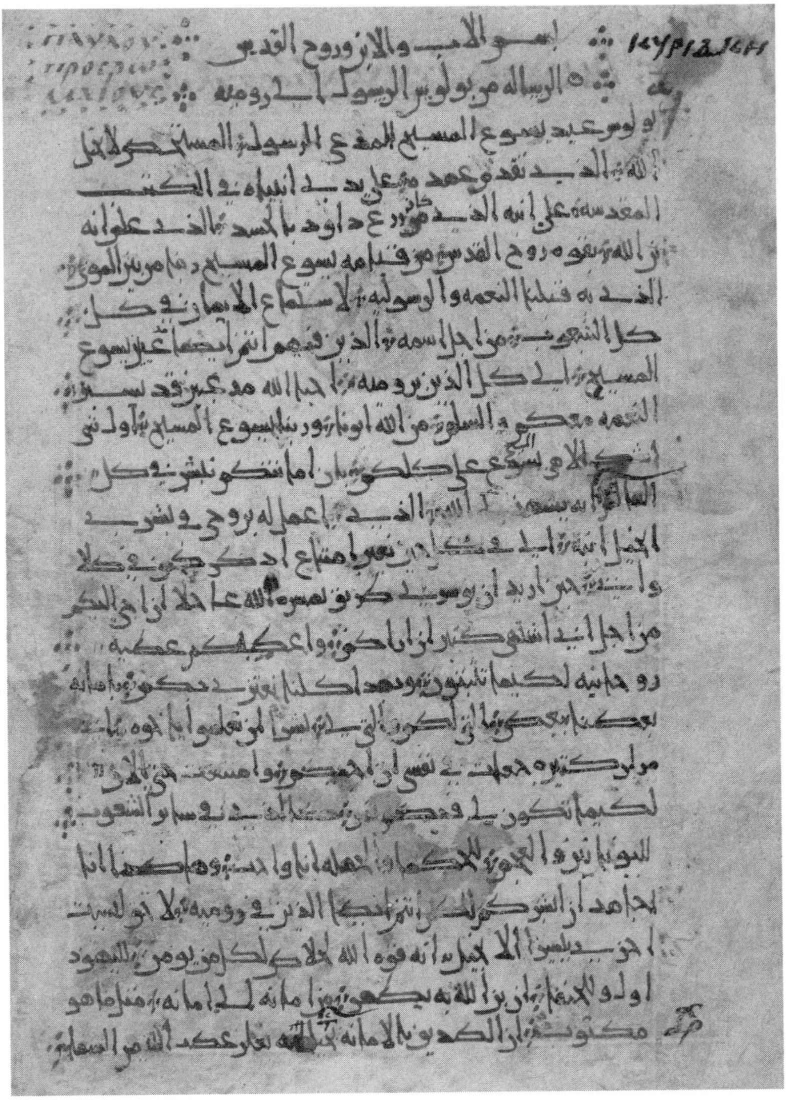

(*b*)

FIGS. 2A AND 2B. Codex Vaticanus Arabicus 13, dated to the third/ninth century, an Arabic manuscript of 179 folios on parchment containing parts of the Gospels and the fourteen letters of Paul. The colophon on the last folio of the manuscript mentions the city of Homs. Fig. 2a shows the hand of scribe b, who ends the letter *alif* with a serif at the top (fol. 15 recto), and fig. 2b shows the hand of scribe a, who extends the bodies of letters horizontally (fol. 87 verso). (Vat. ar. 13, fols. 15 recto and 87 verso, Vatican Apostolic Library.)

(*a*)

(*b*)

FIGS. 3A AND 3B. Papyrus fragment of Wahb b. Munabbih, *Vita and Campaigns of the Prophet,* dated 229/844. Fig. 3a displays extensions of rhyme words of the poems to achieve a justified left border (PB 10), and fig. 3b shows a marginal correction on the left margin within an arch, rewriting clearly the name of Abū Bakr, which is restored in small script between two lines (PB 13). (Papyrus Heidelberg PSR 23, Institute of Papyrology, Heidelberg University.)

ninety-nine sheep, had taken the sole sheep of the other man. David's verdict, addressed to the second man, "He did you indeed injustice" (*qad ẓalamaka*), is however meant for himself, for having organized the killing of the general Uriah (Ūriyā) in order to wed his beautiful widow Bathseba (Batshābaʿ), and one of the angels spells this out: "The man judged himself" (*qaḍā l-rajulu ʿalā nafsihī*). This moment when David realizes his guilt and repents represents a turning point in his vita, and it is possible that the copyist or a later reader drew the frame to highlight it.[65] Nonetheless, the mise-en-page of this papyrus remains relatively plain, and the script mostly lacks vowel signs.

More elaborate is the mise-en-page of the two lexicographical works by Abū l-ʿAmaythal and Abū ʿUbayd. Both contain vowel signs, which are necessary since they are dictionaries for rare and difficult words. As far as the organization of the page is concerned, Abū l-ʿAmaythal's lexicon separates each lemma with a new line, and within the lemma distinguishes the different meanings of an identically written word in the consonantal script (*rasm*) by a space or a paragraph marker consisting of a dotted circle (see fig. 4, Chapter 1). In Abū ʿUbayd's lexicon, each new *ḥadīth* whose vocabulary is explained is introduced after a space on a new line, beginning with the *inquit* formula "He said" (*qāla*) stretched across the full breadth of the text block, so that the word functions like an overstrike. The ensuing text of the *ḥadīth* is separated from the commentary by a paragraph marker (dotted circle). Long *ḥadīth*s receive internal formatting, such as the one of Umm Zarʿ, a fictional story of eleven women who describe their husbands in terse and eloquent language peppered with rare and difficult words. Here each speaker is introduced after a space with a centered new line containing the *inquit* formula (see fig. 6, Chapter 1).[66]

Another dimension is the early codices' scholarly quality; the codex of Shāfiʿī's *Epistle* provides an example. Graphically unsophisticated and almost without vowel signs, it is carefully collated (showing frequent collation marks on the margin) and the text is thoroughly corrected. Marginal suppletion of omissions abound, as do struck-out and corrected words and interlinear rewritings of unclear words. The care to establish an accurate text is evident, though one cannot reliably credit the corrections to the scribe of the codex. Such revisions would become standard in Arabic scholarly scribal practices.[67]

In sum, scribes of the ninth century used the full range of the graphic and editorial options the book medium offered, striving to ensure both visual accessibility and scholarly quality. Nonetheless, the picture remains incomplete; the few preserved specimens may represent some evolving scholarly fields (narrative exegesis, Islamic law, Ḥadīth scholarship, and lexicography), but they say nothing about other disciplines or the actual breadth of the contemporary book production. Excluded here is the bulk of the shorter Arabic papyri, which mostly contain private, commercial, and official correspondence and documents of all kinds, but few literary or scholarly texts.[68]

BIMODALITY

Why so few artifacts survive deserves attention. Their dearth, in view of their (once) massive numbers, is puzzling. Naturally, destruction and reuse of writing materials were major causes, and paper was more vulnerable than the sturdier parchment or papyrus. But two other reasons must be taken into consideration. First, one needs to consider that a "book" in the ninth century was not limited to the physical object. Rather, a book was often conceived orally (in dialogue or by dictation) and then alternated between oral and written modes. It was as often stored in an author's or transmitter's memory as on the written page. A paper codex per se was not an item worth preserving. Since books were made in large numbers, the single copy was often a plain object. What mattered was the content, the reliability of the text, and its clear subdivision and handwriting; fancy ornament was deemed unnecessary. An exception were autographs of known scholars, which would be esteemed for the guaranteed quality of their content. Though Qur'āns would be produced in luxury copies toward the end of the ninth century, it took a while for this to be accepted.[69] Caliph ʿUmar II (r. 717–720) refused to purchase a Qur'ān offered him because he found it unnecessarily lavish and its price exorbitant. The essayist al-Jāḥiẓ (d. 868–869) once criticized beautifully illuminated Manichaean books as a waste of effort and, on another occasion, blamed his patron for having him bind his books, which made them cumbersome to handle and hard to transport.[70] From its very inception, the Arabic book was treated as a practical data carrier rather than a prestigious object, as was the case with early European manuscript codices. Therefore, a book might not have been worth preserving once it had been recopied. Existing in a culture of mixed oral and written communication, a copy was often more appreciated than the original, since Arabic books were constantly optimized, and each copy represented merely one stage of a book before it was again read out or dictated and corrected, glossed, or enhanced with commentary.

In such a culture, a person knowing a book—that is, able to read it and explain its contents—was an indispensable companion to a book, and, one might argue, as important as the book itself. The teaching of any scholarly book required the guarantee of its teacher's competence, by having studied it with its author, transmitter, or other expert, for example. Thus, a book was usually associated with a person in charge of its contents. That a book could replace its author was an idea that sprang up only in the third quarter of the ninth century, as formulated by al-Jāḥiẓ, and this was made possible too by the composition of handbooks on sundry topics by his contemporary Ibn Qutayba (d. 889). This alternating oral and written transmission is unique to Arabic culture and was also made necessary by the reductive Arabic writing system, which is a consonantary (*abjad*); that is, an alphabet in which only consonants and long vowels were written. Expertise in a book's content was therefore vital to supply the missing vowels correctly. This holds particularly true for rare, difficult, or foreign words, proper names, and technical terms. In regular Arabic, the triliteral morphological structure of words (a feature of Semitic languages) dictates the placement of short vowels in many places and allows for easy suppletion by someone familiar with the language. But in difficult texts, expertise in the content is required to interpret the script. To the uninitiated, a book in this script is illegible.[71] A copious literature on frequently made mistakes in speech (*laḥn al-ʿāmma*) and errors in copying, such as setting the wrong diacritical dots or switching between similar-sounding letters (*taṣḥīf*), sprang up in the late eighth and early ninth century and showed that a book in its written form was a medium that, simultaneous to its acceptance, was seen as something in need of constant quality control.

For readers of the ninth century and modern scholars alike, the polysemy of the Arabic language poses further problems in reconstructing the usage of written or oral media. For instance, Arabic does not distinguish between reciting and reading (both expressed by the verb *qaraʾa*). *Qāla* (literally, "he said" in a dialogue) can also refer to the author of a written text, and it serves further as a marker to subdivide narratives into scenes or to return from a dialogue to the frame story (and who exactly said, or wrote, something is not repeated but must be laboriously disentangled from any narrative). *Kalima* may mean a word or an entire speech, *kitāb* a letter, a book, or a piece of writing of any length, and a *ṣaḥīfa* can be a single page, a folded sheet, or a number of these containing a lengthy text. The correct meaning of each of these polysemous words must be inferred from the context. Moreover, many of them derive from the daily lexicon and have come to serve as technical terms in several disciplines simultaneously, with a different meaning in each. *Ḥarf* means a pronouncement of any length in normal speech, but "letter" in orthography, and "particle" in grammar. In the Qur'ānic context the plural *aḥruf* was interpreted as different "readings" of the Qur'ānic text, in order to justify the coexistence of several accepted ways to read the scripture.[72] The Arabic reader of any text needed to know not only the *'arabiyya,* but also the usage of its lexicon in his or her scholarly field of engagement.

Both the reductive writing system and the polysemy of the lexicon turned reading books into something that required linguistic and scholarly expertise. In such an intimate interplay between books and the scholars who taught and transmitted them, every new written iteration of a book became more valuable than the previous, for it had gone through a process of scholarly improvement. There was no particular reason to keep a book once its contents had been superseded by a corrected or enlarged version.

As second factor that made older books dispensable, pointed out by Chase Robinson, was the dynamism of the book culture. The content of older (smaller) books was reworked, combined, expanded, and reordered in later larger summae, often titled "The Great Book" (*al-kitāb al-kabīr*) on such-and-such topic. Knowledge once recorded in writing was seldom left unused. For instance, in grammar and lexicography, later books would combine and synthesize smaller treatises on partial aspects. Lexicography began as short word lists on clouds, camels, weapons, or other semantic groups, and later comprehensive dictionaries assembled these smaller books and sorted their material by meaning or word form (alphabet, phonetics, or morphology). The pinnacle was the *Language of the Arabs* (*Lisān al-'arab*) by Ibn Manẓūr (d. 1311), who prided himself on having merged and recast into accessible form the six largest dictionaries of his time without adding a single letter of his own. Large compendia on a topic would in turn be followed by abridgments, and these again were enhanced with commentary. Readers would obviously prefer the most comprehensive book on any subject, not an earlier and partial treatment. Within the constant process of reorganizing and maximizing knowledge, standard sources emerged which then survived in multiple copies, while earlier books fell into disuse.[73]

These are merely two salient factors, and additional reasons may have been responsible for the scarcity of extant early manuscripts, but in any case, those are only instructive samples and cannot provide a comprehensive view of the cultural practices of which they were part.

BOOK FORMATS, LITERARY SOURCES, AND METHOD

Before moving to literary sources, the structure of the early books containing these requires some remarks. A number of organizing principles existed side by side. Some books were simple transcripts of oral teaching situations, such as the gatherings or dictations (*amālī*) of so-and-so, without any other title than that, no order other than loose association, and no subdivision other than chains of transmitters intervening at the beginning of each account. The order of the text may be either that of the original oral situation or one created by the subsequent redactor. Here the book medium added nothing to the oral form except its materiality. The familiar elements of a redacted book, such as title, table of contents, subdivision into chapters, and cross-references, are wholly absent.

Books that had entered Arabic-Islamic civilization through translation, such as manuals for rulers, were imported together with their structure. A famous example was *Kalīla wa-Dimna,* an advice book in the guise of a fable collection translated in the mid-eighth century, which contained a number of prefaces and was divided into chapters. It is uncertain whether it then already contained a table of contents; its earliest manuscripts from the thirteenth and fourteenth centuries do. However, a list of contents may predate these, since titles and synopses for each of the book's chapters were provided by the historian al-Yaʿqūbī (d. 897), who indicated what type of situation and strategy each chapter covers, and he obviously intended this as case-by-case instructions for rulers. Similarly organized were the scientific works translated from Greek, a process that culminated in the ninth century and not only expanded Arabic into a language of science but also provided the foundation for many disciplines from astronomy to zoology, with philosophy occupying a major share.[74]

A new type of book-composition was the epistle (*risāla*), which grew out of administrative correspondence. It retained the form of a missive, starting with an opening section including the address of a recipient with formulas of blessing and praise and introductory comments, followed by the main text, whose beginning was indicated with the formula "To proceed" (*ammā baʿdu*), which became a standard book formula. The epistle format was introduced by the early state scribes to compose longer treatises, which might or might not have a specific addressee, but which were designed to reach further and subsequent audiences. An example is ʿAbd al-Ḥamīd b. Yaḥyā's (d. 750) letter to the secretaries, in which he expounds on the ethics and duties of the secretarial profession, which had quickly become the backbone of the Abbasid government (although the epistle is extant, its versions differ).[75] Secretaries also constituted an important group among authors, readers, and collectors of early books.

In another book type, the compilation (*taṣnīf*), the texts passed on were already extant, either memorized or in the form of notebooks for private use, and the compiler might arrange these into thematic chapters and even subchapters; this procedure of compiling had its own designation, as opposed to the composition of a book from scratch (*taʾlīf*). A particular type of compilation is the biographical dictionary, which also had its inception in this century, and whose many varieties and exemplars contain entries on a great number of individuals. The vita of a given person can be compared across different dictionaries.[76]

Of all these book types, compilations are the most copious sources for the present endeavor. Within them, smaller independent texts which existed in the form of countless oral accounts, were gathered and compiled. These give ample evidence of the practices of writing and reading and the attitudes of writers and readers, and of the manuscript codex in the various avenues of literary and scholarly life in the ninth century. The reported events often exist in diverging versions, which allows us to approach them from several angles.

One should add that literary and historical *akhbār* from the ninth century do not intrinsically differ from each other, and versions of the same event occur in both types of compilations. In the present book, the focus is on practices as evidenced in such accounts that deal with linguistic scholarship and literature. In regard to accounts of the beginnings of Islamic history, with which the earliest historians (then still called *akhbārīs*) were concerned, one must suppose a great deal of reshaping, especially as the historical collections served not merely to gather these but also to shape a narrative of the origins of the new Islamic polity. The reconstruction of events that had gone through 200 years of oral transmission and creative rewriting poses problems that have led to substantially different interpretations.[77] For investigating practices more or less contemporary to the protagonists, transmitters, and compilers of accounts, or removed only one or two generations, as is the case here, those hazards are somewhat reduced. This does not mean that no reshaping took place, but first, the time span to do so was shorter, and second, the motivations for rewriting were less uniform, since no greater historical agenda was at stake.

In these early compilations, the seams of their assemblage remain visible. The smaller units they were made up of retained their format, so that any compilation enumerates the sources of its discrete elements. Such modules are referred to variously as *ḥadīth, āthār,* or *akhbār,* which differ from each other only in content. Among these, the group of *ḥadīth* (or *āthār*) constitutes a distinct corpus, referred to hereafter with the capitalized and romanized form "Ḥadīth." The two first types contain sayings or events of the Prophet's life (d. 630 C.E.), whereas *akhbār* designate any other content. Such modules are usually brief and bipartite. The first part is a chain of the names of those persons who transmitted the described event (*isnād*) in reverse chronological order from the latest to the earliest person who may have been an eyewitness or protagonist of the related event. It runs like this: so-and-so reported to me (or us) from so-and-so, who reported from so-and-so, who reported from so-and-so, and so on. An *isnād* can be as brief as two names or it can be stretched over several lines, depending how complete it was and how far in the past the related event lay. The scholarly weight of these chains differed according to the subject of an account. In Ḥadīth, which was a source of law and doctrine, the scrutiny of the chains and their evaluation developed into diversified subdisciplines (*ʿilm al-rijāl,* literally, "the science of men," but which also included women and *al-jarḥ wa-l-taʿdīl,* the cross-examination of each transmitter of *ḥadīth*); known and reliable transmitters were superior to anonymous and unreliable ones, complete chains were better than those with gaps, and numerous and differing chains were better than few (or single ones). In the historical or literary *akhbār,* the chains serve more or less to identify the source of the information, and compilers differed in how lax or strict they were in selecting *akhbār;* some might occasionally comment about their truth value, while others did not.

The second part of a *ḥadīth* or *khabar* (sing. of *akhbār*) is the actual content (*matn,* literally "text"), which might be the terse prose of a third-person narrator or a dialogue set in scene. Unlike in Ḥadīth, questionable material need not be left out in *akhbār* if it filled a gap or had entertainment value, and the compiler might then simply express his reservations. The chains of transmitters can be compared to modern footnotes in indicating a source or serving as a disclaimer for events of doubtful veracity. Frequently, several *akhbār* about one event are clustered, and their divergencies either elicit the compiler's evaluation or are left up to the reader's judgement. This juxtaposing of multiple reports about the same event, which differed in detail and style, shows that authors and readers were aware of their literary reworking, and Stefan Leder interprets this practice as an implicit marker of fictionality.[78] In the tenth century, the compiler of the *Book of Songs* (*Kitāb al-Aghānī*), de facto an anthology of poets, singers, and composers, uses *isnād* sometimes in a tongue-in-cheek way—for instance, when he reproduces the *akhbār* on the life of the Umayyad love poet Majnūn Laylā, whose historicity was by then already in question. Nonetheless, the poetry attributed to him was popular and gathered into a *dīwān,* (a poet's collected works) and as such, he deserved an entry. The practice of *isnād* eventually became so ingrained that it was parodized. This was pushed to the extreme a century later in the invention of a genre of picaresque tales in ornate prose (*maqāmāt*), in which the *isnād*-chain became pure fiction.

What evidentiary value may such accounts have? No general answer is possible here, as they oscillate in a gray zone between fact and fiction.[79] Places, major events, and protagonists are usually historical. The same holds true for the transmitters, some of whom were book authors or known collectors of *akhbār.* Scholars such as Manfred Fleischhammer, Walter Werkmeister, and Sebastian Günther have painstakingly traced the sources of major compilations and established that many of the used sources were already extant in writing, either as books or private notebooks, and Günther has proposed a fine-grained categorization of the different functions of redacting and transmitting performed by the individuals in a given chain.[80] As a rule, the compiler would likewise claim historicity, yet this claim must be put down to convention, as overt fiction was not respected. Our own concept of fiction has also evolved, and it is more adequate to speak instead of fictionality, in the sense of Henrik Skov Nielsen, James Phelan, and Richard Walsh, who have defined this as a dimension of many texts, both in literature and everyday speech, that cannot be classified among the genres of fiction and in which fictionality offers strategies to deal with real events.[81]

The singe *khabar* can thus not be tested for its truth value. Even in Ḥadīth, where textual criticism had become a classical scholarly discipline, judgements diverged on many items, and modern scholarship has brought a spectrum of approaches to Ḥadīth, from credulity to summary dismissal, which cannot all be repeated here.[82] However, literary and historical *akhbār* that are collected and fixed in writing close in time to the related events are useful, in their sum, to reconstruct a panorama for human interaction. This of course reflects the view and understanding of the compilers who selected and redacted the *akhbār,* and not of the actual individuals portrayed.[83]

Akhbār also differ in terms of their plot types. Some plots recur frequently, such as a poet's quest to gain access to a caliph or high dignitary or the poet's presentation of a panegyric ode (*qaṣīda*) to him. Copious *akhbār* on one type of plot show the spectrum of possible actions taken in this context, such as the procedure of recitation (by the poet or his transmitter, of full or partial odes, interruptions of an ode, and emotional reactions to an ode); type of rewards given (robes, slaves, horses, estates, coin, or debt payment); forms of payment (coin or cheque), as well as its delay or denial; ranges of prices (from 1 *dīnār* per verse to 100,000 *dirham*s for the whole ode); mediating persons; and so forth. The reaction of the audience depicted and any comments of the compiler give further clues to what was common and what was out of the ordinary. In sum, the changing articulations of a plot type map out the range of actions that were deemed plausible by the compiler.[84]

Other actions or themes do not constitute frequent plots, but the place and function of a given element differs in each instance. These can be more elusive aspects, such as the use of the Qur'ān by poets, or attitudes toward the love lyric (*ghazal*). Here it is the diversity of ways in which such aspects are built into a plot that shows a spectrum of possibilities, and again, depicted reactions of audiences (members of a gathering, bystanders) and comments of the compiler help to gauge where a protagonist's actions are to be situated within the range of familiar and acceptable versus unusual and controversial behavior.[85]

In the particular rendition of an event, one must take into account the agenda of the compiler, who felt entitled to emphasize certain aspects and, at the very least, to edit the narrative style.[86] Most intentional shaping of a *khabar* can be assumed to be directed toward its main message. Such is the success or failure of a particular poet, the positive or negative reaction of his poem's addressee, or the criticism directed at the poet and his defense. A classic example of a partisan compilation would be al-Ṣūlī's (d. c. 946) *Life and Times of Abū Tammām* (*Akhbār Abī Tammām*), the earliest comprehensive collection of *akhbār* on this controversial pioneer of the modern style of poetry that had sprung up in the Abbasid period. Al-Ṣūlī devotes his longest chapter to illustrating the poet's positive reception by dignitaries of his time, countering any criticism with profuse commentary. Toward the book's end, he cites *akhbār* about former opponents who recanted their earlier attacks. His stance is clear throughout (after all, he was right, and Abū Tammām has since joined the canon of the greats). Nonetheless, this does not discredit al-Ṣūlī as an intimate expert of poetry, and notably his incidental remarks on what he counted as originality within the reuse of former poetic motifs. These accurately reflect a concern of his time, and he was the first to set down, in unsystematic fashion, the principles of evaluating poetic borrowing, long before these were laid down systematically by al-Khaṭīb al-Qazwīnī (d. 1338) as part of the "standard theory" of language.[87]

The situation is different with the circumstantial detail that is added in *akhbār* around the core event to give it the flavor of reality. The procedures and props of an action carry no message in and of themselves, other than filling out the story. Such narrative detail can be more reliably taken to reflect familiar and accepted circumstances. It is in this way that information from *akhbār* can be utilized. The single *khabar* does not suffice here; rather, a group of *akhbār* about a plot type, or a cluster of *akhbār* around a particular action or event, can contribute the facets for a larger depiction of contemporary social mores.

It is actually in the course of trying to understand the social functions of literature from *akhbār* that the idea to write the present book first arose. Literary *akhbār* focus on a number of events outlined above. However, the use of media, who wrote, who read, what material was written on, and who produced it are very rarely at the core of any account. They seem not to have been of interest to compilers of *akhbār*. Writing material is mostly referred to as "folio" (*waraq*, pl. *awrāq*), without specifying whether it was parchment, papyrus, or paper. Few types of events relating to media form the core of plots. A protagonist's amazing feats of memory is one rare example (see Chapter 1), but such cases are few. Letter writing serves in some *akhbār* as a connective element to link the steps of a plot, but letters, numerous and varied as they are, deserve their own treatment and are not a subject of this book.[88] Most often, however, the objects and actions related to media are props and minor details of larger events. The disadvantage is that these bits of information have to be carved from a multitude of *akhbār,* but the advantage is that because of their ancillary roles, they are least likely to be elaborated or tampered with.

However, in a number of *akhbār* persons or actions related to media cause controversy. Such *akhbār,* in their variations and with relevant background information, are assembled in this book to paint as complete a picture as possible. These *akhbār* are of the greatest interest, as they show where different or changing attitudes and sensibilities clashed, such as over the ways to use a book (Chapter 1), over the evidentiary role of notebooks (Chapter 2), or over access to scholarly books (Chapter 3).

While the narratives in these sources have doubtlessly been "improved," repeated similar instances of events and their circumstantial detail (the part least likely to be tinkered with) have in their sum a representative value. For example, the great urge a certain caliph or a certain secretary had to consult Abū ʿUbayd or al-Aṣmaʿī is shown by having them transported with the mules of the postal service (as in Chapter 1), and thus refers to existing logistics. The nature of early prose goes hand in hand with this in avoiding the overtly fantastic. Rather, all (even invented) accounts are presented as historical fact, and authors strive for verisimilitude with real events; a particular feature of early *akhbār* is precisely their realistic appearance.[89] This means that detail added by the compiler to an extant account would be designed to give a realistic gloss by referring to actual practices or familiar material objects. Such "realism" is a literary device of early Arabic prose, and what one should look for is not an elusive factuality but the historical plausibility of a narrative. In this, *akhbār* differ from popular literature that delved into the fantastic and cannot be adduced for such analysis. Contemporary scholars also held popular literature in low regard; in their view, books were supposed to serve useful functions, such as scholarship, literature, or commerce, and if entertainment was a side effect, it had to come with instruction.

Literary creations can thus be taken to depict events and circumstances as they were familiar and plausible to their contemporary redactors. More detailed stories draw out what many similar shorter ones attest to in brief, and both will be used to construct a comprehensive narrative and provide exemplary depictions by selecting such individuals whose activities the sources have preserved in greater detail. Based on this nature of the sources, I have chosen to trace in each chapter salient personages on whom clusters of *akhbār* in early compilations exist, and who best serve to illustrate attitudes that are also documented for numerous others in less detail. These rounded-out narratives about a few individuals yield a more multifaceted and comprehensive picture, but one which is representative for numerous similar instances. This procedure is preferable to aggregating a mosaic of small texts with a host of different names, which would make for choppy reading.

OVERVIEW OF CHAPTERS

This book is divided into four chapters, with the first three each focusing on a group of agents in the Abbasid book revolution, and the fourth discussing the usage of books and reigning concepts of the book.

Chapter 1 is devoted to scholars, illustrating attitudes to books ranging from resistance to endorsement, as evinced in particular in the linguistic sciences. Here in the new writing space of the book, layout played a role, as did the effect of the book in breaking down borders between disciplines, creating a wider readership. Examples discussed juxtapose an oral performer and a book-writing scholar, depict a fight between an author and profiteering stationers, and describe the career of an independent book author who achieved recognition as a writer of reference works on sundry subjects, rather than as a specialist in one discipline.

Chapter 2 treats poets' relationship to the book, for instance in accessing their predecessors' work in the form of edited collected works, composing their own verse in writing, and writing books about their art and profession, propagating a certain concept of poetry. This coincided with the rise of an abstract and sophisticated poetic style, spawning a debate about its aesthetics. The availability of poetry in written form made rampant the reuse of motifs as well as the quest to detect reuse, and the phenomenon of plagiarism (or borrowing) became a theme in literary gatherings and the emerging field of poetics, for which cases of poetic composition, recitation, and reception in salons hosted by caliphs or high dignitaries provide abundant records.

Examples discussed include a case of alleged plagiarism between two poets in which notebooks are adduced as evidence. This is placed in the context of the types of books written by both poets: databases for reuse and normative poetics.

Chapter 3 is devoted to stationers, in an attempt to form an impression of these little recorded makers of books. Scarcely figuring in literary accounts, they were also on the fringes of the population biographical dictionaries would include. Yet, the sheer number of stationers' (often minimal) biographical entries yields collective evidence, as does their presence in the book markets in Near Eastern cities, which became venues for these cities' elite and upper middle classes. Some of them, however, were also either students or employees of scholars and received biographical entries on that basis. The massive number of these (however brief) snippets about stationers yields quantitative evidence. A typology of stationers is proposed based on biographical entries. Here contentious issues arise around intellectual property, fraudulent access to books, or commercial promotion frowned on by scholars, and these entries are matched with analogous cases from literary accounts. Examples analyzed in detail include a scribe's orchestration of the reproduction of a scholar's entire works (without permission), a stationer's demonstration of professional pride, and the stir caused by an anonymous stationer recommending a book. The case of a book transmitter illustrates this new career option for persons who possessed sole copies of books—and shows, too, that the mere existence of a book was no guarantee of its dissemination. Conversely, the withholding of a book from written circulation owed less to reservations about the medium than to an intention to maximize one's own profit and prestige from it.

Chapter 4 turns to owners and readers of books. Members of the elite spent considerable funds and effort (often including the services of a librarian or book agent) to assemble vast and comprehensive personal libraries. Yet, book possession could constitute a risk for individuals who fell foul of the authorities, and whose secrets, beliefs, and attitudes could be investigated by requisitioning their books. This last chapter reveals that the Abbasid book revolution not only brought advantages but simultaneously created new opportunities for abuse and hazards for one's life. And despite the proliferation of books in their diverse types, certain ideas about what a book should be still prevailed. Examples discussed include library owners concerned about the completeness of their libraries and other individuals investigated for the books they owned. Finally, the chapter examines the case of a book that failed to meet the contemporary standards of this medium.

In sum, the volume and variety of book production supported the flourishing of an Arabic language-based culture, which was characterized by a crossover between different scholarly disciplines, a blurring of boundaries between experts and amateurs, a prestige of knowledge that made using and dealing in books lucrative, and an audience that expanded beyond the educated elite to form a new urban reading class.

CHAPTER ONE

SCHOLARS

A clash over the book as a new medium occurred between two major philologists at the end of the eighth century, al-Aṣmaʿī and Abū ʿUbayda.[1] Together with Abū Zayd al-Anṣārī (d. 830) they formed the triumvirate (*al-thalāth*) of the Basran school of grammarians. The rocky relationship of the first two, recounted in this chapter, encapsulates phenomena that recurred throughout their generation.

DRAMATIS PERSONAE

ʿAbdalmalik b. Qurayb, known as al-Aṣmaʿī (d. 828), commanded several talents that made him an ideal performer of his knowledge.[2] He expressed himself in flawless *ʿarabiyya*. This was no one's native language, but rather the literary tongue of pre-Islamic times (sixth century C.E.), newly codified by scholars of his kind. To speak it required learning and presence of mind. Even scholars occasionally slipped up, and the grammarian al-Farrāʾ describes it as an acquired skill: "For Bedouins inflection is natural, but for settled people erring [in inflection] is natural. When I learn [something by heart], I do not err, but when I then speak naturally again, I err."[3] With "inflection" he referred to the fact that the colloquials spoken in the Arab cities at his time differed from the *ʿarabiyya* most noticeably in lacking the grammatical endings of words. Inflection was referred to as *iʿrāb* (literally "making [something] Arabic"), and it had been protected and preserved in the classical poetry by its quantitative meter.[4] These case and mood endings were not written in the Arabic script and had to be added by the speaker. Therefore, their correct realization formed the initial subject of most early Arabic grammars: "The first thing that became deficient in the speech of the Arabs and required study was inflection, because error [*laḥn*] appeared in the speech of converts and arabized people from the time of the Prophet."[5]

Al-Aṣmaʿī was gifted with a prodigious memory. Good memory was not uncommon, and people's minds were well trained, but even in his time, al-Aṣmaʿī's abilities stood out. One could learn to recall things by memory simply by listening, as did al-Farrāʾ, who rather than writing things down had his teachers repeat them, as his classmates observed. He would later dictate his books, without notes, instead of writing them.[6] But al-Aṣmaʿī's retention must have been near-photographic and astounded even his contemporaries, and it applied to any kind of text, even administrative documents. Once in a court session that included the presiding secretary's answering to submitted petitions, al-Aṣmaʿī was provoked to prove his skill. He proceeded to recite the texts of the petitions and the verdicts upon them one by one (they were nearly fifty) in their original order, which even the treasurer, who had been handed them for follow-up, had forgotten.[7] Nearly finished, al-Aṣmaʿī stopped only because someone warned him that he was tempting fate.[8]

Al-Aṣmaʿī used his gift to memorize classical poetry. What we now term "classical" meant either pre-Islamic or early Islamic verse composed until the end of the Umayyad period in 750, which constituted the raw data for the disciplines of grammar, lexicography, genealogy, and history. There are quibbles about which exact poet was considered the last worthy to supply linguistic proof in the form of verses (*shawāhid,* literally "witnesses"). The poetry of al-Aṣmaʿī's own Abbasid era was no longer considered linguistically pure enough for this purpose. He in turn devoted particular attention to the thorny and lexically intricate *rajaz* poetry, a half-verse type composed in the *rajaz* meter, and claimed to know by heart 16,000 poems, some of which ran between 100 and 200 verses.[9]

His feats of recitation made his colleagues despair. A younger philologist from the rival Kufan school, Ibn al-Aʿrābī (d. 839 or 844), reports: "I once witnessed al-Aṣmaʿī reciting circa 200 verses, not a single one of them we knew."[10] The legendary Kufan transmitter Khalaf al-Aḥmar (d. 796) lost a competition with al-Aṣmaʿī and conceded: "Only a madman confronts you in lexicon."[11] Even those native doyens of poetry, the Bedouins, marveled at this "city-dwelling expert of Arabs' speech."[12] He once eavesdropped on a Bedouin poetess mourning over the tomb of her sweetheart, and he recited the entire lamentation back to her, upon which she asked him: "Are you perhaps al-Asmaʿī, whose news has reached us?"[13]

He excelled not only in the extent but also in the quickness of his memory. On any given subject, he cited on demand verses and accounts, even placing them in historical context. Such appositeness was an asset in the literary gatherings that caliphs and viziers hosted, where typically verses were requested on any theme of the ongoing conversation, or on the setting's context, such as the cold weather or a distant fire in the night. The host would open the floor with the question "Has anyone composed poetry about this?" and those present were expected to respond. Another way to solicit verses was by giving a model and inquiring about earlier or different renditions of the motif it contained. One such case is a session of the Barmakid vizier Jaʿfar b. Yaḥyā (d. 803), in which someone cited a couplet on a lover's desire to delay the sunset to hold off the departure of his beloved:

> Is it not amazing that our neighbors
> readied tears [*ghurūb*] for the time of sunset [*ghurūb*]?
>
> If I had power over the sun
> I would forbid the sun to set [var.: the sun would take long to set].[14]

Al-Aṣmaʿī was jokingly invited to give precedents. Taken aback for a moment, he composed one himself and then relayed formulations of the motif spanning contributions from the great sixth-century poet al-Nābigha al-Dhubyānī to a panegyrist of the third Abbasid caliph al-Mahdī (r. 775–785). The host, a famous patron of the arts who had seen no small number of brilliant men in his time, commented, "Could you have dreamt what happened? Did you think something like al-Aṣmaʿī existed in the world?" and the narrator added: "One of the wonders of the world."[15]

Al-Aṣmaʿī's oral knowledge was broad, as one infers from the literary account of his introductory meeting with Caliph al-Rashīd (r. 786–809), who tested him for an entire night across the whole spectrum of classical literature, for which the caliph used notes: rhymed prose (*saj*ʿ), *rajaz* poetry, *qarīḍ* poetry (in two hemistichs separated by caesura), proverbial sayings (*amthāl*), and anecdotes (*nawādir*) that gave rise to verses. Just before sunrise al-Aṣmaʿī began to recite a long poetic description of camels, and the attending vizier asked him to shorten it. This excursus into desert animal depictions offered little excitement for the Persian statesman, but the caliph made him listen as a literary replay of the Arabic conquest of Persia with the aid of camels.[16] On another occasion, however, al-Aṣmaʿī's unfathomable depth of memory fatigued even the caliph, and at a recitation of verses showing the different plurals of the word *mother*, he moaned, "Enough! Enough!"[17]

These skills of diction, memory, and appositeness appeared in a man who was of Arab descent (he belonged to the East Arabian tribe of ʿAbd Qays) and had impeccable morals. Al-Aṣmaʿī carefully avoided bringing his lexicographic expertise to bear on Qurʾān and Ḥadīth, the respective domains of exegetes and traditionists.[18] He was also attuned to courtly etiquette. In a much-repeated anecdote, according to which he and Abū ʿUbayda were invited to a meal by the vizier al-Faḍl b. al-Rabīʿ (d. 824), al-Aṣmaʿī thankfully praised modest pickles, while Abū ʿUbayda cried that pickles were precisely what made him flee from Basra to Baghdad.[19]

Al-Aṣmaʿī proved a quick study in court manners. Once asked at a public audience to explain an absence, he used an unusual turn of phrase that dumbfounded the caliph. After everyone had left, al-Rashīd took him aside: "You should not speak to me before people except with what I understand, but when I am alone, then teach me. It is unseemly for a ruler not be knowledgeable. Either I remain silent, and people know that I do not understand when I have not responded, or I respond wrongly, and those around me know that I did not understand what you said." Al-Aṣmaʿī appreciated the lesson: "He taught me more than I taught him," he said, and he promptly put this learning into practice.[20] At the dramatic event of the caliphate in 803, when al-Rashīd liberated himself overnight from the tutelage of his Barmakid advisors, he summoned al-Aṣmaʿī from his bed to look at the severed head (or, in a shorter variant, the corpse) of the caliph's erstwhile favorite Jaʿfar b. Yaḥyā. He gave no instructions but recited three verses on the inescapability of death (in the variant he remains silent). Al-Aṣmaʿī understood that he was to interpret the Barmakids' fall as caused by their own hubris and composed his ode: "O deceived one, will you take a lesson from the House of Barmak? / Keeping accounts on tablets deceived them over the decree of

God."[21] The later grammarian Thaʿlab (d. 904) probably thought of this political acumen when he said, "Al-Aṣmaʿī came to Baghdad and stayed there for a while, and on the day he left the city he was many times more learned than when he arrived."[22]

Despite all his success, al-Aṣmaʿī was wary of competition and did not stop short of faking knowledge to cut out competitors. No display of erudition, it seems, made him feel safe. Indeed, the type of scholar-performer that he tried to perfect was no longer the only model. His stylization in the sources likewise makes him something of a throwback in a world that could not resist the influx of books. In his dealings with al-Abbās b. al-Aḥnaf (d. 804 or after 808), whose sunset couplet was mentioned above, al-Aṣmaʿī once misused his scholarly authority and jeopardized the poet's reward. Ibn al-Aḥnaf claimed to have invented the motif of two lovers melting into each other in a kiss, and al-Aṣmaʿī forged on the spot a precedent.[23] With the musician Isḥāq al-Mawṣilī (d. 849–850), who studied with him, al-Aṣmaʿī behaved in a disingenuous and intellectually stingy manner. He taught him part of a poem, withholding many verses, and when it pleased at court, he publicly embarrassed al-Mawṣilī by reciting the long sequel that the musician had (apparently on good authority) denied existed.[24] The event backfired, and the student's revenge would be consequential: he suggested inviting to court al-Aṣmaʿī's rival Abū ʿUbayda, whom the musician vaunted as a scholar who had broader knowledge and was more generous with it.

Abū ʿUbayda Maʿmar b. al-Muthannā (d. 822–828) was in many ways the opposite of al-Aṣmaʿī. He was no lesser scholar, and some, such as Abū Naṣr al-Bāhilī (d. 846), would argue that he was the better scholar: "When seekers of knowledge went to the gathering of al-Aṣmaʿī, they bought dung in a pearl market, and when they went to Abū ʿUbayda they bought pearls in a dung market." The meaning was clear: "Al-Aṣmaʿī shone in reciting and embellishing lousy accounts and poetry to make the ugly become beautiful, but there was little benefit in it. Abū ʿUbayda had bad exposition, but the benefit from his ideas was great and his scholarship boundless."[25]

Abū ʿUbayda was indeed a bad oral performer.[26] Partly of non-Arab origin (he admitted to a Jewish father), he erred in meter when reciting poetry and made mistakes when he read the Qurʾān off the page. He could not produce eloquent *ʿarabiyya* on the spot, but did not care, for his concern was the written form of scholarship. Abū ʿUbayda was aware of his audience, and perfect grammar was a function of the addressee. In a letter of recommendation for a student to a potential employer, he instructed the writer to insert some errors (*laḥn*) in the inflection, "for [people's knowledge of] syntax is sparse."[27]

This less-than-perfect oral performance stood in contrast to the encyclopedic breadth of his knowledge. Besides poetry and lexicography, he mastered accounts of the ancient Arabs and genealogy. He claimed, "No two heroes met in the *Jāhiliyya* or Islam without my knowing."[28] This vast knowledge had prose as its dominant style. He collected in addition to poetry the prose accounts of Arab history and set these down in book form. His student Abū Ḥātim al-Sijistānī (d. c. 869) compares the two men: "Abū ʿUbayda was a greater scholar than al-Aṣmaʿī, he had more accounts and more books, while al-Aṣmaʿī had a greater presence of mind, was better liked by people, and not accused of anything in his religion. Poetry belonged to al-Aṣmaʿī, and accounts to Abū ʿUbayda."[29] Ibn al-Aʿrābī put it succinctly: "The *dīwān* of the Arabs was in his [i.e., Abū ʿUbayda's] house," while his colleagues had mere "pickings."[30] *Dīwān,* a Persian loan word meaning both "office" and "payroll, register," was adopted into Arabic in both meanings, and it acquired a third—namely, the collected works of a poet or tribe. Metaphorically the word appears in the famous saying "Poetry is the *dīwān* of the Arabs," implying that the written registers of historical data were to the Sasanians what poetry was for the ancient Arabs.[31] Applied to Abū ʿUbayda, this meant that he mastered the whole of Arab history before Islam.

Abū ʿUbayda demonstrated his breadth of knowledge by laying it down in a number of books. Some he imparted in the form of notes, such as his proverbs, of which it is said he shared 14,000 items, but "He had many books about the Arabs' battles and wars, such as *Fatal Fights of Heroes* [*Maqātil al-fursān*] and [other] well-known books about the *ayyām*."[32]

To make something the subject of a book was not necessarily Abū ʿUbayda's idea. His most controversial work resulted from a conversation in the palace. Perhaps to trip him up, a secretary asked him a question about the use of the word *satans* in a divine threat uttered in the Qurʾān and wondered how one can threaten with something unknown. Abū ʿUbayda responded, "God spoke to the Arabs according to their language," availing himself of the concepts inherent in it.[33] In the same way, he explained, the pre-Islamic poet Imruʾulqays (d. c. 550 C.E.) had used ghouls as a threatening image in one of his verses, without anyone ever having seen such creatures. Abū ʿUbayda treated scripture as a specimen of the Arabic language, no different from the pagan poetry, and he felt entitled to understand the Qur'ān through the *ʿarabiyya*. As his explanation pleased both the secretary and the hosting vizier, Abū ʿUbayda conceived the project of assembling explanations of such problematic passages into a book. "From that day on I decided to devise [*iʿtaqadtu an aṣnaʿa*] a book about the Qur'ān for this kind [of question] and similar cases, and when I returned to Basra I produced [*ʿamiltu*] my book that I called *Explanatory Re-writing of the Qur'ān* [*Majāz al-Qur'ān*]."[34] Many early books were thus inspired or commissioned by the court, and the subjects ranged from grammar to history and religious tradition.[35] That this work offended the sensibilities of exegetes was another matter.

Books were popular at the court before they would become a staple on the teaching circuit or among the educated lay public in the latter half of the ninth century. For courtiers, the book served as a convenient reference tool for the kinds of knowledge that they had no time to delve into, but wished to have at their fingertips. This relieved them of having to summon and consult a specialist, which only high officials could afford, and even they might find it time-consuming and cumbersome and prefer a book instead.

Abū ʿUbayda, however, was prolific. The tenth-century *Catalogue* of Ibn al-Nadīm lists 109 titles. The polymath Yāqūt al-Rūmī al-Ḥamawī (d. 1229) lists eighty-two titles in his thirteenth-century *Biographical Dictionary of Authors,* but estimates their total number at 200.[36] The following is but a selection of Abū ʿUbayda's book titles to show the range of his subjects.

Some covered linguistic issues of the Islamic Scripture and the Prophetic tradition (surviving and edited works are marked by an asterisk):

**Explanatory Re-writing of the Qur'ān*[37]
Rare Vocabulary of the Qur'ān
Explication [*Maʿānī*] *of the Qur'ān*
Rare Vocabulary of Ḥadīth

Others treated pre-Islamic and Islamic history:

The Brocade [on battles, or *ayyām,* of the Arabs]
The Fatal Fights of Heroes
**Battles of the Arabs*[38]
Literary Accounts [*Akhbār*] *of the Tribe ʿAbd Qays*
[*The Tribes of*] *Aws and Khazraj*
Deeds of [*the Tribe*] *of Ghaṭafān*

The Battle of Marj Rāhiṭ
Arab Brigands[39]
Conquests of Armenia
The Story of the Kaaba
Basra
Khurasan
Accounts of [the Umayyad governor] al-Ḥajjāj
Judges of Basra
The Vices of [the Tribe of] Bāhila (a polemic treatise against Arabs)

Poetry and proverbial lore were the subjects of:

Poetry and Poets
**Flytings of Jarīr and al-Farazdaq*[40]
The Proverbs

Grammatical works treated issues of morphology, including dialectal forms and commonly made mistakes:

Verbal Nouns
Plural and Feminine Gender
The Faʿala and Afʿala Verbal Stems
Linguistic Errors of the Arabs
Dialectal forms

Lexical works comprised rare words and words from a specific semantic subfield, such as, mankind, flora, fauna, or objects of Arab Bedouin material culture:

Words That Signify a Term and Its Opposite [Aḍdād]
Rare Words (Nawādir)
The Human Body
*[*Words for*] *the Horse*[41]
Camel; The Falcon; The Dove; Snakes . . .
The Sword; The Bucket . . . [42]

To place this written output into context, Abū ʿUbayda was not the only prolific author of his time. Many of his titles (which often simply denoted the book's topic) were also used by other authors for their books, and only a few, like *The Brocade,* received an ornamental title. A majority of his books were probably small fascicles, as they dealt with narrowly defined lexical, grammatical, and historical issues. Since most of Abū ʿUbayda's writings are lost, with the exception of *Explanatory Re-writing,* [*Words for*] *the Horse,* and *Flytings,* we can say little about their original shape; that is, which of these were actual redacted books, and which were simple transcriptions of collected data without an overall concept, which would make their way into the books of later generations of scholars, such as Abū ʿUbayd (d. 838).[43] Neither did the author of the *Catalogue* see these in person or list folio numbers for any of them, as he did with later works. However, enough of Abū ʿUbayda's material survived in attributed citations in subsequent, redacted books by later authors to give a sense of his enormous productivity.

THE INCIDENT OF THE HORSE

The memory of al-Aṣmaʿī and the book writing of Abū ʿUbayda clashed in one incident at the court of al-Rashīd, which must have taken place around 804, when Abū ʿUbayda was summoned to the city by the new vizier al-Faḍl b. al-Rabīʿ. The event is recorded in two variants, both contained in the *History of Baghdad* by al-Khaṭīb al-Baghdādī (d. 1071), where they appear in each man's vita, and they are reproduced here in their entirety. In the vita of Abū ʿUbayda, the grammarian al-Māzinī (d. 863) relays Abū ʿUbaya's telling of the event as follows:

> I was ushered into the presence of al-Rashīd who said to me: "I have heard you have a beautiful book on how horses are described, I want to hear it from you." Al-Aṣmaʿī said: "What will you do with books? A horse shall be brought and we place our hands on each of its limbs, name them, and mention what [poetry] exists on it." Al-Rashīd said: "Servant, a horse!" A horse was brought. Al-Aṣmaʿī rose, began to place his hand on it limb after limb and to say: "This is such and such, and a poet said such and such about it," until he had finished. Al-Rashīd said to me: "What do you say about his words?" I said: "He was right in some [places] and erred in others. Whatever he was right in he learnt from me [*minnī taʿallama*], and what he erred in is something he got I know not where."[44]

In a later citation of this account, the compiler Yāqūt followed it up with another (that had appeared elsewhere in the earlier sources on Abū ʿUbaya's vita) about al-Aṣmaʿī's fear of his rival: "When al-Aṣmaʿī wanted to enter the mosque he used to say: 'Make sure that that one [meaning Abū ʿUbayda] is not there,' out of fear of his tongue."[45] By placing both reports contiguously, the compiler implicitly made al-Aṣmaʿī the loser in the encounter.

In this version, Abū ʿUbayda carried the day. Al-Aṣmaʿī dismissed the book per se as a detour and distraction from tangible reality. Al-Aṣmaʿī was a known expert in verses about the fauna and flora depicted in ancient Arabic verse. In his introductory meeting with the caliph he had amply displayed this, and the caliph had relished his long recitations of camel and onager descriptions. But on this occasion the scholar misread the caliph's curiosity, which was not merely for the subject matter of horses. Instead, the caliph's question aimed at how this material was presented in "a beautiful book."

Word lists of specific animals, objects, or polysemous words, explaining their meanings and documenting the words' use with verses, were a common early book form and forerunner of the later comprehensive thesaurus (see fig. 4).

For lexica, different ordering principles had already been invented: phonetic order by the last letter, alphabetical order by first or last letter, or logical sequence of the theme (e.g., from head to toe). In the lexical monographs, the semantic order predominated, following the logic of its subject.[46] Al-Aṣmaʿī's surviving monograph on the human body, for instance, lists one group of words in chronological sequence from birth to death, and another in the physical order from head to toe. The anatomy of the horse from ear to hoof (as it appears in the next version of the story) allowed searching for specific terms for the animal's limbs without reading (or listening to) the entire book. It was typical for the time that the caliph still wished to "hear the book" read to him.

In addition to chapter sequence, Arabic books of the third quarter of the ninth century had the advantage of a legible layout. Different from the *scriptio continua* of European medieval codices, well-spaced words and set-off paragraphs made passages easy to find and saved the reader having to scan the book from beginning to end. In the *Transmitted Polysemous Words* (fig. 4), for instance, lemmata are marked with indents at the beginnings and paragraph signs at the end. Paragraph signs (dotted circles) or word-long blanks in the middle of the line separate the different meanings of a term within one lemma, and proof verses are recognizable by being placed on a separate line and spaced as two hemistichs with a caesura (subsequent verses thus show a graphically prominent end rhyme, as in figs. 3a and 3b). The early book already presented a "user-friendly" face that enabled the reader to search for specific information.

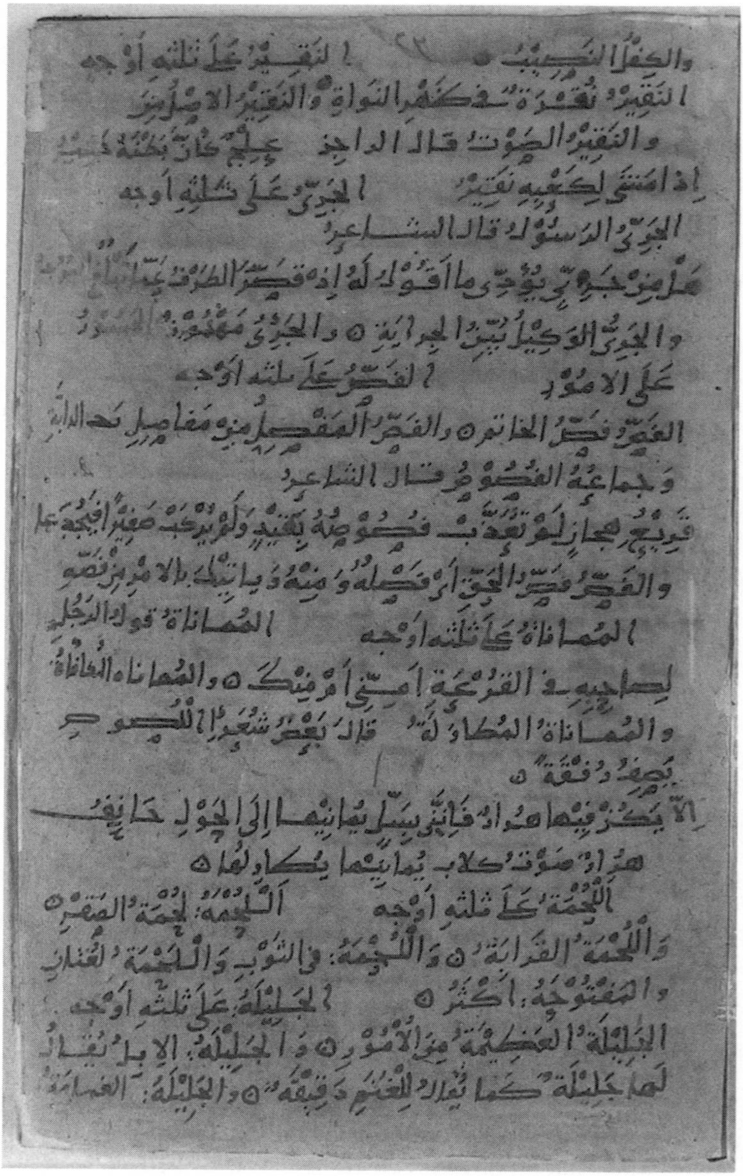

FIG. 4. Parchment codex of Abū l-ʿAmaythal, *Transmitted Homonymous Polysemous Words* (*al-Maʾthūr fīmā ttafaqa lafẓuhū wa-khtalafa maʿnāhu*), dated 280/893, a short collection of words that have multiple meanings. The page contains seven lemmata, each with three to seven meanings (*awjuh*),

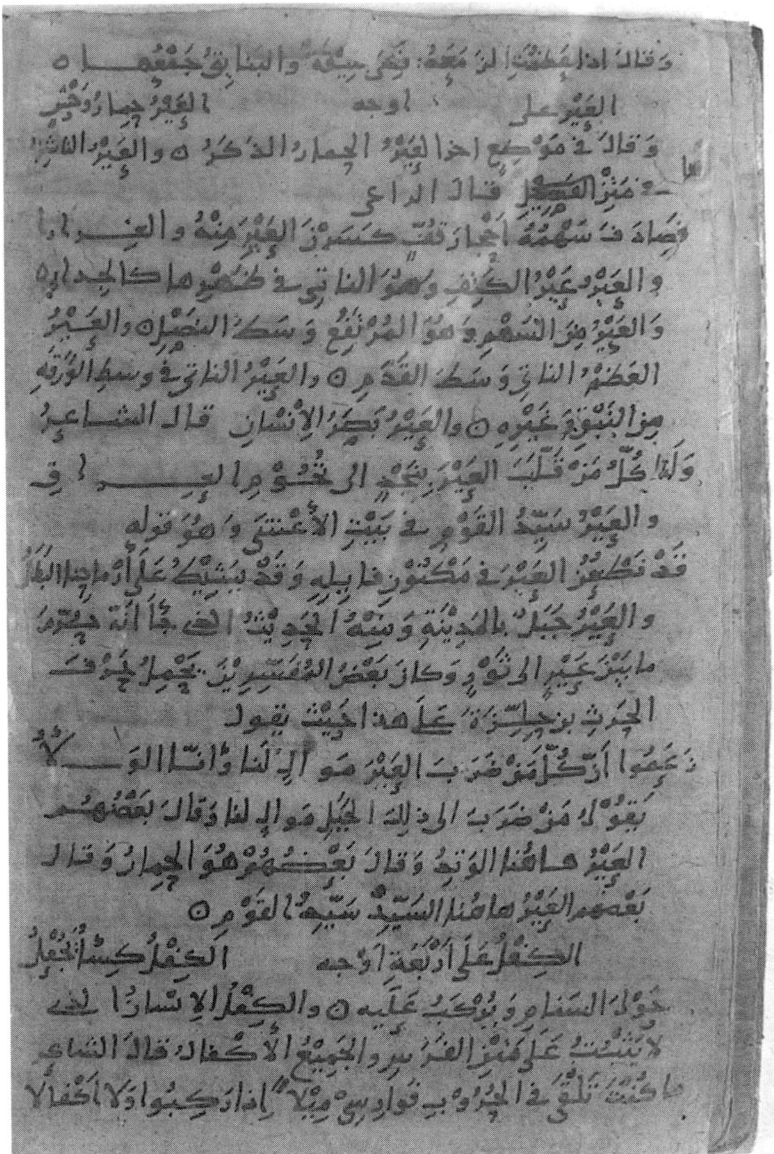

occasionally indicating a different vocalization, forms of the plural of each, explanations by synonym and paraphrase, and sometimes a verse or *ḥadīth* in which a particular meaning is attested; difficult words in example verses are also explained. (Veliyeddin Efendi 3139, fols. 21 verso and 22 recto, Beyazit State Library, Istanbul.)

One of the earliest self-described "reference works" was the *Rhyme Dictionary* by al-Bandanījī (d. 897), who arranged rare words alphabetically by last letter, adjusted to the mono-rhyming Arabic poetry.[47] In his prefatory instructions he explained the reason for this order as follows:

> If he [i.e., the author] would assemble all these words without consistent order, and if then an unknown word appeared whose meaning someone [*al-rajul*] needs to learn from our book, it would be difficult for him to retrieve it, because the lexicon is vast and voluminous. Therefore he composed the book in a coherent and systematic way [*taʾlīfan mutanāsiqan mutatābiʿan*], to make it easy for the reader who consults it for something he needs to know [*li-yashula ʿalā l-nāẓiri fīmā yaḥtāju ilā maʿrifatihī*].[48]

The addressed user was expected to consult the book for purposes of information, as implied by the technical term *naẓara fī,* which means "to study" (literally "to look into something"). For the semantic order, the earliest preserved example is the *Classified Rare Words* (*al-Gharīb al-muṣannaf*) by Abū ʿUbayd, and this order was the one expected by the caliph, as shown in the next version of the story. This appears in the vita of al-Aṣmaʿī in the *Taʾrīkh Baghdād.* The courtier and man of letters Abū l-ʿAynāʾ (d. 896) relates al-Aṣmaʿī's telling of the event:

> I and Abū ʿUbayda entered into the presence of al-Faḍl b. al-Rabīʿ, and he said: "O Aṣmaʿī, how many [volumes] is your book on horses?" I said: "One volume [*jild*]." He asked Abū ʿUbayda about this, and he said: "Fifty volumes." So he ordered that both books be brought, then he ordered a horse to be brought and said to Abū ʿUbayda: "Read your book word by word [*ḥarfan bi-ḥarfin*] and put your hand on [the horse] place after place." Abū ʿUbayda said: "I am not a veterinarian [*laysa ana bayṭār, sic*], this is something I heard and took from the Arabs and put it in writing [*allaftuhū*]." The vizier said to me: "O Aṣmaʿī, rise and put your hand on place after place of the horse." I rose, bared my forearms and legs, then jumped up to reach the ears of the horse, then I put my hand on its forelock and proceeded to touch item after item of it and say: "The word for this is so-and-so," and I recited [poetry] about it, until I reached its hoof. He ordered me to receive the horse, and when I wanted to anger Abū ʿUbayda, I visited him riding it.[49]

Al-Aṣmaʿī's argument is both erroneous and preposterous. He made himself the advocate of a reality that his book-writing rival had supposedly lost.

But his own material, though presented orally, was no closer to the actual animal it treated. It was likewise vocabulary about horses taken from odes that idealized them and their riders. Neither was he interested in the animal for its own sake, its biology, way of living, domestication, and so forth. For him, as for Abū ʿUbayda, the depiction of the horse was part of the *ʿarabiyya* and a topos of poetry. Al-Aṣmaʿī utilized the animal (in his physical demonstration) as a mere prop to "attach," by touching it limb by limb, the various quotations to their relevant parts. Both he and Abū ʿUbayda had collected extant early poetry about the subject. But al-Aṣmaʿī stole the show from his bookish colleague by performing his repertoire live and having just enough knowledge of the realia to strike a convincing pose. What he produced was as mediated (through the artistic eyes of the poets he quoted) as Abū ʿUbayda's written descriptions.[50]

The salient changes in the second version are that both scholars have books (even if Abū ʿUbayda's was more voluminous), and that Abū ʿUbayda freely admitted his lack of concern with the horse's anatomy, while al-Aṣmaʿī connects book knowledge to realia. Here he wins the day, and the story has him triumph symbolically by receiving the living animal as a prize for his live performance. Which of the two versions is closer to the truth (if the meeting took place at all, as the host varies between a caliph and his vizier) is impossible to tell. Both appear in the same chronicle and the participants may even have told the different versions of the story themselves. What matters is the controversy, the competition between the display of knowledge by voice and in the form of a book. Al-Aṣmaʿī used the argument that knowledge must remain alive and connected to its object, while Abū ʿUbayda declared his project to be the gathering of information from previous scholars and linguistically knowledgeable Bedouins in written form. His chosen medium was to prevail (and al-Aṣmaʿī profited from it too, as we will see).

The fortune of history has preserved both horse monographs, and their different makeups validate the opposing positions sketched in the anecdote. This can be ascertained, however, only for the structure and content of the text, and not the book's graphic layout, because the edited versions are based on later manuscript copies. Both works come divided into chapters (though the separation of the chapter beginnings for use as headings in Abū ʿUbayda's book is the editor's doing). All of al-Aṣmaʿī's chapters also figure in Abū ʿUbayda's book, such as those on horses' colors and markings and the names of famous steeds. Some chapters of al-Aṣmaʿī, such as those on the horse's body (*khalq*) are further divided by Abū ʿUbayda into breeding behavior, the anatomy of the front half of the animal from ear to front hoof, and the back half from rump to rear hoof. Instead of al-Aṣmaʿī's three chapters on the horse's merits, defects, and paces, Abū ʿUbayda subdivides the merits into performance and pedigree, and the defects into inborn and acquired. Then he discusses all four conditions as manifested in the horse's stance, trot, and gallop, resulting in twelve chapters. Other chapters of Abū ʿUbayda's book that are completely absent in al-Aṣmaʿī's treat the horse's behavior: fieriness, neighing, and differences between the genders. The same goes for cultural aspects, including the Arabs' and the Prophet's esteem for the horse, commands used for it, and natural versus trained racehorses. Here his deeper interest in Arab tribal history and folklore comes to the fore, as he was a recognized authority on the subject. Furthermore, Abū ʿUbayda structured some chapters internally. In anatomy, he grouped the vocabulary into body regions, such as the head, neck, back, and so forth, beginning with a preestablished list of terms, which he explained in detail thereafter—a procedure termed in later rhetoric "wrapping and spreading" (*laff wa-nashr*) or "summary and explication" (*ijmāl wa-tafsīr*). There are two long, remarkable chapters by Abū ʿUbayda, "What Arabs Love in Horses" and "What Poets Say about Horses," replete with quotations of twenty-some verses' length, which make the book a veritable compendium of early Arab horse poetry. Let us remember that al-Aṣmaʿī was the "devil of poetry," famed for his sheer interminable memory of poetry on any subject.[51] Abū ʿUbayda, by contrast, deployed his exhaustive knowledge in the written form. Lastly, two paratexts have him speak in the first person as the book's author. In one, he contrasts the ideal horse as a virtual sum of merits that never came together in any real horse, and in another passage, he summarizes the attributes of the perfect horse in a two-page, systematic list, a veritable synopsis of his book.

Though al-Aṣmaʿī's name appears repeatedly in his book, it is only in the third person ("al-Aṣmaʿī said"), which shows the text to be a redaction of a student who acknowledged al-Aṣmaʿī as a source of oral information that was later compiled. The student produced the received text from dictation, and subsequent dictations resulted in different variants of the same book.[52] The preserved edited version carefully lists two paths of transmission, one through al-Aṣmaʿī's nephew and Abū ʿAbdallāh al-Yazīdī (d. 922), the other through his student al-Sijistānī and Ibn Durayd (d. 933).

Al-Aṣmaʿī had been able to shine in an ad hoc performance. One can imagine him telling one of those anecdotes placed at the end of his book: at a horse race organized by the Kufan governor ʿAbdarraḥmān b. Umm al-Ḥakam (alive seventh century), a Bedouin of the tribe of Asad called Ibn Uqayṣir predicted the winner out of a thousand steeds. When asked how he could do so, he simply described the steed's motions in rhymed prose, "I saw her walk and she moved her shoulders, then trot and she raced, then gallop and she swept [like the wind]." She won as foretold.[53] But to the eye of the reader, Abū ʿUbayda was the one who realized the potential of the book medium. His voice is that of a conscious book author, and his reasoned and sophisticated presentation was superior to al-Aṣmaʿī's secondary transcript, once it no longer came with the impersonation by the "teller of jokes" (*ṣāḥib mulaḥ*).[54] In form, al-Aṣmaʿī's book fell behind the planned order of his rival's, and in volume his less than 4,000 words paled next to the over 30,000 words of Abū ʿUbayda. This falls short of the dramatic one-versus-fifty-volume difference of the anecdote, but it confirms the general idea. To summarize, Abū ʿUbayda evinced a sophisticated holistic approach to the subject from biological to cultural aspects, and from the real to the ideal animal. He used proof materials in diverse ways, from chapters going completely without them to others consisting only of uncommented examples, and those included all of Prophetic traditions, historical accounts, and poetry. As an author, he organized his information, explicitly distinguished the real from the ideal, and inserted for the convenience of his reader a digest of the book.

In the described incident, al-Aṣmaʿī and Abū ʿUbayda still clashed over the merits of the Arabic manuscript book, and although the winner of the day remains undetermined, history would soon prove Abū ʿUbayda right.

A BOOK AUTHOR

The early Arabic book functioned on different levels. Within the regular teaching circuit, which was conducted in a circle (*ḥalqa*) or session in a mosque or outside a teacher's house, the change from dictation (*imlāʾ*) to reading (or having a student read) aloud from a book did not essentially alter the procedure. But the oral performance of the *ʿarabiyya* was a taxing business, which was admitted even by the grammarian al-Farrāʾ, who dictated entire books from memory, and it sometimes also went beyond the comprehension of the addressee, as some caliphs conceded (who had little to lose by doing so).[55] To produce and receive scholarship in written form relieved it from the burden of immediacy. More fundamentally, the existence of the book gave access to different audiences beyond the control of the author. This had advantages, such as the caliph hearing about and requesting Abū ʿUbayda's book. It further allowed an author to address different audiences or members of various disciplines, who would not frequent the same venue or who held different interests, as Abū ʿUbayda would do with his *Rare Vocabulary of Ḥadīth.* But the existence of a book could also harm its author, because foes who did not dare confront him face to face availed themselves of a copy. Al-Aṣmaʿī borrowed a copy of Abū ʿUbayda's *Explanatory Re-writing of the Qur'ān* (*Majāz al-Qur'ān*) from a student in order to pick out mistakes for criticism, and the scribe Ismāʿīl b. Ṣubayḥ al-Ḥarrānī (alive late eighth and early ninth century) had all the books of Abū ʿUbayda reproduced without his permission.[56]

If, in the preceding example, the book could be faulted for losing the connection with reality that the living scholar retained, precisely this disconnected status opened new avenues. This is the case with a new type of genre that bridged the boundary between two groups of scholars, philologists, and exegetes—namely, Abū ʿUbayda's *Explanatory Re-writing.*

Abū ʿUbayda was widely credited with committing to writing the battles (*ayyām*) of the ancient Arabs: "He was the first to set down in book form [*rasama kitāban*] [the names of] pre-Islamic and [early] Islamic munificent men, heroes, and so forth, and people called it *The Brocade* [*al-Dībāj*]."[57] Although he was not the first historian, the use of the term *rasama* "to outline, to conceive [a plan]" implies that he framed the subject in a fundamentally new way. Indeed, there were other early historians, but the grammarian Thaʿlab states: "Abū ʿUbayda is best in literary accounts of the time before Islam [*Jāhiliyya*], al-Madā'inī best in those of Islam."[58] Al-Wāqidī and al-Madā'inī focused indeed on the early Islamic phase of history, and Ibn al-Kalbī (d. 819) devoted himself to genealogy. The term *rasama* had been earlier applied to Abū l-Aswad al-Du'alī's (d. 688) first rough sketch of the rules for inflectional syntax, and *ʿamila* ("to produce") was the term Abū ʿUbayda used to describe his innovative composition of the *Explanatory Re-writing of the Qur'ān.*[59] The regular terms for writing books were *ṣannafa* ("to compile") and *allafa* ("to compose"), which until the time of the *Catalogue* still

meant two different things: the former stood for assembling and arranging preexisting material according to the author's vision, and the latter for a more integrative treatment, though hardly any text of this period dispenses with quotation. Some entries in the *Catalogue* separate one author's compilations (*taṣnīfāt*) from his compositions (*ta'līfāt*), as with the historian al-Madā'inī, or qualify one author as turning a predecessor's *taṣnīf* (or transmission, *riwāya*) into *ta'līf*.[60] Likewise, letters of a state scribe collected as models by a successor are distinguished in the *Catalogue* from such collections prepared by the letter writer himself (and nearly every early scribe had one to his name).[61] Abū ʿUbayda's codification of the *ayyām* was seen as a paradigm shift, the laying of a new foundation, or an act of *rasm*. The work is lost, but the material credited to him dwarfs that of any other source.[62]

With his *Explanatory Re-writing,* however, Abū ʿUbayda inaugurated a genre that raised eyebrows.[63] Many philologists were also Qur'ān scholars, but for Abū ʿUbayda this was not the case. He was a philologist who dared to discuss the Qur'ān, the domain of exegetes and their prerogative. His colleagues did not mince their words. Al-Farrā', precisely one such double expert (his *Explication of the Qur'ān* is discussed in the section after the next), declared that Abū ʿUbayda should be given twenty lashes, whereas Abū ʿUbayda's student Abū Ḥātim al-Sijistānī declared that he would prefer to be whipped himself rather than teach this book, because "it is a book that is not allowed for anyone to write, and until today, nothing was harder for me than to read it."[64] The request to do so came from a newly arrived student from Khurasan, who was unconcerned with scholarly sensitivities.[65] He kept pestering al-Sijistānī, who wavered, saying yea and nay, until he finally succumbed and read the book in class. Its very existence had become a factor that forced it on the resisting pedagogue. But since the author "erred and explained the Qur'ān in a manner one must not do," al-Sijistānī saw it as his duty to pinpoint places where Abū ʿUbayda had gone wrong, and he advised others to do likewise.[66]

The biographical sources do not cite the exact passages that met with disapproval from al-Sijistānī and a visitor to his class, the brother of the poet Ibn al-Muʿadhdhal (d. 854), and the text of the *Explanatory Re-writing* evinces a variety of strategies, such as word-for-word substitution and paraphrase of syntactically obscure or idiomatic expressions.[67] One criticism by al-Aṣmaʿī is exposed by his student as gratuitous nitpicking. The very same explanation (of *shakk,* "doubt," for Qur'ānic *rayb,* "uncertainty") al-Aṣmaʿī objected

to in Abū ʿUbayda's book he had apparently once used himself, as the student remembered, and the teacher was silenced.[68] The actual motives for the criticism may have been variously the protection of scholarly turf, pious sensibilities, wariness against subjectivity (*raʾy*) in exegesis, an unwillingness to treat God's word as regular *ʿarabiyya,* or a combination of all these. Confronted to divulge the authority for his exegesis—"From whom did you take this, Abū ʿUbayda? For it contradicts the exegesis of theologians [*fuqahāʾ*]"—Abū ʿUbayda countered, sharp-tongued, "It is the exegesis of the Arabs who piss on their heels. If you like it, take it, if you don't, leave it."[69] Ignoring the person-to-person teaching convention of Qurʾānic exegesis, Abū ʿUbayda innovated by using as a basis of explanation the *ʿarabiyya* as he had gathered it from his Bedouin informants. According to his logic, if God had used the speech of the Arabs, and the Arabs used idioms, then the Qurʾān contained these as well, and it was licit—or, rather, necessary—to resort to the *ʿarabiyya* if one wanted to understand the Qurʾān correctly.[70] In a more polemic fashion, he tricked the unsuspecting al-Aṣmaʿī into explaining the word *bread,* which also appeared in the Qurʾān. Caught out, the pious philologist defended himself: "This is something that was clear to me, so I said it; I did not explain [the Qurʾān] using my opinion [*raʾy*]," and Abū ʿUbayda gloatingly claimed the same defense for his own book: "All of which you blame us for is something that was clear to us; we did not explain it with our opinion."[71]

Being conceived as a book, not a lecture to be delivered before students, the text bypassed the scholarly control of exegetes and traditionists and addressed the Qurʾān in a neutral and, some thought, irreverent linguistic manner. This disengaging of the method from the conventions of transmission had advantages and drawbacks. In his biography of the Prophet, the historian Ibn Isḥāq had used poetry of doubtful authenticity, which was ill received by the philologists, who then still acted as poetic critics by default, and who could (mostly) tell authentic from forged poetry.[72] In Ibn Isḥāq's case, the weakness of the quoted verses remained a blemish on his work, for poetry had proof value for the names, places, and events it contained. Poetry, together with the Qurʾān, constituted the corpus from which classical Arabic was drawn by the philologists who systematized it and poured it into the mold of manuals of grammar. But it also supplied data on places, genealogy, and tribal wars, for which reason Abū ʿUbayda used it in his book on the subject (*al-Ayyām*). A verse served as a witness (*shāhid*) for a linguistic or

historic fact.[73] Ibn Isḥāq's uncritical selections were thus devoid of evidentiary power. In the case of the *Explanatory Re-writing*, whose popularity among the student generation legitimized it, the "misdemeanor" of treating the Qur'ān simply as a product of Arabic language was objective scholarship, and it triumphed by being included almost completely in the chapter on Qur'ān exegesis (*tafsīr*) of the classic tenth-century Ḥadīth compilation by al-Bukhārī (d. 870).[74]

INESCAPABLE, IMPERFECT BOOKS

Returning to the two archfoes, al-Aṣmaʿī cut a good figure, thanks to his exceptional memory and courtly savoir faire. In public he kept up the image of a scholar who relied on oral methods. To a student visiting from Khurasan who asked him which books he owned, he pointed to a tiny bundle in the corner of the room, which turned out to be the Qur'ān.[75] During a move of the caliph's retinue to the temporary capital Raqqa, al-Aṣmaʿī asked his fellow-courtier and student, the musician Isḥāq al-Mawṣilī, how many books he was taking. Isḥāq described his selection of eighteen boxes as (literally) "light reading" (*khaffaftu*), while the scholar marvelled at his traveling so burdened.[76] But even someone scorning books, like al-Aṣmaʿī, could not escape using them. To track his adversary's writing, he borrowed from one of his students a copy of the *Explanatory Re-writing* and studied it at home from beginning to end (*naẓara fīhi ḥattā intahā ilā ākhirihī).*[77]

Al-Aṣmaʿī's reservations against the book were not unfounded, as this format harbored the risk of misunderstanding if it was not accompanied by a teacher reading it aloud and commenting on it. He once corrected a student's question as being either a misreading of the questioner or a scribal corruption (*taṣḥīf*) in his source.[78] Indeed, scribal error abounded, and it was identified and remedied early on in a number of ways. One was the invention of a vocabulary of paraphrase (*ḍabṭ*) for such vowels of a word that were left out in the script, which only denoted consonants and long vowels. Moreover, the Arabic alphabet has only twenty-two letters to express twenty-eight sounds. This had been solved by giving several graphemes multiple functions and distinguishing these with diacritical dots. In practice, however, these dots were not always used, and if they were, they might occasionally be misplaced. The remedy for this was the compilation of particular books that

listed words with frequently misplaced diacritical dots or misspelt letters. This type of book was comparable to another genre for orally made mistakes in words whose unaugmented morphological form (i.e., simple nouns), rare occurrence, or foreign provenance gave no guide on how to supply the missing vowels left out in the writing system. Common titles of this sort were *Solecisms of the Commoners, How Commoners Misspeak,* and *The Rectification of Speech* (*Laḥn al-ʿāmma, Mā talḥanu fīhi l-ʿāmma, Iṣlāḥ al-manṭiq*).[79] Pronunciation of Arabic text, which required an interpretation of morphology and syntax, was more prone to error than writing or reading it in silence. Still, however imperfect, the book's existence per se was not in question. Rather, the new medium had to be optimized, new sources of error remedied, specific mistakes corrected, and some authors refuted. A frequent early book title was the *Retort to So-and-so* (*Radd ilā* [*Kitāb*] *Fulān*). Curiously, this tolerance of error in the book format would resurface as an argument in its favor.

By the time of al-Aṣmaʿī, the awareness of books had reached far beyond scholars and educated urban readers. The usually illiterate Bedouins (though a few of them lived in cities and became scholars, such as Muḥammad b. Ziyād al-Kilābī, d. end of eighth century, and Abū Misḥal, d. mid-ninth century) were keen to deploy salient information with those people they understood to possess a new way of preserving it—namely, offices that kept written records (*dawāwīn*).[80]

Al-Aṣmaʿī's own language reveals the ubiquity of books in his time (as far as one can rely on the wording of the following literary accounts in their transmitted form). In gnomic sayings about the ideal student, he describes learning for someone with a bad memory as "writing on water," a metaphor imported through the translation of Greek literature.[81] Elsewhere, he is summoned to assess the knowledge of two slave women given to the caliph al-Rashīd (the vizier has him rushed to court on official post mules from Baghdad to Raqqa). He examines each of the women on the catalogue of subjects with which a cultured individual is expected to be familiar—poems, types of polite letters (*adab*), literary accounts, and lexicon of the Qurʾān—and finds the first woman's responses to be so fast and accurate "as if she were reading the answer from a book."[82] Ironically, the idiom highlights a book's accuracy, which al-Aṣmaʿī elsewhere distrusted.

However impressive he was as a scholar-performer, al-Aṣmaʿī's very resistance confirms the book's omnipresence. Not a few titles are preserved in

his own name, though their final shape was largely provided by his transmitters. In this incipient phase, the redaction process of a book could easily take two to three generations of teachers and students. Al-Aṣmaʿī's *Great Poets* (*Fuḥūlat al-shuʿarāʾ*) tells its own redaction history in the preface. Toward the end of al-Aṣmaʿī's life, his student al-Sijistānī asks him to name the best early poet. As the teacher noticed al-Sijistānī writing down the answer, he sat up and began to dictate in a question-and-answer format whether or not each poet which al-Sijistānī named deserved the label of a "great poet" (*faḥl*):

> I often heard al-Aṣmaʿī, ʿAbdalmalik b. Qurayb place al-Nābigha al-Dhubyānī above the other poets of the time before Islam, so I asked him as the last thing shortly before his death: "Who is the first of the greats [*fuḥūl*]?" He said: "al-Nābigha al-Dhubyānī." Then he said: "I think no one in the world has words like Imruʾulqays:
>
> > Their ancestors guarded them with the sons of their fathers
> > in al-Ashqayn, where the vultures were.
>
> Abū Ḥātim [al-Sijistānī] said: When he saw me write down his words he mused, then he said: "Indeed, the first of them all in excellence is Imruʾulqays, he has the acclaim and the precedence. All of them took his words and followed his way, so he in fact made al-Nābigha al-Dhubyānī one of the greats."
>
> Abū Ḥātim said: I asked: "What is the meaning of 'great' [*faḥl*]?" He said: "One means by that a feature that singles out [one] from others, like the feature that distinguishes the stallion [*faḥl*] from [ordinary] adult male camels."[83]

The transcript of al-Sijistānī was redacted in turn by his student Ibn Durayd, who kept the question-and-answer format as it survives today in this earliest book on poets. This redaction of an extant transcript was typical of Ibn Durayd's way of working, as he belonged to that group of later scholars who used extant books as models or references for their own writings. In this case, the creator of the core text, al-Aṣmaʿī, had accepted that this would be recorded. But this was not always the case with transcripts from audition. Some texts appearing as books derived from lectures by scholars who had no idea or intention of giving their material written form. In this vein, the same Ibn Durayd commented that he recognized a teacher's oral comments made in class, written down as a new book under the name of a student.[84]

A MIDDLE POSITION

The contemporary grammarian al-Farrāʾ, already mentioned as a critic of the *Explanatory Re-writing,* occupied a middle position. He stood between Abū ʿUbayda and al-Aṣmaʿī by embracing the book form as a teaching tool without using books himself. Famously, he learned only from hearing and kept no books. At his death his private papers amounted to a couple of baskets containing a memo with questions and verses of poetry, but he left a written oeuvre of 3,000 sheets. Al-Farrāʾ produced his books by dictation. This was done with two kinds of audiences. One of his books, *The Definitions* (*al-Ḥudūd*), a compendium on the basics (*uṣūl*) of syntax and the *ʿarabiyya,* was commissioned by Caliph al-Maʾmūn (r. 813–833), who provided him with all logistical support:

> He had him placed in his own room in the palace and charged female and male servants with tending to his needs, so that his heart would not want nor his soul lack anything; even the prayer times were announced to him. The caliph appointed stationers [*warrāqūn*] for him and delegated treasurers and buyers to him. Al-Farrāʾ would dictate, and the stationers wrote till he had compiled [*ṣannafa*] *The Definitions* over several years [var.: over two years], and al-Maʾmūn ordered his volumes [*kutub*] to be placed in the treasury [var.: to be copied in the treasury].[85]

The "publication" of al-Farrāʾ's second book may have been a reaction to this first one, whose composition was not his choosing, and over which, once written, he had no control. It was copied and shut away in the treasury of the caliph, to whose sole readership it was confined. He preempted such a fate for his next book by producing it before the ears and eyes of the public. Gregor Schoeler proposes a similar reasoning for the traditionist al-Zuhrī (d. 742), who followed up a palatial commission to produce a Ḥadīth collection with another broadly published one.[86] It is unclear whether the move was triggered by his conviction that the public was as deserving of scholarship as the palace or by a calculation that more copies ensured a better survival of his work.

The impulse for al-Farrāʾ's second book came again from the palace, but this time as a suggestion from a lower secretary and companion of his, ʿUmar b. Bukayr, who wrote to al-Farrāʾ: "*Amīr* al-Ḥasan constantly asks me about things from the Qur'ān to which I have no answer. It would be good if you assembled the basics and made that a reference [*kitābun yurjaʿu ilayhi*]."[87] In two close versions of an account, a class of students received the dictation on an appointed day: "Al-Farrāʾ came out to us, dressed in formal attire, in the mosque in Khandaq ʿAbbūye. He wore a tall cap [*qalansuwwa*] on his head. He sat down and Abū Ṭalḥa al-Nāqiṭ recited [*qaraʾa*] a tenth of the Qurān, then al-Farrāʾ said to him: 'Stop,' and dictated from his memory to the assembly."[88] A third version, narrated by Abū Budayl al-Waḍḍāḥī on the same book's genesis, has the dictation taken by a large crowd: "Al-Farrāʾ went out to the people and began [to dictate] the book *The Explication* [*of the Qur'ān*]. His two copyists were Salama [b. ʿĀṣim] and Abū Naṣr [Muḥammad b. al-Jahm al-Simarī]. The transmitter said: "We wanted to count the people who had gathered for the dictation and could not put a figure to them, so we counted [only] the judges, who were eighty, and al-Farrāʾ did not stop dictating until he completed it."[89]

Al-Farrāʾ sits on the fence by not using books for his own scholarship and displaying an excellent memory while orally creating books for different audiences and endorsing their distribution. Indeed, his first book, *The Definitions,* disappeared forever in the caliph's treasury, whereas the text of the second, *The Explication of the Qur'ān,* survives in later copies and has been edited.[90] But public dissemination did not necessarily increase an author's control.

INTELLECTUAL PROPERTY VERSUS ENTREPRENEURSHIP

By making his second book widely accessible, al-Farrāʾ faced another phenomenon of the new world of books: to wit, the copyists, booksellers, and book agents.[91] The designation of their trade, *warrāqūn,* derives from the Arabic word for folio (*waraq*). The folio was both a formatting and volume unit. The *Catalogue* routinely defined book sizes by numbers of sheets, rounded to tens, specifying the folio as "paper of the *Sulaymānī* type with twenty lines to the page," named after Sulaymān b. Rashīd, director of finance in Khurasan under Caliph al-Rashīd (r. 786–809), when paper was first brought from that region to Baghdad.[92] Unless specified, *folio* referred to all three contemporary writing materials—namely, papyrus (*qirṭās*), parchment (*riqq*), and paper (*kāghadh*), the last of which increased in use throughout the ninth century.

In this book I translate *warraqūn* as "stationers," adopting from Adrian Johns the Early Modern English term for the craftsmen producing and dealing in printed books.[93] I chose this term because the range of functions of the seventeenth-century London stationer was as broad as that of the early Arab makers of manuscript books, including the production of paper and the sourcing, storing, selling, and assessing of books, even though not every stationer would engage in all of these activities. Resorting to a term from early print culture may seem unjustified, but apart from the absence of movable metal type, the cultural phenomena commonly associated with the "printing revolution," such as the codification of a shared language and the growth of a reading public, do apply to the Baghdadian manuscript book culture of the ninth century. In her study of early Arab printing, Dana Sajdi puts it plainly: "If we take the case of Arabic, things simply happened the other way round."[94] Arabic indeed had a book culture before book print, and this partially explains the lack of urgency in introducing printing technology, before the demands of the daily press in volume and speed made it indispensable.

In the case of al-Farrā', though he himself parted with his information for free, he witnessed the attempt by his two students, who acted as stationers for the abovementioned second book, to sell copies for an unusually high price of five folios per *dirham.* The public balked at this and complained to the author, assuming that he retained control over the fruits of his intellect.

What was an "author" in the ninth century? Authorship existed as an established concept in Arabic literature, though different roles need to be distinguished: the author as the creator of a new text; the author as collector and compiler of existing texts in which he felt free to intervene; and the author as the rightful beneficiary of his intellectual product's material countervalue.[95] The meaning of authorship differed in the various spheres of knowledge—namely, poetry, indigenous scholarship, and popular fiction.

In poetry, the poet was the creator of the text, and a line of poetry had an "owner" who could give it as a gift, or, in panegyrics, expect and receive a reward for it. Standard rates for odes to caliphs were 1,000 *dīnār*s or 10,000 *dirham*s (in gold and silver currency, respectively); the conversion rate between the two currencies was one (gold) *dīnār* to twenty to twenty-two (silver) *dirhams* at the beginning of the ninth century, rising to twenty-five *dirhams* per *dīnār* by the middle of that century.[96] During this period, some trained professionals earned fifteen to twenty-four *dirhams* a month (less than one *dīnār*) and others between one *dīnār* and a quarter and two *dīnār*s. The authorship pertained foremost to the formulation, given that themes and motifs were constantly revisited. This does not mean that poetic authorship (as intellectual ownership) was not violated, but that was an infraction, labelled "theft" (*sariqa*) or "rip-off" (*salkh*). These were evolving concepts that were still hard to grasp in the ninth-century sources. But a basic difference already existed between a "ripped-off" verbatim formulation and a borrowed reformulated motif. The word-by-word copy was frowned on (unless it was a quote of a famous verse), whereas a degree of reformulation changed the discourse from ownership to literary inspiration, or what we today call intertextuality. The conventional nature of poetry made the reworking of motifs inescapable, or, rather, desirable. An ode by the poet Abū Tammām to be presented to a Ṭāhirid governor passed muster only because the screening literati, to whom he had to submit it before, found within his hard-to-understand novel style two reused familiar motifs.[97] These were the only lines they easily understood and became the cause for the ode's acceptance. Yet it would take another two centuries for a proper system and nomenclature of *sariqa* to evolve. Then, the way a model was used determined the evaluation of its outcome: a later superior rendition transferred the right of authorship (*istiḥqāq*) to the second poet. Quality eclipsed chronology, and glimpses of this already appeared in the practical criticism of the early ninth century. For instance, Abū Hiffān al-Mihzamī (d. c. 869–871) deemed the poet Diʿbil al-Khuzāʿī (d. 859 or 860) more entitled to a motif that he borrowed from his teacher Muslim b. al-Walīd (d. 823) and improved. A century later, al-Ṣūlī would defend the poet Abū Tammām against accusations of plagiarism and demonstrate his creative reuse of older models.[98] But any accusation of *sariqa* must also be looked at in its context, as the competitive atmosphere of the court invited a self-serving use of it as a libel.

In scholarship, the case was different. In many scholarly books (excluding the exact sciences and the literature translated into Arabic) the body of the text often contained little in the way of in the actual words of the "author," whose contribution was memorizing, collecting, arranging, commenting, and transmitting of preexisting sources. This dealing with extant text made a scholar no less of an author in the eyes of his contemporaries, as he provided a repository of the knowledge that they needed. Material benefit was, however, not immediately connected with this type of authorship. For Ḥadīth scholars, piety forbade them to take payment. Philologists were occasionally reported to receive payment for classes (al-Aṣmaʿī accepted from one student agricultural produce from his estate, whereas Abū Zayd al-Anṣārī turned it down).[99] More often, a philologist's source of income (if at all related to his expertise and not deriving from another trade he engaged in) was tutoring the offspring of a ruler or a high official, or serving him in an official function, such as a judgeship. If employed in the court service, he might receive the same stipend as a boon companion (*nadīm*). The case of a stipend defined explicitly as support for an author of books, such as the one paid by governor ʿAbdallāh b. Ṭāhir (d. 844) to Abū ʿUbayd, was rare.[100] With the increase of book writing, it was more common to dedicate a book in the preface to a patron, who rewarded the author with a remuneration, like the way an addressee of a panegyric would reward its author. In both cases, reward might be refused, and the poet or book author might rededicate his work to another recipient.

The book format changed this dynamic by turning scholarship into a sellable good. Yet, with the production of books, the author or compiler of the contents was no longer the only one to lay claim to the proceeds, for the one creating the physical object also demanded his share. An antecedent was the transmitter of poetry, who in Abbasid times accompanied or represented the poet and took 10 to 20 percent of what a poem earned. An intermediary stance was taken by the *rāwī* of the poet ʿUmāra b. ʿAqīl, who was asked by the poet to hand over in writing his oral repertoire, and demanded a 50 percent cut.[101] But with the business of books, the *warrāq* became a more important financial partner than the *rāwī* of oral poetry had ever been.

A third situation occurred in popular literature, where no author existed by definition, and the person who reproduced a text, or translated it from Greek or Middle Persian, became its author by default.[102] Books of this kind were often ignored, or defamed, by the writers of highbrow literature; Ibn al-Nadīm called the *Thousand Nights* "a shabby book in poor language," but it is precisely this work from which the earliest literary paper fragment survives, reused for writing exercises.[103] Another fragmentary paper of a popular tale, datable to the ninth century based on the paper and the script, is illustrated with two tombs shaded by a tree (see figs. 5a and b). The legible remainder of the text above the tombs reads, "[Till] death did them part. This is their tomb, God have mercy upon them," suggesting that it belonged to one of the copious tales of lovers who were separated in life but united in death. The heroes of these tragic love stories are Umayyad poets and their beloveds, but the accounts about them date to the Abbasid period, when these stories became very popular.[104] Ibn al-Nadīm relegated them into the last chapter of his *Catalogue,* but for booksellers, popular literature was a much-demanded and lucrative category. It is a paradox that to this type of "authorless" book Ibn al-Nadīm sometimes applies the label of forgery: "Tales serving for nocturnal entertainment [*asmār*] and fantasy stories [*khurāfāt*] were desired and coveted in the days of the Abbasid caliphs, particularly those of al-Muqtadir [r. 908–929], and stationers compiled and invented them."[105] It is probably because of such products that the profession was associated with forgery, such as the type of the "lying and fabricating stationer" (*kadhibun mukhtaliqun mina l-warrāqīn*) and "stationers' compilations" (*taṣnīf al-warrāqīn*), intended as an insult.[106]

Returning to al-Farrā', who belonged to the second-mentioned group of book-producing scholars, his authorship was undisputed for the orally delivered text of *The Explication of the Qur'ān.* But, as in other periods of changing media, once the work was transferred into the new data carrier, it fell into a gray zone, where gain had to be renegotiated. This is exactly what happened to al-Farrā'. He was the author of the oral text but lacked authority over its written form, which he had turned over to others. The student-stationers were well aware of the potential benefit from the book and argued, "We assist you precisely to benefit from you; and from everything that you have compiled [*ṣannafta*], people need nothing more than this book. Let us have an income from it!" But al-Farrā' no longer actually retained control and needed to bargain: "'Make a compromise, so that you profit [yourselves] and let them profit [var.: and they, i.e., the people, profit].' But the stationers refused, so he said; 'I will show you.'" The option he chose was to strip the written version of commercial value by announcing that he would dictate "a more detailed and more accessible version." The stationers therefore lost the monopoly of their "master copy" and relented to sell it at half of the originally demanded price, ten folios per *dirham,* which was a more common rate.[107] This clash between author and stationers was only one of the many risks and potentials in the yet uncharted commercial terrain of early Arabic book culture.

(***a***)

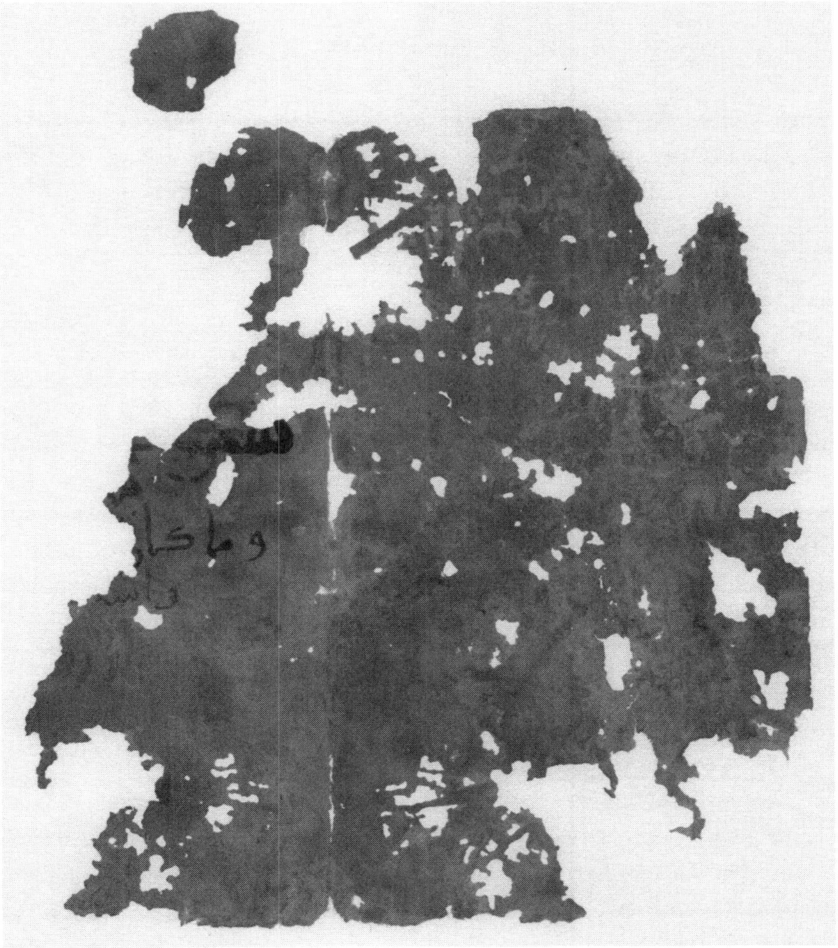

(*b*)

FIGS. 5A AND 5B. Paper fragment of an anonymous illustrated Egyptian popular tale from the late third / ninth century, showing two adjacent tombs shaded by a tree. The text of lines 2–4 (left side) reads "[Ttill] death did them part. This is their tomb, God have mercy upon them." (*[ḥatt]ā faraqa l-mawtu baynahumā fa-hādhā qabruhum raḥimahumū Llāh*). The tree (painted in green, yellow, and red colors) is a motif symbolizing lovers' posthumous reunion. (*ÖNB / Wien, A. Ch. 25612 Pap,* Austrian National Library.)

BOOK PRODUCTION

With a scholar of the next generation, Abū ʿUbayd al-Qāsim b. Sallām (d. 838), a student of both al-Aṣmaʿī and Abū ʿUbayda, the debate would be drowned in the flood of books. Looking back from the later ninth century, the prolific al-Jāḥiẓ, who would elevate book writing to yet another level, commented on Abū ʿUbayd: "People wrote no books more accurate or more useful than his."[108] Already contemporaries realized Abū ʿUbayd's importance: "We need him, and he does not need us."[109] The archfoe of books, al-Aṣmaʿī, in his old age reportedly endorsed Abū ʿUbayd. Seeing a man approach his gathering, the aged, weak-sighted philologist asked about his identity and, on hearing it was Abū ʿUbayd, commented, "The world will not go astray, that is, people will not go astray, as long as this man approaching us is alive."[110] The direction of endorsement had been reversed. The traditionist Yaḥyā b. Maʿīn (d. 847) rephrased a question posed to him about the reliability of Abū ʿUbayd: "Is someone like me being asked about Abū ʿUbayd? Abū ʿUbayd is the one to be asked about [other] people."[111] The traditionist Ibn Rāhawayh (d. 853) candidly admitted Abū ʿUbayd's superiority: "God loves the truth and Abū ʿUbayd is a better scholar than me, Ibn Ḥanbal, and al-Shāfiʿī combined."[112] The later Thaʿlab placed Abū ʿUbayd's oeuvre on par with another time-honored book culture: "If Abū ʿUbayd lived among the Israelites, he would be [regarded] a miracle."[113]

With Abū ʿUbayd, book redaction appeared on the radar as an aspect of scholarship. He highlighted himself the skill of composing books among traditionists, giving special credit to Ibn Abī Shayba (d. 849), who authored a thematically classified collection of traditions.[114] In turn, his colleagues placed Abū ʿUbayd in a quartet of the most meritorious scholars of Ḥadīth of their time, shoulder to shoulder with the systematizer of legal reasoning al-Shāfiʿī (d. 820), the incorruptible traditionist Ibn Ḥanbal (d. 855), and the expert on transmitters Yaḥyā b. Maʿīn.[115] His book on the rare vocabulary in Ḥadīth (*Gharīb al-ḥadīth*) counts among the few codices preserved from the ninth century (see fig. 6).[116] The difference between those scholars and Abū ʿUbayd was that he also authored foundational works in other fields in addition to the language of Ḥadīth discourse. His new brand of scholarship was book composition. The governor of Baghdad and dedicatee of the *Classified Rare Words* placed Abū ʿUbayd therefore among the polymaths of all ages of

Islam—namely, the Prophet's cousin Ibn ʿAbbās (687), the Umayyad jurisconsult al-Shaʿbī (d. 721), and the Abbasid lexicographer al-Qāsim b. Maʿn (d. 791 or 803).[117]

Esteemed in Abū ʿUbyad was not the fact *that* he wrote books, but *how* he wrote them. The new medium had become so current that differences in usability were noticed, and the layout mattered. Various styles were more or less popular. Abū ʿUbayd was called a "well-composing book compiler [*muṣannif ḥasan al-taʾlīf*]," combining both abovementioned terms of compilation and composition.[118] His *taṣnīf* consisted of gathering for the convenience of the reader all that had been written on a certain topic. Such were his *Famous Proverbs* (*al-Amthāl al-sāʾira*).[119] Hardly a philologist lacked a book on the subject, but Abū ʿUbayd assembled in his work all that had been written before. Rudolf Sellheim's history of the genre shows that Abū ʿUbayd's work became the basis for all major subsequent collections; he established the foundation. In addition to gathering the material from different sources, Abū ʿUbayd organized it accessibly in chapters (*bawwaba*).[120] These are both semantic and formal; the latter including types of idioms, such as a chapter on someone's possessing a certain quality to greater degree than a character legendary for it (*afʿal min fulān*). He appears as a consummate author, defining the proverb in the preface as a pithy, general, and analogical saying, legitimizing his undertaking with reference to the Prophet's use of proverbs, and then explaining his sources and arrangement. The book follows the sketch plan of the preface point by point (which is not always the case in early Arabic books).

In his thesaurus, titled *Classified Rare Words* (*al-Gharīb al-muṣannaf*), he again used extant material and gave it a written form. Here he adopted the structuring principle from a predecessor (either a man of the Banū Hāshim or al-Naḍr b. Shumayl, d. 819).[121] The type of the synonymic-semantic thesaurus is documented in the titles of seven earlier (lost) books, either as *Classified Rare Words* or [*Book of*] *Qualities* (*Ṣifāt*).[122] Of one them, the chapter headings survive in the *Fihrist* and show that Abū ʿUbayd developed the idea and reordered and expanded his model fivefold to twenty-five chapters, each containing up to 180 subheadings.[123] As with the *Famous Proverbs,* he did not slavishly adhere to the semantic system, but included headings based on formal features (morphological types, synonyms, and lexical roots; chapters 17–20, 25) as necessary to complete the collection. Into this structure, Abū ʿUbayd poured the most comprehensive set of data of his time, raising

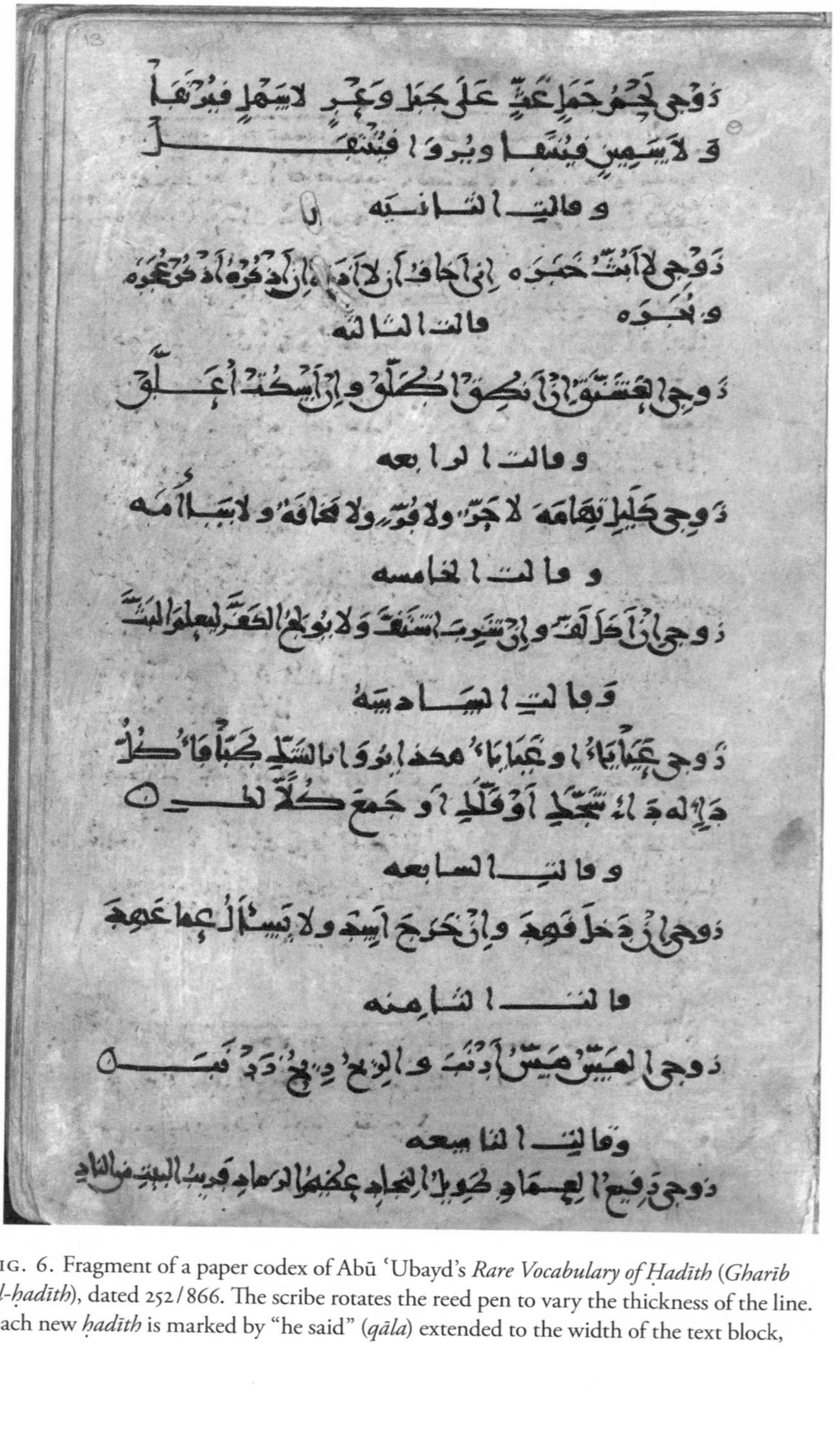

FIG. 6. Fragment of a paper codex of Abū ʿUbayd's *Rare Vocabulary of Ḥadīth* (*Gharīb al-ḥadīth*), dated 252/866. The scribe rotates the reed pen to vary the thickness of the line. Each new *ḥadīth* is marked by "he said" (*qāla*) extended to the width of the text block,

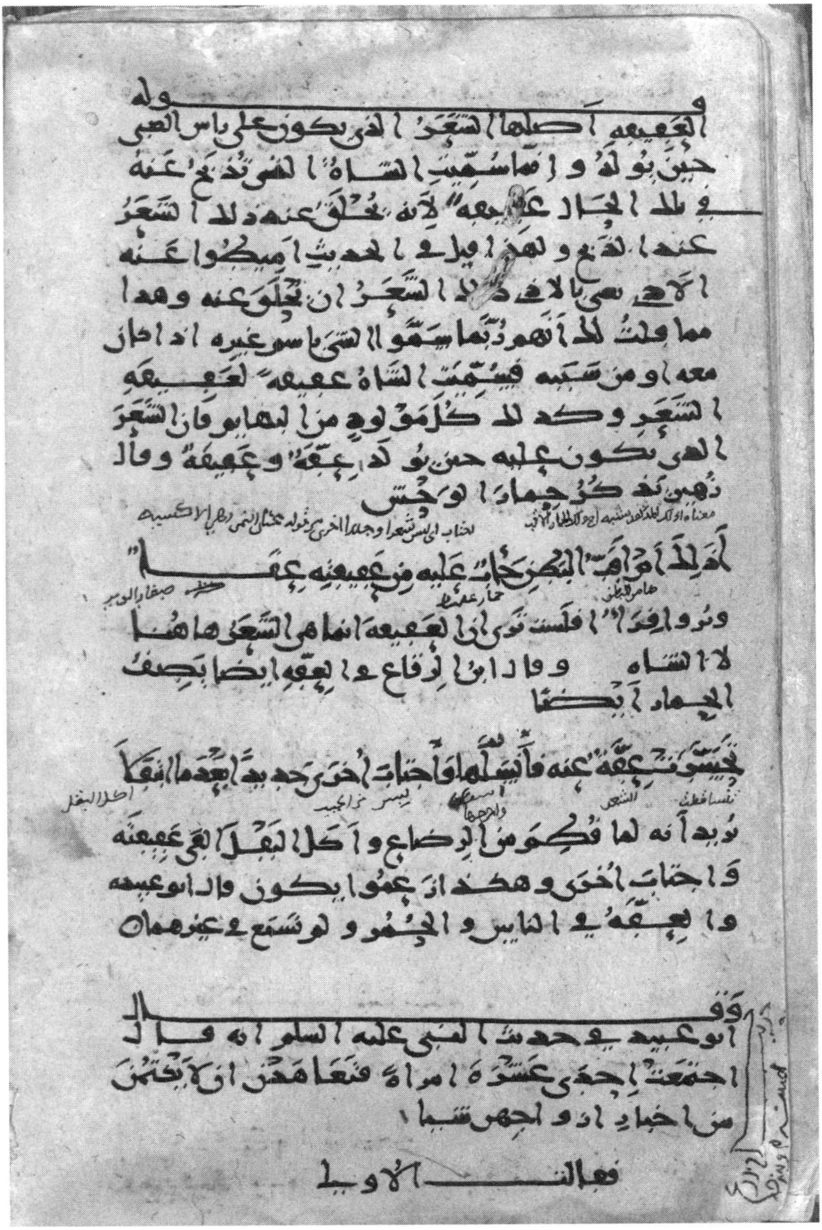

and within the *ḥadīth* of Umm Zarʿ (beginning on the lower right), each woman's statement is introduced by a shorter centered line with "she said" (*qālat*) and sometimes ended with a dotted circle. (Cod. Or. 298, Leiden University Libraries, fols. 12 verso and 13 recto.)

the genre to an unprecedented level. The great number of carefully credited oral sources amply disproves the allegation, made in some vitae, of a sole reliance on one predecessor.[124] The *Classified Rare Words* firmly established synonymic-semantic lexicography and it was fully excerpted in all subsequent major dictionaries. The following list of the lexicon's headings (and select subheadings) illustrates Abū ʿUbayd's exhaustive outline:

1. The human body (including morals, behavior, reproduction, genealogy)
2. Women
3. Clothes
4. Foods
5. Illnesses
6. Tents [*dūr*] and terrains
7. Horses (qualities in anatomy and paces, their cries, herds, defects, stance, wild vs. tamed horses, riding gear)
8. Weapons
9. Birds and insects / reptiles [*hawāmm*]: such as, bee, cricket, and queen bee [*yaʿsūb*], locust, lizard, snake, turtle, frog, scorpion, ant, louse [*qaml*], fly, tick [*ḥalam*], camel tick [*qurd*])
10. Pots [*qudūr*] and vessels [*awānī / āniya*] heavenly bodies, including sun, moon, fire, and anecdotes about these
11. Mountains
12. Shrubs and plants
13. Bodies of water and canals [*qinā'*]
14. Palm trees
15. Clouds and rain
16. Times (days of the week, months, climate, and winds)
17. Morphological noun types [*amthilat al-asmā'*]
18. Morphological verb types [*amthilat al-afʿāl*]
19. Terms denoting a thing and its opposite, including also metathesis, gender, dialectal variants in sound and meaning, foreign words [*mā dakhala min ghayri lughāt al-ʿarab fī l-ʿarabiyya*], commoners' diverging uses [*mā khālafat al-ʿāmma fīhi lughāt al-ʿarab*], inflection of names, etc.
20. Synonyms [*asmā' mukhtalifa li-l-shay' al-wāḥid*] in thematic order
21. Camels
22. Goats and sheep

23. Wild animals (gazelle, antelope, their flocks, onager, ostrich) and how they move
24. Predatory and other animals (lion, jackal, fox, hyena), lizard and hedgehog, rabbit, dog, polecat [*ẓaribān,* a stench-emitting animal], cat, ibex; females, copulation, pregnancy; quadrupeds [*bahā'im*], their offspring, cries, burrows, genitals [*qaḍīb,* "stick," and *ḥayā',* "vulva"], chasing them away, epithets, hunting them, and how they move
25. Homonyms and polysemous roots [*ajnās;* no internal subdivision][125]

Abū ʿUbayd's effort to capture the universe by means of the Arabic language was not the first attempt. Decades earlier the lexicographer al-Khalīl b. Aḥmad al-Farāhīdī (d. 791) had devised a dictionary and used a formal approach through the letters of the alphabet in all their permutations. This turned his lemmata into a total transcript of the Arabic lexicon, but they were lacking in data. Abū ʿUbayd conversely took reality as his starting point and divided it into chapters, and then filled them with everything he, his contemporaries, and their predecessors had gathered.

His second method of book writing, original composition (*ta'līf*), can be seen in his *Types of Dues* (*Amwāl*), in which he conceived an entire system of taxation.[126] It consisted of a tripartition of types of dues, namely, those owed by non-Muslims (*fay'*), by Muslims on war booty (*khums*), and by Muslims on their income (*zakāt*). The first type was further subdivided in to poll tax (*jizya*), land tax (*kharāj*), and tolls (*maks*). The third was split into dues on cattle (*ṣadaqa,* excepting horses) and agricultural produce (*ʿushr*). The respective tax rates are given, some of them in a staggered way, depending on personal income (e.g., for *ṣadaqa*). Others depended on treaties (*fay'*) and might be lowered if people were unable to pay them.[127] The agricultural tax rate (*ʿushr*) varied depending on the cost of irrigation (5 to 10 percent).[128] Standard deductions (i.e., nontaxable minimum income) applied, and a "poverty line" was set at personal possessions worth forty *dirhams*, below which the individual did not owe tax but instead became entitled to receive alms tax (*zakāt*). The receipt of alms tax, however, was dependent on the individual's ability to work and his effort to find employment.[129]

This book was produced from scratch—Abū ʿUbayd did not use any models (he was unaware of the few extant books on land tax)—and it represents a remarkable intellectual achievement.[130] Some aspects certainly grew out of Abū ʿUbayd's professional experience as a judge, and noteworthy is his concept of mutual duties between ruler and subjects. Their loyalty was made conditional on on the ruler's being a good Muslim and fulfilling his own duties toward them.

The changed status of the book author was also reflected in his remuneration.[131] Previous commissions were not usually connected to a reward. Al-Farrāʾ had been paid as a tutor of the caliph's sons, not for the book he was commanded to write. Abū ʿUbayda's books were copied by his student without the author's own knowledge or permission. Had he been aware, "he would not have allowed it."[132] As for Abū ʿUbayd, the governor of Baghdad once gave him a reward (comparable to the sum paid for a panegyric ode), but on another occasion he allotted him a stipend with the express purpose of freeing him from financial need in order to devote himself to book writing. In one of two variants of the account, the figure of 500 *dirhams* a month dwarfs in comparison what the famous grammarian al-Mubarrad (d. 898) once allotted to a promising student to allow him to devote himself to scholarship full time—namely, thirty *dirhams*.[133]

Abū ʿUbayd also knew the market. He employed a stationer to increase production and geared his product toward two audiences, and it flourished among both of them.[134] One group was rulers, but it was no longer they who commissioned a book on a certain theme. Abū ʿUbayd came up with the subject for a book and offered it on completion: "He went with his compilations [*muṣannafāt*] to the wealthy and powerful and they remunerated him, therefore his compilations abounded."[135] A frequent willing taker was the governor: "When he used to compose [*allafa*] a book, he dedicated it to ʿAbdallāh b. Ṭāhir, who sent him a lot of money in appreciation."[136] This elite audience was responsible for the fact that his books circulated, and indeed, many of them are preserved, among them the oldest surviving paper codex of Arabic civilization, his *Rare Vocabulary of Ḥadīth* (see fig. 6).

But his books were likewise "esteemed and demanded in every town [*balad*]" by the scholars of every discipline in which Abū ʿUbayd was active.[137] Those were many, for as his biographers observed, he "reunited various disciplines [*ṣunūf min al-ʿilm*] and compiled [*ṣannafa*] books in every scholarly discipline and literary genre [*fī kulli fannin min al-ʿulūmi wa-l-ādāb*]."[138] He also mastered the feat of serving simultaneously two audiences with one book. Here Abū ʿUbayd used composition strategically to reach with one book different audiences that would not come together in one gathering. In his *Rare Vocabulary of Ḥadīth* he combined the material from lexicographic models with the structure of legal works—to wit, the chapter division of collections of traditions and the grouping of information under the name of the guarantor (Companion or Follower) to whom it was traced. At the same time, Abū ʿUbayd restored the chains of transmission, the part that was necessary to assess their evidentiary value, which lexicographers had left out in their works (as being of no interest to them), but without which a *ḥadīth* was worthless to a traditionist. The dictionary thus became popular among three groups of scholars, "Traditionists, jurisconsults, and lexicographers desired [the book] because it assembled what they needed."[139] In the view of some colleagues, Abū ʿUbayd's manifold interests as well as his judgeship came at a cost, for in subjects that required one's total and exclusive attention, such as Ḥadīth, he did not excel.[140] He himself may not have thought this a sacrifice. He was interested in too many things to be limited to acquiring exhaustiveness in a field that would have kept him from pursuing others, and his judgeship acquainted him with practical matters that enabled him to devise a systematic manual on taxation that separated the essential from the superfluous.

By the time of Abū ʿUbayd, the standards of oral transmission for book authors had also loosened. He engaged in both lexicography and jurisprudence without becoming a target of criticism, although he had not received many of the prophetic traditions used therein through audition, as usually required.[141] His *Types of Dues,* with its careful cross-references and many addresses to the reader with "don't you see [*a-fa-lasta tarā*]" and "as I told you [*ka-mā aʿlamtuka*]," was certainly meant to be read outside of the teaching circuit.[142] The existence of Abū ʿUbayd's product in book form, however, did not replace or discard the oral framework of imparting knowledge. His books were still "heard." When he came to Baghdad, people audited his *Classified Rare Words.*[143] Though existing in writing, his books were still audited as well. Traditionists in particular insisted on hearing the *Rare Vocabulary of Ḥadīth* from him in person, with full chains of transmission to authenticate, for them, their audition of it, as opposed to readers, who possessed the book but not the license to teach it (*ijāza*).[144] Abū ʿUbayd, however, differentiated among his hearers and privileged the public that ensured his income and safeguarded his status. The first to have Abū ʿUbayd's *Rare Vocabulary of Ḥadīth* read to him was the caliph al-Maʾmūn (to whom he also dedicated it).[145] Governor ʿAbdallāh b. Ṭāhir had to come to the scholar's house, but he still received an individual reading. Having a governor receive knowledge from his lips in his own home was a stark contrast to the beginning of Abū ʿUbayd's career, tutoring a boy in a Basran alley. This son of a Greek slave who spoke broken Arabic had come a long way, and his books had been the reason.[146] Lesser scholars were told to "sit in with the public" in the general session. Out of reverence, Abū ʿUbayd made an exception for two Ḥadīth scholars, personally carrying the book to them for daily readings.[147] Twenty-some of his books were thus transmitted, and their written existence actually bolstered their oral circulation.[148] An unusual number of his books survive today—one of them, the *Rare Vocabulary of Ḥadīth,* as a paper codex from the same century (see fig. 6). His *Types of Dues* exists in near original form, and the *Famous Proverbs* and *Classified Rare Words* are each preserved in multiple manuscripts, and of the former, an autograph existed.[149] Others that may have been redacted by his students are the *Virtues of the Qurʾān* (*Faḍāʾil al-Qurʾān*) and *Abrogating and Abrogated Verses in the Qurʾān* (*al-Nāsikh wa-l-mansūkh fī l-Qurʾān*).[150] Books of his that had disappeared in Ṭāhirid palace treasuries reappeared occasionally as bequests sold on the market.[151]

Indicative of the change of tide was that even though Abū ʿUbayd's less-than-perfect oral performance still was noted ("His knowledge of inflection was deficient"), it was given less weight than his superior skill in setting things down in writing, which to his numerous readers mattered more: "Abū ʿUbayd did not have that eloquence, but when he fixed something [in writing], he fixed it."[152] Equally telling was another change in attitude. With Abū ʿUbayda's *Explanatory Re-writing of the Qurʾān,* the reaction had been to point out the work's "errors," some of which, to be sure, was nitpicking on doctrinal issues or motivated by personal jealousy. Abū ʿUbayd, made aware of errors in his *Classified Rare Words,* placed their number in proportion with the book's size: 2,000 wrong words in 100,000, or 20 [200] in 10,000, or 1,000 in 100,000, as different variants of the account have it.[153] The biographer of grammarians, al-Zubaydī (d. 989), noted the divergence in these accounts and counted the work's words himself, ascertaining their number at around 17,000. Unflustered and forgiving—a stance the famed book author and former judge could afford—Abū ʿUbayd remarked that his margin of error was negligible (ranging between 0.2 and 2 percent), and allowed that the mistakes could have easily been added in the transmission, and that some might be debatable.[154] He did not deny potential faults, but doubted that these, being relatively few, invalidated his book. Rather, he defended the book as a data carrier that tolerated a margin of error. His argument would be repeated by al-Jāḥiẓ a generation later, regarding less-than-perfect translations.[155] For Abū ʿUbayd, the price of faulty detail allowed the bulk of the information to survive the slings and arrows of transmission across time, and this resilience to error vindicated the new medium for him.

Abū ʿUbayd inaugurated a new type of author. Instead of striving for exhaustiveness for its own sake in composing a book on any subject, he contented himself with marshaling the essential for the purpose at hand. He also wrote each book in a different way. The spectrum of his authorial techniques can be gauged by the contrast between his *Famous Proverbs,* in which he pooled and systematized data already available, and his *Types of Dues,* in which he conceptualized in an unprecedented manner the principles of taxation. He composed books on subjects that were needed and used extant models for structure and material as far as those were available. When excellent and copious work by his predecessors and contemporaries existed, he felt no need to reinvent the wheel but satisfied himself with assembling and presenting it for easy use for the broadest possible readership. His *Rare Vocabulary of Ḥadīth* has less than 200 of his own words.[156] But when needed, he would compose a book from scratch and create a structure and a system, such as he did in his tax book.[157] There he used Prophetic traditions selectively, as required, to formulate and motivate general rules. He adduced, for instance, only thirty traditions on a point for which fifty existed, because his goal was to compile not an exhaustive Ḥadīth collection on the theme but rather a handbook on the different types of dues, how these were to be calculated, who was entitled to collect them, and who were the ultimate beneficiaries. He also brought to bear his experience as a judge and even conducted an experiment to test the commensurability of units of volume and weight measurement. It was a practical book. In an anecdote he tells a scribe not to copy it with golden ink but rather with the more modest and durable gall nut ink (*ḥibr*).[158] The inconsistent appraisals of the tax book, either as the "best and most excellent [book] compiled in jurisprudence" or as his weakest book, because of the selective (some thought nonchalant) usage of Ḥadīth, is more a reflection of his contemporaries' struggle with his approach than of quality of the investigation itself.[159] Unlike Abū ʿUbayda a generation earlier, he was held to observe extant methods but permitted himself to select whichever among them suited his subject best. This modus operandi could not have succeeded without a growing openness to knowledge presented in book form, but it also indicated an individual of versatile mind and little vanity who felt no urge to put himself forward and who faced criticism with equanimity. Not supposing himself faultless or above criticism, Abū ʿUbayd admitted his own errors as well as those that arose from the transmission process. His popularity as an author as well as his status as a city judge doubtlessly aided such self-assuredness. One gains the sense of a man who saw no need to prove anything to anybody.

CONCLUSION

The journey of the book in the ninth century had barely begun, and the book—like all new media—had not yet been developed to its full potential. A generation later the polyphony of the single book would be vaunted as being "many books" at the same time (*wa-in kāna kitāban wāḥidan fa-innahū kutubun kathīra*), and al-Jāḥiẓ would highlight its capacity to replace the author in space and time.[160] Some people turned into veritable "book addicts."[161] Thereafter, a host of "books on books" would arise (compilations, digests, retorts, appendices, commentaries, and so forth). The critical mass of books led to private libraries, book markets, and the profession of the stationer, which allowed individual intellectuals to ply the trade of authorship without patronage. The profession quickly diversified into the maker or dealer of paper, the palace copyist, the stationer attached to an author, the part-time scholar-stationer, the full-time stationer-craftsman, and the maker, dealer, or assessor of books.[162] Commercial opportunism and fraud abounded, demonstrating how lucrative book production had become. Finally, the book as an instrument of knowledge changed the nature of scholarship toward a new concept of knowledge. All this would occur with breathtaking speed and be "old news" at the close of the ninth century, a rapidity of change that is puzzling in comparison with a process that in Europe took 300 years, from the twelfth to the fifteenth century. Abū ʿUbayda had anticipated this development, al-Farrāʾ had accepted it more passively than actively, but Abū ʿUbayd became its declared advocate and successfully made his mark as a book-writing scholar.

CHAPTER TWO

POETS

Grammarians had made poetry a subject of their expertise and a building block of their careers in teaching, performance in courtly gatherings, and composition of books. But what about the suppliers of their subject matter, the poets themselves? They surely carried on an oral commerce observing conventions that protected their authorship and income, whatever the uncertainties inherent in serving influential clients. They had successfully made recited verse a proprietary and payable commodity. But what about its written form? Were they merely passive subjects of the emerging book market? Or did they have an active share in this new medium? And which, if any, books did they use or produce themselves?

DIʿBIL, A POET WITH OPINIONS AND AN AVID WRITER

In fact, two major poets in the first half of the ninth century engaged actively in the book culture. One of them, Diʿbil b. ʿAlī al-Khuzāʿī (d. 859 or

860), is noteworthy as much for having written the first book on poets by a poet as for his bad temper. He began his career by robbing (perhaps killing) a man and had to flee his hometown Kufa and stay away until the victim's relatives had passed away and no one was left to demand retribution.[1] He got into brawls over wine drinking and into fights with door keepers who denied him entry.[2] He was quick to satirize when temporizing would have achieved the desired result, and, once enraged, he would reject what he had initially asked for, even if it was offered. Protests from lampooned individuals, or attempts to arrest him, only egged him on to further satire.[3]

A lover of risk, he chose satire over praise for its greater efficacy in assuring income:

> One cannot benefit except through fear. . . . Someone who fears you for his honor is more common than he who wishes you to propound his nobility, because people's defects outnumber their virtues. Not everyone whose nobility you have propounded in poetry is truly noble. . . . But if he sees you damage the honor of another [man] and expose him to scandal, the [former] man fears you for his own sake and takes care to avoid what befell the other. . . . Reviling satire strengthens a poet's arm more than meekly offered praise.[4]

This was a practical calculation, and Diʿbil kept blank satires ready for potential enemies.[5] In this vein, he once forewarned a patron of what had happened to an underpaying predecessor, and the patron sent reward and asked not to be mentioned further.[6] But not all of Diʿbil's satire was self-serving. He wagered his life more than once for the luxury of an opinion. More often, poets adopted (at least overtly) the politics and religious persuasions of their patrons. Diʿbil, however, did not hesitate to satirize the Abbasid caliphs when they turned their back on the succession of the Alids (closer in relation to the Prophet than the Abbasids), since he felt that they had therewith forfeited their legitimacy. Once, he used the Qurʾānic legend of the Seven Sleepers as an analogy to call the eighth caliph al-Muʿtaṣim (r. 833–842) a dog, and stated that history had foreseen only seven caliphs.[7] Such satire had an aspect of bravado, since potential consequences ranged from imprisonment and exile to execution. The secretary and man of letters Ibn al-Mudabbir (d. 892–893) was impressed by Diʿbil's courage in reminding Caliph al-Maʾmūn that he gained his throne through fratricide.[8] He disapproved, however, of Diʿbil's obscene satire of a chief judge.[9] The forbearance of some victims and the intercession of highly placed friends repeatedly came to Di'bil' rescue. But eventually, his diehard stubbornness caught up with him in a ghastly end. Having satirized Mālik b. Tawq al-Taghlibī (d. 873–874), the governor of Western Mesopotamia, as a son of a whore, Di'bil fled to Basra, but the local governor had him beaten severely and pardoned him only on the condition that he eat his own excrement. This gave him a reprieve, until the offended patron had him located in Syria and poisoned for a fee of 10,000 *dirhams*, the prize usually given for a praise poem.[10]

Though hot-tempered, Di'bil stayed true to his convictions, among them his loyalty to the appointed Alid heir of the Abbasid caliphate, whom he went to praise personally in faraway Khurasan.[11] Another point of honor was his friendship with personages from the Baghdadian underworld, whose company he had kept before fleeing, and whom he invited and hosted at his house on his return from exile as a famous poet.[12] To his teacher, the poet Muslim b. al-Walīd, he remained faithful till a financial affair caused a falling-out on Muslim's side. From his apprentices he likewise expected loyalty, and he called an ungrateful student "a dog who bites his trainer."[13] This "demon of the poets" (*shayṭān al-shuʿarāʾ*), as Ibn Rashīq (d. 1070) nicknamed him, was a tough character with attitudes that were curiously incongruous, but to which he remained true.

Knowing the power of the word, he feared poets more than caliphs and warned in the preface of his book against antagonizing any poet, because even a random strike from untalented quarters might stick forever, as he experienced himself as a newcomer in Rayy and Qumm.[14] In his book he relates that the Persian-born Bashshār b. Burd (d. 783–784), himself a feared satirist, paid grudgingly his yearly 200 *dirhams* of poll tax to a Muslim colleague to keep the latter's satire of him under wraps. Di'bil availed himself of the many uses of writing current at the time. Next to his authorship of books, he used writing for numerous informal and personal occasions.

Doors

To protest the theft of his rooster, which neighbors' boys had chased and cooked, he inscribed a shaming quatrain on the door of the Friday mosque. This was a place where scholars and the people consulting them regularly gathered. In the quatrain, he called the rooster a "muezzin" and threateningly described his killers as having won a Pyrrhic victory: "They swallowed him [without chewing], for they lost their teeth, the backs of their heads being crushed against the wall." The father of one of the boys urged them to buy up all of the neighborhood's roosters for Diʿbil, to evade irreparable and lasting denigration.[15] The well-placed graffito had had an instant effect. Satire would also be spread by street boys, but then it had to be kept simple to facilitate memorization.[16]

Letters

A ubiquitous format of writing was the letter (*kitāb*), or written note (*ruqʿa*).[17] Invitations to gatherings were usually extended in writing.[18] When his own teacher gave him the cold shoulder on gaining the governorship of Jurjan, Diʿbil dispatched a satire by letter, which effectively ended their relationship. On another occasion he was on the receiving end: having arrived in Rayy, a note of satire was slipped into the hallway of the house where he was staying, calling his poetry "as cold as the snow" that had just fallen. "Cold" was a common insult for bland and insipid verse. This warned him that he was encroaching on the local poets' turf to his own detriment, and he turned on his heels.[19] But sometimes letter writing could backfire, as, for instance, when Diʿbil and his brother provided themselves with letters of introduction to the Egyptian governor al-Muṭṭalib (r. 813–815) before traveling there. A man joined them en route and won their trust as a travel companion—so much so that they "ghostwrote" a panegyric poem for him to present to the governor. To their surprise, the unknown man revealed himself to be an excellent poet and upstaged the brothers with a brilliant recitation of his own poem in which he belittled their letters of introduction (all the while using them as props). To add insult to injury, he called such written aids a diversion and instead threw himself (alone) upon the mercy of the Egyptian sovereign: "I single him out with my hope and do not place connections next to him or meet him with letters." Al-Muṭṭalib was pleased by such endorsement of his power and distinguished the interloper above his better-prepared colleagues.[20] The incognito poet had used the fact that in public audience, the spoken word held sway over writing. Diʿbil himself had once successfully invoked the sole "bond of culture" (*ḥurmat al-adab*) with the Baghdadian governor ʿAbdallāh b. Ṭāhir, implying that there was a connection between men of letters stronger than any ties of blood, which should make an introduction through a third person unnecessary.[21] A member of the Ṭāhirid dynasty, which ruled nearly independently in Khurasan and supplied the governors for Baghdad, was a fitting addressee for such a claim, because the Ṭāhirids lavishly sponsored both Arabic and Persian literature. ʿAbdallāh's son ʿUbaydallāh, likewise governor of Baghdad, was one of the major patrons of the poet Ibn al-Rūmī (d. 896).[22] Another letter by Diʿbil was even more destructive. Having being appointed to the governorship of the city of Aswan by the same Muṭṭalib, whom Diʿbil had lost no time in lampooning after the above described event, he received his own written dismissal just as he was about to ascend the pulpit to give his first Friday sermon.[23] His satire had reached al-Muṭṭalib. Diʿbil was deposed literally at the instant of assuming his duties. To return the humiliation, the governor had orchestrated the letter's delivery in the great mosque right before the public eye.[24]

Legal Documents

Letters had legal power. After a brawl over wine drinking which resulted in a false accusation against Diʿbil, he wrote to the prosecuting judge defending himself on theological grounds. A judge from the adversary's clan accepted the argument and opined the charge should be dismissed.[25] Diʿbil's continued satirical exchanges with Abū Saʿd al-Makhzūmī (alive 813–833) led to legal contracts. Satire often broadened to include an individual's entire tribe, and afraid of this, his own kin, the Banū Makhzūm, stripped Abū Saʿd of his tribal membership to escape Diʿbil's tongue. They drew up a document to this effect (*katabū ʿalayhi kitāban*), and he had to wear a seal ring with an inscription documenting his ouster (*katabū l-ṣakka ʿalayhi*), which inspired Diʿbil to further lampoons.[26]

Poetry in Draft

Writing also came to serve as an interim mode for the composition of poetry. Once at home, Diʿbil was composing a satire of Abū Saʿd, writing it on a sheet (*ṣaḥīfa*), and it so happened that his foe came to visit to make up with him. They exchanged politenesses over a dinner of leftovers, but inebriation led Abū Saʿd to request to listen to a bawdy satire of himself, and on his return home he sent a similarly obscene retort in ink on papyrus (*qirṭās*). Angered in turn, Diʿbil ended where he started, sitting at home with parchment and inkwell (*jild wa-dawāt*), composing satire, and when the two met by chance some days later, neither one greeted the other.[27]

Diʿbil also used writing to record sudden inspirations. Watching the funeral parade of a caliph, he asked his friend standing next to him: "Do you have something to write on you?" So the friend produced a scrap of papyrus from his sleeve. Diʿbil dictated: "A caliph dies whom no one mourns and another rises in whom no one delights."[28] Written drafts also served to submit a new poem to a trusted critic. Marwān b. Abī l-Janūb (d. after 854 or 861) had this done orally, whereas Diʿbil showed a fresh composition written on a sheet to a colleague, and when this poet gave it bad marks, Diʿbil tore up the sheet (*mazzaqa*).[29] Writing paradoxically allowed the destruction of a text in a way memorization did not. Listeners made and kept their own transcripts of poems, and these were worth more when proofread by the author. Late in Diʿbil's life, a young admirer, armed with such a transcript, asked the poet to listen to a recitation of his own ode for correction. But instead of spotting errors of transcription, Diʿbil used his knife's edge to scratch out (*jarrada*) a verse offensive to the Quraysh, which means that the material was either parchment or papyrus, since ink could not be erased from the porous paper.[30] Although paper had been available for a couple of decades, papyrus and parchment were still in use. The secretary and *adīb* Ibn al-Zayyat (d. 847), while listening to Diʿbil's recitation of an ode, chewed absentmindedly on a parchment scroll, and Diʿbil lampooned him for this lack of etiquette as a "parchment roll kisser," employing sexual innuendo.[31]

Such written drafts were temporary, and the publication of poems still took place by recitation at court and subsequently in literary gatherings. At such an event in the palace, the caliph al-Ma'mūn, who secretly relished the poet's outrageous verses, mostly those composed at others' expense, relied on the memory of those attending.[32] Much of Diʿbil's poetry also circulated as songs, which his friend and companion, the court musician Aḥmad b. Yaḥyā al-Makkī (d. 862), set to music.[33] Thus Diʿbil heard his first ode again after many years as a song.[34]

Notebooks

Another format of interim writing in literature and scholarship was the notebook (*daftar*). This appeared foremost as a personal tool, whose existence was not advertised. When al-Buḥturī (d. 897) did not understand someone's

FIG. 7. Papyrus notebook from the second / eighth century. Photograph by Adolf Grohmann of Papyrus Cairo Dār al-Kutub, Inv. no. 765. (Reproduced from Grohmann, *Arabische Paläographie,* vol. 1 [Vienna: Hermann Böhlau, commissioned by the Austrian Academy of Sciences, 1967–1971], pl. 9.)

criticism of a modern poet he was visiting, he silently consulted his written notes on the poet when he returned to his own home.[35] Such notebooks were kept at home and circulated, if at all, only within one's teaching circuit, as had been the case since the last quarter of the eighth century in Ḥadīth scholarship.[36] They preserved, for instance, the earlier poetic repertoire, which philologists and contemporary poets were expected to know, but newer poetry came to be recorded too. Diʿbil's foe Abū Saʿd consulted his father's *Nizāriyyāt,* praise poems on the northern Arab tribes, in a notebook that a certain Aḥmad b. Marwān had kept. Caliphs often had poems praising them written down after the oral delivery and kept them as records. The written form also allowed for a panegyric of Abū Saʿd to fall into Diʿbil's hands, and he satirized the verses.[37] Diʿbil thus used manifold forms of writing, mostly for day-to-day purposes and his immediate professional needs, and in this he did not differ much from other literati of his time.

But with the exception of legal contracts, these written forms were impermanent records or props for spoken delivery, and very few specimens have come down on us. With one format, however, this was about to change.

NOTEBOOKS AS EVIDENCE IN THE AFFAIR OF THE "FALLEN MOON"

An incident about the man who would steal the aging Diʿbil's limelight, the innovative Abū Tammām (d. 845 or 846), shows that notebooks had acquired a new public status. This is connected to another facet of Diʿbil's persona: the poetic critic. This "poet of scholars and the scholar-poet" was considered an authority.[38] Any information Diʿbil gave on poets' identities and his transmission of poems were considered absolutely dependable. Contemporary and later critics furthermore relied on his judgements of poetry's aesthetic value. Ibn al-Jarrāḥ (d. 908) cites Diʿbil in many entries of his *Book of the Folio* (*Kitāb al-Waraqa*) on poets. But Diʿbil was not infallible. The following is one known case in which his personal interests skewed his otherwise incorruptible poetic standards.

His book on poets survives only partially in scattered later quotations, which have been assembled by Leon Zolondek.[39] But Diʿbil's achievements as a critic were not confined to his book. He also acted as a critic in literary gatherings and in his own circle, which can be gleaned from descriptions of these settings that contain phrases such as "We passed poetry of So-and-so back and forth" (*tajāraynā fī shiʿri fulān*) and "We were in Diʿbil's circle and Abū Tammām was being evoked."[40] In such a conversation between Diʿbil and the transmitter Khalaf al-Aḥmar, Khalaf claimed that he himself had composed the pre-Islamic brigand-poet Ta'abbaṭa Sharran's (alive first half of the sixth century C.E.) famous boast of accomplished revenge, which begins "At the mountain pass that is below Salʿ / there is a slain man, whose blood shall not stay unavenged" (*inna bi-l-shiʿbi lladhī dūna Salʿin / la-qatīlan damuhū mā yuṭallu*).[41] The ode breathed a "dark spirit of vengefulness," as described by the German poet Johann Wolfgang von Goethe (d. 1832), who produced a German version in his *West-Eastern Divan*.[42] Authentic or not, this quality made the ode a perfect sample of pagan Arab values. Abū Tammām nonetheless credited Ta'abbaṭa Sharran in his *Ḥamāsa* anthology, though most early compilers sided with Diʿbil in casting doubt on his authorship. Diʿbil's oral pronouncements in such gatherings are more colorful and stinging than his more sober written assessments. He volunteered opinions about famous contemporaries, such as al-ʿAbbās b. al-Aḥnaf, whom Diʿbil judged to have composed a few good verses among a generally inferior output, a statement made in a session hosted by the secretary Hārūn b. ʿAbdallāh al-Muhallabī.[43] This poet was indeed rather limited, specializing in a new kind of courtly love lyric (*ghazal*), even if it enjoyed popularity in the highest quarters. Diʿbil carefully kept such polemics against living competitors out of his book, and they survive only from separately transmitted oral occasions.

The Accusation, Version One

To this polemic type of literary criticism belongs Diʿbil's accusation of Abū Tammām, whose meteoric rise and new style eclipsed other poets' fame. Abū Tammām had his first breakthrough with a lament for the general Muḥammad b. Ḥumayd al-Ṭūsī (d. 829), who fell in the battle against the rebel Bābak al-Khurramī (d. 838), and the poet then became popular among generals, e.g., Muḥammad b. Yūsuf al-Thaghrī (d. 851). Later he was noticed and championed by Caliph al-Muʿtaṣim, for whom he composed the famous victory ode on the battle of Amorium in 838.[44] But Abū Tammām received the greatest acclaim among Abbasid officials and literati, notably the secretaries al-Ḥasan b. Wahb (d. c. 862), and Muhammad b. ʿAbdalmalik b. al-Zayyāt, who prized his intellectually challenging style.[45]

Diʿbil scathingly described the bulk of Abū Tammām's verse as either absurd or stolen, but in one gathering he charged Abū Tammām with a specific act of plagiarism.[46] The event occurred in Diʿbil's house four years after Abū Tammām's death in 845 or 846, and it is relevant for a new kind of "mixed media": a face-to-face dispute corroborated with written documentation. The man from whom Abū Tammām allegedly stole, Abū Sulmā Muknif al-Madanī (alive late eighth or early ninth century), was an obscure descendent of the great pre-Islamic poet Zuhayr b. Abī Sulmā (d. 609).[47] Diʿbil made the case by showing a notebook of Muknif's original poem. The narrator of the following account was the expert on reports Muḥammad b. Mūsā b. Ḥammād al-Barbarī (d. 902 or 907):[48]

I was with [al-Qāsim and] al-ʿAmrawī [or: al-ʿAmrāwī] at Diʿbil b. ʿAlī's place in the year 35 [var.: 235, 850 C.E.], when he had returned from Syria. We were discussing Abū Tammām, and Diʿbil began to insult him and accuse him of stealing poetry [var.: and Diʿbil said: "He is an arch-thief (*sarūq*) of poetry"]. "Hand me that sack," he said to his servant Nafnaf [var.: Thaqīf]. The servant brought a sack full of notebooks. Diʿbil rummaged through them [*yumirruhū ʿalā yadihī*] and pulled one out. "Read this!" he said. We looked at the notebook, and it read:

> Muknif Abū Sulmā, descendent of Zuhayr b. Abī Sulmā [his home was Qinnasrīn], had lampooned Dhufāfa al-ʿAbsī in verses, including the following:
>
> > Tribe of Qaʿqāʿ, your lucky star rose in *al-Durāṭ* [literally "flatulence"]
> > pride yourselves on the fart [*ḍarit*]!
> >
> > [The notebook continued. with:] Later [Dhufāfa died and] Muknif mourned Dhufāfa:
> >
> > Can fate [var.: poetry] taste sweet after Abū l-ʿAbbās?
> > After him fate is all bad [var.: has no reconciliation] and has no excuse.
> >
> > [If decree and fate were to be blamed after him,
> > they could not make amends, as long as the mimosa greens.][49]
> >
> > You who announce the death of Dhufāfa, the death of generosity,
> > Perish! May all your ten fingers wither!
> >
> > Are you announcing the death of a rock of the Qays ʿAylān
> > which pulverized the mountains of our enemies?
> >
> > When Abū l-ʿAbbās leaves his place,
> > no female shall be fertile or conceive
> >
> > Rain shall not water the earth, nor stars travel,
> > no wine delight the drinker!
> >
> > *On the day he died, the Banū l-Qaʿqāʿ were like stars in a sky
> > from whose midst the full moon had fallen.[50]
> >
> > *Hope died with him [var.: with Dhufāfa],
> > now travelers [*al-safr*] have no reason to travel [*safar*].
> >
> > *[Consoled (*yuʿazzawna*) for a man dwelling (in a tomb)
> > for whose loss Greatness too must be comforted (*tuʿazzā*),
> > and over whom Magnanimity, Bravery, and Poetry weep.]
> >
> > *[He was but the wealth of him whose wealth was little,
> > and the treasure of him who had none.]

> "Abū Tammām stole most of this ode and incorporated it into his poetry," asserted Di'bil [var.: into his ode, beginning "There! Let the blow of fate be enormous and the matter crushing—no excuse for an eye whose water does not run over" (*kadhā fa-l-yajilla l-khaṭbu wa-l-yafdaḥi l-amru / fa-laysa li-'aynin lam yafiḍ mā'uhu 'udhru*)].

This was not the only occasion on which Di'bil made this accusation. In a variant of the account in al-Āmidī's (d. 987), *The Weighing between the Poetry of Abū Tammām and al-Buḥturī* (*al-Muwāzana bayna shi'r Abī Tammām wa-l-Buḥturī*), the narrator Abū Muḥammad al-Yazīdī expresses amazement at Di'bil's revelation that the verses were Muknif's: "Di'bil recited this ode to me and made me wonder about Abū Tammām with his claim against him and his accusation of some of the verses."[51]

Assessment of the Charge

The seventh to tenth verses above (marked by asterisk) indeed are contained nearly verbatim but in a different order in an ode by Abū Tammām.[52] They appear in Abū Tammām's *Dīwān* as follows (the changes are italicized):

> Hope died with *Muḥammad,*
> now travelers have no reason to travel.[53]
>
> He was but the wealth of him whose wealth was little,
> and the treasure of him who had none. . . .
>
> On the day he died, the Banū *Nabhān* were like stars in a sky
> from whose midst the full moon had fallen.
>
> Consoled for a man dwelling [in a tomb]
> for whose loss Greatness too must be comforted,
> and over whom *Generosity,* Bravery, and Poetry weep.

The changes are minimal: "generosity" (*jūd*) replaces "magnanimity" (*majd*) in the last verse, and the name and tribe of the eulogized differ. If Abū Tammām had tried to conceal a theft, Di'bil caught him here red-handed, despite that fact that Abū Tammām had chosen his victim well, because Muknif's verse was too obscure for his *dīwān* to survive, and his ode is preserved solely in anecdotes connected to the present dispute about its origin.

The Accusation, Version Two

But there was another side to the story in a variant on the above account. It includes the secretary al-Ḥasan b. Wahb, a fervent admirer of Abū Tammām. Al-Ḥasan kept notes for his own use, such as his selections of Abū Tammām. But he also used them as pieces of argument. The variant is placed behind the previous by the compiler al-Ṣūlī and related by the same narrator, but missing in all the other citations of the event:

> Muḥammad b. Mūsā [al-Barbarī] told me this story [i.e., al-Ṣūlī] another time and added: I told al-Ḥasan b. Wahb this. "I know this poem of by Muknif," he responded, "and I own a copy of his poetry. Abū Tammām used to recite it to me. None of [Muknif's] poem appears in Abū Tammām's ode. Rather, Diʿbil mixed up the odes, since they have the same meter and both are laments, in order to falsely accuse Abū Tammām.[54]

Al-Ḥasan's defense is as ingenious as it is dubious. He once delivered an oral defense of Abū Tammām's Amorium ode in the form of an abridged recitation, but here he chooses the written form as a more powerful method of proof. The idea to put the notebook to this new use was possibly derived from Diʿbil, as he stored his research in this manner. Diʿbil's goal, however, was a book on poets' lives and works, so he needed their *dīwān*s as a database. Al-Ḥasan b. Wahb probably used notebooks to aid his memorizations of Abū Tammām's odes, for he intervened in the odes by excising them and preparing optimized digests of their highlights, which he then recited.[55] This form of creative excerpting was focused, however, on his ideal, Abū Tammām, and designed for strictly personal use. Regarding the case at hand, al-Ḥasan admitted writing down his proof against plagiarism from the mouth of the very man who had been accused of the act. Since he was a champion of Abū Tammām, it is implausible that al-Ḥasan would have kept a notebook on an obscure contemporary poet such as Muknif, other than for the purpose of counteracting the said charge. His notebook is dependent on, and an accessory to, the debate. Moreover, the information was received orally and then fixed in writing, and apparently this change of medium endows it with greater evidentiary power. This is thus prepared evidence, adopting a novel and scholarly format for polemic purposes.

Al-Ḥasan adduced a further line of defense, which, however, weakens the first, for he admitted the two poems' prosodic similarity, which facilitated an exchanging of lines back and forth between them. But al-Ḥasan reverses the agency and accuses the accuser Diʿbil of having mingled the two texts. In satires, such counteraccusations were common when an author wanted to offload his responsibility onto the shoulders of his enemy and have him bear the consequences. The same occurred, for instance, between Muslim and al-Ḥakam b. Qanbar (fl. beginning of the eighth century), when the Quraysh, the tribe to which Muḥammad had belonged, and the Helpers of the Prophet (Anṣār) got dragged into a satire match.[56] The specific charge of plagiarism was not novel, either; it had often been leveled against Abū Tammām by others.

The notebooks were a Janus-faced instrument of evidence. Their written form was given higher authority than the spoken charge, both in corroborating and disputing it. In both cases, they were not finished, published books but rather personal records. Diʿbil simply shared his not-yet-redacted research notes, to which others were not usually privy. Yet his actual charge is made orally and did not become part of his book on poets, as he "excluded Abū Tammām from it."[57] In al-Ḥasan's case, the notebook is a dictation taken down from Abū Tammām, who was not a reliable transmitter; on the contrary, he took liberties with the poems he included in his anthology, titled *On Bravery* (*al-Ḥamāsa*), excerpting and editing them.[58] In both accusation and defense, writing notebooks served different ends, scholarship versus polemics, but in both they were interim media and used as a trump cards in an oral debate. The mere transformation into the written medium had thus gained credibility. The argument of an oral debate was usually judged by the scholarly standing of its proponents, and while Diʿbil was considered reliable, Abū Tammām was not. By taking the debate from persons to pieces of writing, al-Ḥasan managed to square with his opponent at eye level. One notebook stood against another. We cannot retrieve the historical facts. But what matters is that the *daftar* as a format had acquired evidentiary power regarding authorship. Such a line of argument could succeed only with an audience that was familiar with, and accepted, such written proof. Notebooks had evidently moved beyond the stage of a mere prop for the exercise of one's memory to become a recognized source of information in their own right.

POETIC BORROWING VERSUS "RIP-OFF"

What about plagiarism, the substance of the charge? Given what we know of Diʿbil, a completely invented charge was unlikely. Neither was the accusation far-fetched, because Abū Tammām's thefts were a general theme; the *Muwāzana* lists various collections of them.[59] But not all thefts were the same. What exactly constituted a blameworthy theft was still unclear in the ninth century. While the charge was often leveled and certain labels were current, no general theory had as yet been formulated. The spectrum was vast, ranging from a vague reuse of a common theme to a partial or whole adoption of the wording or meaning, and the verdict varied. To wit, in a verse that reused older ideas, one could look either at what had been taken or what had been altered and added. It was a case of the glass half-empty or half-full, depending on the stance one took. For instance, Diʿbil's most famous line, "Do not wonder, Salm, about a man whose hair is laughing while he weeps," which became his signature verse, encountered such a charge.[60] He had produced it as a young apprentice, upon which his teacher Muslim declared him ready to "publish" his work. The grammarian al-Aṣmaʿī desperately tried to credit more distant precedents; the narrator of another report, Abū Hiffān, credited Muslim with the original motif but opined that "[Diʿbil] improved it" and "was entitled to it" (*jāʾa bihī ajwada min qawli Muslimin wa-ṣāra aḥaqqa bihī minhu*).[61] This argument was based on the principle that the superior wording or metaphoric recasting of an extant idea was praiseworthy and transferred the idea's authorship to the more recent poet. Unconcerned with the literary genealogy of Diʿbil's verse, Caliph al-Rashīd, on hearing it put to music, invited the poet to court and allotted him a stipend.[62] Inversely, Diʿbil accused Abū Tammām of having stolen one of his motifs (*maʿnā*), but a man attending his circle asked to hear both verses and judged Abū Tammām's rendering to be better and that poet as more deserving (*awlā*) of the motif (the editor al-Ṣūlī rephrases it as "more entitled to it," *aḥaqqu bihī*).[63] To eloquently rewrite a verse demonstrated skill. Thence there was an extensive gray area that allowed for subjectivity and polemics and invited gratuitous attack and elbowing for personal advantage. Some of the alleged instances of borrowing were certainly tendentious and intended as a slight to Abū Tammām. This poet's success spurred his colleagues' envy, and his difficult abstract style was an easy target for the gripes of old-fashioned critics.[64]

The Need for Classical Poetry

As popular as the new style of poetry might be, there was no way around the classical poetry (i.e., poetry composed in pre-Islamic and early Islamic times until the end of the Umayyad period). It is true that minute poetic descriptions of things as they really were, or comparisons of them, however articulate, had gone out of fashion. This was true particularly in panegyric, which mattered to poets as their main source of income. Caliphs not infrequently conveyed exact models of how they wished to be portrayed, often staged as competitions or entry exams, to crowds of poets waiting for admission at the palace gate.[65] Hyperbole of cosmic dimension was much in vogue. The philologists, the default critics of the classical verse, still carped about the lacking verisimilitude of the novel tropes with reality, but they were being sidelined as arbiters of taste by the intellectually and artistically more open literati of the court. This notwithstanding, poets could not afford to leave the old corpus aside, for audiences and critics still expected and relished familiar themes and topoi. This is precisely what Abū Tammām succeeded in: the combination of the Bedouin heritage with startling, sometimes intricate, abstract conceits.

To return to the ways of borrowing, one end of the spectrum, the verbatim takeover of a whole verse (or more), called *salkh,* was clearly frowned on, unless it was a well-known and recognizable quotation. The incident of the theft of the fallen-moon verse belonged to this kind. It constituted a verbatim "rip-off," which was an infringement of authorship, if authorship could be proven. The lines supposedly came from an unknown poet, and the verbatim repetition could therefore not pass as a recognizable quotation.

Other Criticism

The ode with the disputed verse, a lament for general Muḥammad b. Ḥumayd al-Ṭūsī had earned Abū Tammām fame, so much so that the Arab general and patron of the arts Abū Dulaf al-ʿIjlī (d. c. 840–843) regretted that it had not been composed about him. On receiving his own panegyric from Abū Tammām before a mixed assembly of Persians and Arabs, he had the entire lament of the late general recited to the applause of those present, and he admitted his envy of the eulogized, saying, "A man lamented with such poetry is not dead."[66] The plagiarism accusation does not come up in this context, as it would be made only some years after the poet's death.

Other criticism was leveled against the verse as well. A certain Aḥmad b. ʿUbayd b. Nāṣiḥ confronted Abū Tammām directly: "Did you want to describe the [Banū Nabhān's] good or bad situation after his death [i.e., of General al-Ṭūsī]?" Abū Tammām responded, "By God only their bad situation, because their moon has vanished." But Aḥmad countered, "By God, the stars are never more beautiful than when the moon is not with them," and then cited an allegedly superior verse by the poet al-Khuraymī (d. 829): "When one of their moons fades or is eclipsed another moon appears on the horizon, shining," silencing Abū Tammām.[67]

Al-Ṣūlī appended to the above-related positive reception of the notebook's evidence a similar account of "some people's" nitpicking about the motif of the disputed verses, but he disqualifies them as poetic critics.[68] Those individuals likewise found that the analogy of the surviving tribe with "the stars from whose midst the full moon had fallen" made them shine stronger after the addressee's death and therefore had the effect of satirizing rather than praising the deceased. The poet was faulted for confusing genres. Instead, the critics proposed the same verse by al-Khuraymī as a better motif. Al-Ṣūlī comments at great length, citing evidence from pre-Islamic parallels, that the philologists and their followers (those were the ones advancing the criticism, he explains) missed the poet's point, which was to portray not the tribe's glimmer in the dark but the greater glamour of the addressee in their presence, in analogy with the moon's outshining the stars. However, this second type of motif criticism was at odds with the former charge of plagiarism, for if the verse was not Abū Tammām's, he should not be the one blamed for it. Ironically, Abū Tammām earns censure for a verse of which his authorship is later disputed. The two contradictory cases of criticism document either the double shame of a plagiarist who picked his model badly, or the mutually invalidating polemics against an upsettingly successful pioneer.

BOOKS BY POETS

Let us now return to the major written format current at the time. The incident of the notebook had pitted two writing poets against each other. Private writing was common in the first quarter of the ninth century. The fact that Diʿbil's many uses of writing are particularly well documented may be a coincidence of the sources. But he had certainly felt the adverse effect of writing against his own person, and perhaps he therefore took control of his craft by composing a book about it. He wrote what became a much-cited standard work, and he therewith placed on the map poets and verses that he deemed important. With this act he was the first poet to appropriate a genre that had heretofore been the realm of philologists.

Books on poetry and poets were frequent titles in the *Catalogue,* and a number of philologists had made selections of poetry in written form. But the subject antedates the book format to which it was transferred from conversation. In literary gatherings people "cited poetry and poets to each other" or focused on the poetry of one individual as an educated entertainment, such as in a session held at the court of al-Maʾmūn on the poetry of Diʿbil, or another, hosted by the governor ʿAbdallāh b. Ṭāhir, on pre-Islamic and Islamic poets.[69] This sort of practical criticism went on not only before caliphs and viziers but also among literati and book merchants.[70] Books on the subject began as transcripts of, or cramming sheets for, precisely such recitation sessions. As shown in Chapter 1, the earliest extant book on poets still shows its transition from a conversation to a book: the aging al-Aṣmaʿī was questioned by a student about a list of names and received in reply short comments about their rankings as "great" or not, with occasional explanations of the reason. The answers were dictated, but it took a third person, a student of the following generation (Ibn Durayd), for them to be edited as a book (as with al-Aṣmaʿī's book on horses).[71] The question-and-answer format was retained in the surviving redaction (based on later manuscripts) of this forerunner to biographical dictionaries on poets. Conversation continued to be a popular literary device long after books were being conceived in writing. The next book about poets that has been preserved (again, in later manuscripts) from the early ninth century, authored by Muḥammad b. Sallām al-Jumaḥī (d. 846–847), already displays a systematic treatment—to wit, a chronological and thematic arrangement of poets into classes, with an intervening geographical section on the poets of Mecca, Medina, Ṭāʾif, and Baḥrayn, and a section on Jewish poets. It opens with a preface tracing the development of the discipline of linguistics and the art of poetry, as well as a definition of criticism as a profession based on experience. Poets had thus become a subject of philology.

Diʿbil's Book

Diʿbil was the first poet to turn the tables on the philologists as arbiters of good poetry and write a book from the purview of a practitioner. In it he formulated identifiable aesthetic standards, and it documents a professional vision and consistency unusual for his time. He captures poets' real-life circumstances, their tribal status, local provenance, posts, and affiliation to the government. Poetic passages he selects are often snapshots from real life, such as a dog bite, satirically explained by the host's dog being unused to the good smells of meals cooked for guests; brawls at a banquet and on a bridge; a rich man's argument that he is actually poor ("They think I have wealth and envy me, for the poor may resent the rich [*yughrā bihī*], but if they added up my new and old wealth, my debt, and my [tax] obligations [*farḍ*], it wouldn't be worth half a *dirham*"); and a sardonic comparison of matrimony and a cross: "O tree trunk [carrying] a crucified [man] [*jidhʿu maṣlūbin*], will you, full thirty years past his crucifixion, ever exchange him? / You have not been keener [*aghraḍu;* var.: "more disgruntled," *aḍjaru*] on the burden you have born than I am on mine [i.e., my wife]."[72] One quoted passage laments the change of the owner of a palace through its purchase.[73] Other selections complain about poll tax, or make a claim for a share of tax revenues. One poet defends the standard 4,000 *dirhams* he usually demanded for a poem as his *sunna.* Veracity is an issue in the suitability of praise for the person who received it, as well as in the praise of God.[74] A poet of the era of Caliph al-Mahdī is cited emphasizing his truthfulness: "He who says something other than me lies, antagonizes, and fabricates" (*man yaqul ghayra maqālī fa-laqad qāla zawran wa-taʿaddā wa-kadhaba*).[75] With similar directness, ʿAmr b. al-ʿĀṣ (d. c. 662) requests in verse the governorship of Egypt.[76] Poets Diʿbil approved of had something to say, and they did not beat around the bush.

He also included the new type of secretary-poets, such as the accomplished Baghdadi clan of the Banū Umayya, whom Diʿbil describes with a pun—"This house is the family of the [memorable] verse" (*hādhā l-baytu ahlu bayti shiʿrin*)—and whose best and most prolific member was Muḥammad b. Abī Umayya (alive first half of the ninth century), a client of the dynasty's eponymous ancestor Umayya.[77] Among the secretaries was the only poet whose verse Diʿbil envied, Kulthūm b. ʿAmr al-ʿAttābī's (d. 823 or 835) couplet on the motif that a forbidding man misses the opportunity of being asked for help by his brethren: "The awe before brethren cuts off the one in need from a request to him. / When I am in awe of someone in whom I place my hope, my connection to him fails."[78]

Diʿbil was interested in good poems, not an assemblage of big names whom "one should know," such as the anthology the official Ibn Qutayba would produce.[79] Reflecting the author's own vocation, his book was a "primer for the practicing poet."[80] It included many model verses of the *afʿal* type, each perfecting a specific poetic intent. This was an early epigrammatic form of poetic criticism. Diʿbil selects the "most boastful" verse (*afkharu l-shʿir*) by the Arabs, the "most satirical" verse (*ahjā bayt*), the "truest" (*aṣdaqu bayt*) and the "falsest" verse (*akhdhabu l-abyāt*).[81] Further passages are exemplary in defending succinctly a poet's claim, attitude, or ethics, and in showing poetry to be a "means for getting on in the world."[82] Diʿbil's book thus composed a model corpus for the poetry of his time.

But Diʿbil was a harsh critic. He opined that the poet ʿAmr b. Naṣr al-Qiṣāfī (d. c. 861) produced only a single good verse in sixty years. He deems a poet straddling the period of Islam (*mukhaḍram*) to have produced only mediocre poetry (*shiʿr wasaṭ*), and labels Abū l-ʿUdhāfir's (alive mid-ninth century) poetry "uneven" (*mukhtalif al-shiʿr*), despite his having received a 2,000 *dirham* reward for it.[83] Some literary accounts are just well-told or funny stories and not infrequently referred to as "tales" (*qiṣaṣ*). The deaths of two lovers in Kufa are recounted as a *fait divers,* leading to the fashioning of literary accounts (people did not leave a good love story alone).[84] But such stories are only evoked, not reproduced, as they did not contribute to the substance of the book.

Taken together, the work is surprisingly level-headed. It shows a different side of a man who did not hesitate to satirize high-standing patrons. His authorial persona is that of a rigorous critic of poetry who set a standard to be followed and was forthright, even harsh, in his comments, without being insulting. The book lacks the more acerbic statements he was reported to have made in literary gatherings, where he was prompted into spur-of-the-moment reactions.

Diʿbil on Abū Tammām

Diʿbil must have completed his book toward the end his career, before the time of the alleged theft of the fallen-moon verse, for it includes a lamentation for Abū Tammām but no charge of plagiarism against him, either general or specific. The author simply remained silent on him. Being aware of the status a mention in his book conferred, Diʿbil excluded from his collection the towering rival who succeeded with a new style, which this demanding critic considered beyond the pale of poetry. To his mind, it belonged instead to prose speech and oratory.[85] This exclusion was inconsequential, for Abū Tammām had overshadowed the aging Diʿbil, but it showed that the latter attempted to use his book to skew the record of literary reception and literally write Abū Tammām out of poetic history. In a candid moment, however, Diʿbil endorsed Abū Tammām's genius and conceded that his grudge sprang from jealousy. This was again an oral occasion and left no trace in the book.[86] The poet's new style was simply so far beyond Diʿbil's aesthetic compass that he withheld written judgement and let posterity decide.

How did Abū Tammām fare otherwise as a subject of writing? Though popular in many circles, his poetry was during his lifetime not readily available in writing. The poets in Khurasan, for instance, needed to gather to hear Abū Tammām's verse when he traveled there, which means that they did not have access to it in written form.[87] His poems were taken down in sessions of recitation like those of other modern poets. His reciter, whom he was forced to use, for his own rough voice did not please, must have had many of them memorized and perhaps used a notebook, as did, for instance, the *rāwī* of the slightly earlier poet Muslim b. al-Walīd. Muslim himself still saw no point in perpetuating his oeuvre in writing, and when his *rāwī* presented him a collection of his own poems for correction, he tossed it into a river.[88] In this case it was the *rāwī,* not the poet himself, who saw the value of an authenticated transcript, even if on this occasion it was denied to him. Toward the end of the ninth century, the grammarian Thaʿlab, before joining the literary salon of the vizier Ibn Thawāba (d. 890), still had to ask his secretary friends, the Banū Nawbakht, to prepare a written selection of Abū Tammām for him to prevent the embarrassment of seeming to ignore this fashionable verse.[89] But such poetry collections must have become increasingly current, and shared at least among the literati at the end of the century, because the prince, poet, and poetic critic Ibn al-Muʿtazz (d. 908) states in his biographical dictionary of contemporary poets that most such poetry was available, and he contented himself with listing the first hemistichs of Abū Tammām's well-known odes in order not to waste space with things his reader knew.[90] His book was immediately copied by a secretary from the Banū Munajjim, several of whom also composed books on poetry and poets.

Abū Tammām and His Books

Abū Tammām was also an avid book reader and writer. He kept notebooks, for he, like other "modern" poets, needed to familiarize himself with the classical heritage. This could be done by memory, as the prolific early Abbasid poet Abū Nuwās had still done it, or in writing, as Abū Tammām chose to do by, for instance, keeping in his house notebooks of the *dīwāns* of Abū Nuwās and Muslim b. al-Walīd.[91] A friend once found him in his home, bent over these two *dīwāns* to draw inspiration from them, while composing poetry. Questioned what those notes were, he called them, after two pagan Arab goddesses, his "Al-Lāt and al-ʿUzzā whom I have venerated for thirty years instead of God."[92] Not being of Arab stock and upbringing, he collected his subject matter in written form. But other than Diʿbil who circulated his book, Abū Tammām's notebooks were only designed for his own memorization, composition, and poetry compilations, without any intention of written publication. His ultimate method of publishing was oral.[93]

Abū Tammām was also familiar with libraries, and whiled away several months in one belonging to a patron after a heavy snowfall interrupted his journey home from Hamadhān.[94] Books had become a much-used data carrier for the older poetry, while the more recent poetry, though current among some, required a personal connection to be obtained in writing.

Abū Tammām also became active as a book author, putting together collections on pre-Islamic, early Islamic, and modern poets. Those were not "written" books in the sense of a text composed from scratch; rather, Abū Tammām excerpted extant poems and rearranged the fragments according to an overall structure. He thus reduced poetry to small elements and recomposed those into a thematically searchable database. The arrangement of his *Ḥamāsa* anthology facilitates the search for the specific topic. It breaks down poems into discrete semantic units, or conceits, and assembles these in large thematic chapters (on bravery, lamentation, etc.). What other poets had done in their minds, Abū Tammām did with paper and prepared a repertoire by topic. Later records credit the genesis of this collection to his stopover in the library, and it is plausible that the (un-)lucky occasion of a stay in a well-appointed library greatly supported the anthologies' creation, but Abū Tammām's well-documented reliance on writing makes it unlikely that the idea was born there. However, the completion of the anthology was not followed by its circulation.

Another distinction points in the same direction: different collections by Abū Tammām focus variously on obscure or famous poets—the *Ḥamāsa* and the *Waḥshiyyāt* on the former group, the *Ikhtiyār al-shuʿarāʾ al-fuḥūl* (preserved in a unicate unedited manuscript) on the latter group.[95] In terms of reuse, it was practical to separate the two groups. Obscure poets' verse could be reused with greater impunity than famous verse. Al-Āmidī also latched onto this idea and claimed that Abū Tammām suppressed lesser poets completely to take over their work in toto.

How did Abū Tammām's thefts, then, relate to his book writing? Leaving aside the gray area of the transmitted literary accounts, let us recall that in the theft of the fallen-moon verse we are dealing with an extreme form of verbatim copying. The most damning criticism is the poetic critic al-Āmidī's claim that Abū Tammām's project in his anthology writing was to systematically source and suppress excellent ancient verse by excising it from his selections and then passing it off as his own, while "overwriting" people's memories with the truncated leftovers of such poems. This generalizes the single case of the wholesale "rip-off," of which Diʿbil had accused him, to a premeditated program. Al-Āmidī writes:

> These selections [i.e., his anthologies] indicate his care for poetry and the fact that he occupied himself with it and made it his endeavor [*wukd;* var.: goal] and exclusively focused on it among all the arts and sciences. There is not much pre-Islamic, Islamic, and modern poetry that he did not read and study. Therefore I say that his hidden borrowings are [even] more copious that his apparent ones, despite their copiousness.[96]

Given that we owe to Abū Tammām the preservation of much verse that would otherwise have been lost, and that he is the sole source for much minor verse, the charge can never be substantiated. But the idea is not far-fetched; indeed, burying some poets' identities in a flood of others might be suspected of a pioneering anthologist. His own compositions indeed subsisted on extant motifs and conceits, and it was for their complex recombinations that he became famous, or infamous, depending on the recipient's perspective. In sum, Abū Tammām's book writing was a handy collection of the (by now written) heritage for an artistic purpose. His judgement was intuitive and the selection an arsenal for future creation.

However, an intentional skewing of the historical record holds up only if Abū Tammām had circulated his anthologies in his lifetime, which he did not. He is reported to have transmitted his (later so-titled) *Ḥamāsa* to only one person during his lifetime, and the earliest commentary dates to the end of the ninth century. Only during al-Āmidī's lifetime, one and a half centuries after the poet's passing, did his anthologies and particularly the *Ḥamāsa* become well known. The charge that he intended to change literary history cannot therefore be taken at face value. His anthologies were not a public statement but a private reference. If he reshaped the past, the anthologies' effect was posthumous. For him, they served as an interim written database for his own orally presented compositions.

As for the borrowings that were not verbatim copies but reworked motifs, Abū Tammām was in the same boat with any other poet in not being able to evade the widespread and familiar repertoire of motifs, as al-Āmidī himself concedes: "This is an issue [*bāb*] none but a few poets are free of."[97] However, through his intense study of the written heritage, Abū Tammām became a plausible suspect.

Nonetheless, his transformation of his models had a unique quality, as even his critic al-Āmidī admits, and his contemporaries the composer and litterateur Isḥāq al-Mawṣilī (d. 849–850) and the philosopher al-Kindī (d. 866) stress the poet's self-reliance on his intellect in producing his novel verse (al-Kindī prophesied an early death for him due to overexerting his brain).[98] And while collections of his borrowings abounded (such as the one by Ibn Abī Ṭāhir, reproduced by al-Āmidī), he incurred greater criticism for the unusual twists in motifs and wording to which he subjected his models.

Criticism of this creative but hard-to-understand pioneer of Abbasid modernism had become a kind of sport, which was pursued with verve by both those who were experts and those who were not. This can be seen in the moon verse being taken to task with different types of blame, as being a theft, a poor formulation, a spoilt motif, or a misunderstanding of the genre to which it belonged. It appears that certain verses of Abū Tammām were familiar as "frequently criticized," although the exact point of debate varied from one account to another—as if people knew that there was something to be said, even if they might not remember exactly what it was. An outright competitive spirit shows in al-Marzubānī's (d. 994) *The Embroidered [Book] on What Scholars Faulted Poets For* (*al-Muwashshaḥ fī ma'ākhidh al-ʿulamāʾ ʿalā l-shuʿarāʾ*), in which he lists objectionable verses and marks, whether the points of critique had been voiced before him or he was the first to make them.

Poets' Split Attitude to Books

Both books were composed with the aim to change poetic history. Abū Tammām overwrote past poets with the interim help of his anthologies (though the publication of these anthologies was an unplanned secondary consequence), and Diʿbil tried to overwrite Abū Tammām. The power of writing had come home to both of them in very different ways. But poets approached book writing with a sort of split consciousness; books served to assemble the greats of the past (editing them for contemporary taste) or to assemble the noteworthy ones of the author's time together with a guiding commentary. The first type of book (Abū Tammām's anthologies) was still produced only for the author's convenience, while the second type (Diʿbil's book), even if completed at the end of the author's life, was intended for circulation.

Neither of those poets, curiously, considered their own oeuvre as a subject of books. Did they regard the ongoing oral transmission as sufficient? It certainly pervaded the educated circles, but it did not reach everywhere, as the grammarian Thaʿlab had to realize. Or did the poets deem those unconnected to their circle unentitled to their own production in a convenient way? It was not until the tenth century and required a poet with the self-assurance of al-Mutanabbī (d. 965) to edit his own collected verse. But regarding the written availability of modern verse of the kinds of Diʿbil and Abū Tammām, the situation would change very soon. Ibn al-Muʿtazz, writing at the end of the ninth century, judged contemporary poets' *dīwāns* to be well known and generally available.[99]

This rapid change occurred within less than half a century, by which time books by and about poets had become commonplace and served as a basis for the nascent sophisticated rhetorical tradition. The affair of the fallen-moon verse revealed the first small but significant step in this direction. Its exact facts (theft, mistaken image, or missed genre) are irretrievably lost, yet the means of committing the crime, if a crime it was, was writing, and both the accusation and the defense relied on the display of notebooks; these were thus trusted to carry the burden of proof. As such, the incident represents a tipping point, when authorship for the first time resorts to writing as proof.

Further Writers among Poets

The man whose couplet Diʿbil had envied, al-ʿAttābī, was known for a rare combination of skills that usually occurred in different people: poetry and prose. He used either as needed for his professional furtherance. An ode of his stopped a punitive campaign against the tribe of Rabīʿa that had caused much bloodshed.[100] Thereafter, one its verses, praising the resolve of the local governor ʿAbdallāh b. Ṣāliḥ al-Hāshimī—"He derives the resolve of the heart from thoughts the space between which and God no one inhabits"—became a benchmark against which other poets were gauged.[101] Another of his couplets became "the rage" (*hijjīrā*) among people.[102] When the circumstances required it, he sent poetry by letter, such as in illness, or on another occasion, in disgrace.[103] His prose was outstanding and earned him the kind of rewards usually reserved for poetry.[104] To gain access to Caliph al-Maʾmūn he won the help of a judge with the argument that using one's status to help others was analogous to giving the tithe of one's wealth to the poor.[105] On admittance, he proved his worthiness in a testing conversation with the musician Isḥāq al-Mawṣilī, instigated by and conducted before the caliph.[106] Al-ʿAttābī even once ad-libbed an absurd mock sermon to prove the credulity of the populace.[107] He also combined both registers with success, such as when Caliph al-Rashīd was angered when he entered without permission a session of the *maẓālim* court and recited a plea in prose and poetry, skillfully coopting the crowd of petitioners present: "People brought me back to you and to myself in [what I think about] you." This reconciled the caliph, and the poet went home with a robe of honor and a gift.[108]

Al-ʿAttābī had a punctilious ethic; he was forgiving to those who admitted fault, but merciless with disloyalty, such as that shown by his student Manṣūr al-Namarī (d. before 809).[109] Like Abū Tammām, al-ʿAttābī knew the value of libraries. He read Persian books in the library of Marw, and after having left and traveled ten parasangs beyond Marw, he realized that he had overlooked a book and turned around to spend some further months of reading in Marw.[110]

But al-ʿAttābī differed from Abū Tammām in knowing and fluently speaking another language. The latter poet was of Greek origin but seems not to have read books in this language. Al-ʿAttābī's readings of Persian books led him to the pronouncement, "Are not meanings and eloquence solely in the books of the Persians? Ours is the language, but theirs are the meanings."

Books led inevitably from Arabic to the multilingual late antique cosmos of knowledge, which Arabic readers and writers knew to be relevant to their own careers.[111] The knowledge and culture contained in books was seen by some, such as al-ʿAttābī's neighbor, as a privilege of the rich, and he belittled the poet's reading as pointless. But al-ʿAttābī instead described his reading as looking into "culture and wisdom" (*al-ādāb wa-l-ḥikam*) and as gaining "knowledge" (*ʿilm*) and "understanding" (*fahm*), the good fortune from which the ignorant neighbor was barred.[112]

Though steeped in book culture and writing for utilitarian purposes, al-ʿAttābī, like Diʿbil and Abū Tammām, seems not to have considered gathering his own verbal art in book form. The idea came instead to his patron. The Barmakid vizier Yaḥyā b. Khālid who appreciated the pithiness of al-ʿAttābī's conversation. Finding him rather quiet on one day, he remarked, "If your words are few, their benefits abound," and advised his sons to take down the poet's utterances (*anfās*) in addition to his verses and epistles.[113] Yaḥyā was an educated administrator who suggested giving contemporary literature a written form, yet it was still the poet's spoken word, "his breath" (*anfās*), to which the authorship and ownership belonged. Proprietary issues only arose with other poets, and al-ʿAttābī reminded his student al-Namarī that there was "nothing beautiful or handsome you pronounced that does not derive from me, though you might deny it."[114] As for members of the government, his prose and verse were a service provided and remunerated with rewards and a stipend (*rizq*); their use of it was therewith paid for. Written literature and gain still moved on separate planes. The value was inherent in the spoken word, irrespective of what happened to it afterward. But it was the written form in which knowledge would be deposited and whence it was mined. For al-ʿAttābī that mine was still a free database, not anything relevant to the market. In this sense poetry still differed from scholarship, such as grammar, whose written form created an opportunity for gain where none had existed.

CHAPTER THREE

STATIONERS

Having outlined the scope of how scholars and poets of the ninth century used books openly and in private, a third type of agent remains to be considered, less visible perhaps but indispensable; these are the craftspeople who manufactured the increasing numbers of books.

There are still open questions about the beginnings of Arabic book production. It is uncertain how the technique of papermaking arrived in Transoxania (modern Uzbekistan; at the time, part of the governorate of Khurasan in northeastern Iran), whence it made its entry to the Arabic-Islamic world.[1] A much-cited account of Chinese papermakers taken prisoner at the Battle of Talas (or Taraz) in modern Tajikistan in 751 and forced to reveal the secrets of their craft has been consigned to the realm of legend; the know-how came most likely through monks and traders traveling along the network of trade routes commonly referred to as the Silk Road.[2] Paper, though invented in China in the second century B.C.E., was used primarily as writing material only by the third century C.E. This technology then gradually spread westward along the Silk Road and arrived in Central Asia by the eighth century C.E. Archeological sites containing paper from the period between the fourth and the ninth centuries C.E. are found (from east to west) in the Tarim Basin, situated between Dunhuang and Kashgar in the Chinese section of the Silk Road, at Mount Mugh, a fortress southeast of Samarqand across the border of modern Tajikistan, and Moshchevaia Balka in the Caucasus, the site furthest west, where paper from the eighth to ninth centuries C.E. was discovered.[3] This was still imported Chinese paper, for paper was not produced in Central Asia until the eighth century. All this suggests that the technology moved westward. Better documented is the subsequent transfer of paper from Transoxania to Baghdad, where it became known and used at the end of the eighth century and quickly diversified into five types, named after contemporary Iraqi and Khurasanian officials, including "al-Jaʿfarī," named after the vizier Jaʿfar b. Yaḥyā al-Barmakī (d. 808), who introduced it in Baghdad, after his brother al-Faḍl b. Yaḥyā had spotted the new writing material in Khurasan during his brief governorship there (793–795).[4] The existence of a paper factory, however, allegedly founded in the Dār al-Qazz quarter of Baghdad, has not been reliably proven. Documented instead are numerous individual craftspeople, often clustered into markets, who produced the new writing matter and also copied and sold the finished books. There were a hundred booksellers in Baghdad alone. The ninth-century historian al-Yaqūbī mentions them as part of those markets that were relocated from the central city to what came to be called al-Sharqiyya, that is, the eastern part of al-Karkh, the suburb extending south and southeast of Baghdad.[5] Mosul, Kufa, Basra, and Ahwaz featured their own thriving book markets.[6] Besides the copious local production, imported paper from Khurasan continued to be considered superior in quality for a long time.

As for the technique of Arabic book manufacturing, the know-how was closer at hand: Christian communities in Palestine and Egypt had since the fourth century been active in the production of Greek and Syriac books, and a number of early Arabic books and book fragments of the ninth century contain Christian texts, such as collections of the New Testament (containing the Gospels, Acts of the Apostles, and Pauline letters), the lives of saints and martyrs, monastic anthologies, and theological treatises, which largely emerged in the context of monastic life.[7] That this technique was passed on from monasteries to the urban stationers, though not documented, is possible, given the close contact between cities and their surrounding monasteries. Material links are Christian texts copied in Arabic but with the numbering of the codices' gatherings, liturgical calendar dates, and reading notes in Greek.[8] In Arabic literary sources, the contact between cities and monasteries is illustrated in, for instance, the frequent *akhbār* type of poets' outings to monasteries to enjoy wine, song, and verse in their gardens, resulting in ample poetic descriptions of such scenes, as recorded notably in the *Book of Cloisters* (*Kitāb al-Diyārāt*) by al-Shābushtī (d. 1008 or earlier).[9]

Irrespective of how Arab stationers had come by their expertise, they emerged as a well-attested profession in the urban economy beginning in the late eighth and early ninth century. In short time, the book trade became sophisticated and diversified, as is evident in its numerous designations (a bookseller or dealer is referred to as *ṣaḥḥāf, bayyiʿ al-kutub,* or *kutubī*) and its degree of specialization. In terms of content, copyists of the Qur'ān (*maṣāḥifī*) and assistants who added the vowel markers (*nāqiṭ, naqqāṭ,* both of whom usually specialized in this) differed from copyists of other books (*nāsikh*) and calligraphers *(khaṭṭāṭ*). There were ink makers and sellers (*ḥibrī, ḥabārī*), papermakers and sellers (*kaghghād, kāghadī*), and bookbinders (*mujallid, saḥḥāf*). The draft copy produced by a scholar was clean-copied in larger script by a *muḥarrir,* and finished copies would be proofread by a hired collator (*muʿāriḍ mustaʾjar*).[10] However, the most common denomination was *warrāq,* or "stationer" (literally "folio maker"), whose expertise might include everything from producing the paper to disseminating the finished product, including finding authors or buyers for potential books to be copied, sourcing books for scholars' research, and assembling or assessing entire libraries for purchase by wealthy clients.

The sources that inform about stationers differ from those on scholars and poets. Craftsmen do not constitute per se a category of people on whose lives writers in the ninth century would spill any ink. In literary sources, they seldom make an appearance, unless they figure in a tellable story next to more noteworthy people, such as men of letters, secretaries, scholars, or dignitaries. Such accounts are often rich in detail, but, because of their rarity, of insufficient representative value. The few identified cases certainly illustrate singular occasions but they do not add up to a comprehensive view of the stationers' profession. Another more fruitful source in this regard is biographical dictionaries, a major genre in Arabic literature. Having initially been devoted to members of this or that scholarly discipline, or the notables of a certain city or region, such dictionaries reached an unprecedented breadth of coverage in the Mamluk era (1250–1517).[11] They now included anyone, male or (less often) female, who gained some degree of notoriety (*shuhra*), as noted by al-Dhahabī (d. 1348), who produced the summa of biographical compilation. His *History of Islam and the Classes of the Famous and Illustrious* (*Taʾrīkh al-islām wa-ṭabaqāt al-mashāhīr wa-l-aʿlām*) preserves the names of around 30,000 individuals of the Arabic-Islamic world, spanning the period from pre-Islamic times (sixth century C.E.) to his own fourteenth century.[12] Though still selective and not what one might term a statistically valid source, his work nonetheless broadened the panorama enormously.[13]

Different from the character of the detailed literary accounts, which have served as a basis for the two preceding chapters, the data al-Dhahabī supplies on a given person are terse and matter-of-fact. After the full name and the death date (and occasionally the birth date) of the biographee, there are lists of the person's teachers and students and his (or her) degree of reliability in transmitting scholarly texts. This is akin to the format of books on transmitters of the Prophetic tradition (Ḥadīth), titled "books of men" (*kutub al-rijāl*), which also included women to a varying degree.[14] Al-Dhahabī is an invaluable source for the existence of types of people who had gone unrecorded in prior compilations of this genre. And not a few of his biographees carry the professional label of stationer (*warrāq*) or papermaker (*kāghadī*). The latter denomination derives from the exact technical term for the new paper, *kāghad*, a word of Sogdian provenance that had been imported together with the writing material, but which was not frequently used. Though concise on the single individual and lacking in literary color, al-Dhahabī's work includes a massive number of individuals who together cover a spectrum of stationery activities during the ninth century.

The benefit of his work is that through its wealth of single cases, it allows us to recognize recurring types of stationers, even though each one does not receive much individual detail. Those stationers described in greater depth tend to be remarkable personages, as we will see, and the same is true for those who gave rise to literary accounts. By matching the predominant types with single cases fleshed out into palpable portraits in the accounts, one can draw more detailed professional profiles, pinpoint where tensions and conflicts arose in the exercise of this new craft, and gauge what effects its practitioners had on the acquisition, dissemination, and material value of written text and the conventions of scholarly transmission.

Al-Dhahabī arranged his biographical entries by death dates, grouped into decades, which he labelled "generations" (*ṭabaqāt*), listing at the end of each decade those individuals whose exact year of death within the decade he could not ascertain. What follows is an analysis of the biographies of all stationers with death dates between 200 and 350 A.H. The latter date has been chosen because some of the stationers were long-lived (two reached their eighties and one nearly a hundred) and were thus active for many decades prior to their deaths. Where aspects of the biographical entries coincide with literary accounts, I juxtapose the former with the rounded-out versions of individual representatives from the latter sources. In order not to overburden the text with names (which tend to be long), I refer to each stationer in the following analysis by his shortened name and his generation with his sequential number within it; for example, "23 / 1" is the first stationer in the 23rd generation (i.e., those who died between 221 and 230 A.H.). The full name is given when a biographical entry is discussed in detail. The following is a full chronological list of the stationers' names, as grouped in al-Dhahabī's *Taʾrīkh al-Islām* in decades of death dates (volume and page numbers refer to the edition by ʿUmar ʿA. al-Tadmurī). For those stationers who can be assigned to specific subtypes, this is added in parentheses in gray shading:

20TH GENERATION (death dates 191–200 A.H.)

Abū l-Ḥasan Saʿīd b. Muḥammad al-Thaqafī al-Warrāq al-Kufī *nazīl* Baghdād (traditionist-stationer) (20 / 1, vol. 13, 188–189)

21ST GENERATION (death dates 201–210 A.H.)

Abū l-Ḥārith Naṣr b. Ḥammād al-Baṣrī al-Bajallī al-Warrāq al-Ḥāfiẓ (traditionist-stationer) (21 / 1, vol. 14, 410–411)

22ND GENERATION (death dates 211–220 A.H.)

Ismāʿīl b. Abān al-Warrāq, Kūfī, d. [2]16 (traditionist-stationer) (22 / 1, vol. 15, 71–73)
al-Ḥasan b. ʿAnbasa al-Warrāq, d. 213 (traditionist-stationer) (22 / 2, vol. 15, 117)
Abū Muḥammad Salm b. Ibrāhīm al-Baṣrī al-Warrāq (traditionist-stationer) (22 / 3, vol. 15, 177)

23RD GENERATION (death dates 221–230 A.H.)

Abū Jaʿfar Ahmad b. Muḥammad b. Ayyūb al-Bagdādī al-Warrāq, d. 228 (copyist of a vizier) (23 / 1, vol. 16, 52–54)
Abū ʿAlī Maḥmūd b. al-Ḥasan al-Warrāq (poet and author-stationer) (23 / 2, vol. 16, 404)

24TH GENERATION (death dates 231–240 A.H.)

Abū ʿAlī al-Ḥasan b. Ḥammād al-Ḍabbī al-Kūfī al-Warrāq, d. 238 or 239 (traditionist-stationer) (24 / 1, vol. 17, 129)

al-ʿAbbās b. ʿAbdallāh al-Baghdādī al-Warrāq, d. 233 (traditionist-stationer) (24 / 2, vol. 17, 209–210)

al-ʿAbbās b. Ghālib al-Baghdādī al-Warrāq, d. 233 (traditionist-stationer) (24 / 2, vol. 17, 211; (the entry is identical with the previous, but since the duplication is al-Dhahabī's it has been retained.)

25TH GENERATION (death dates 241–250 A.H.)

Aḥmad b. Abī ʿUbaydallāh Bishr al-Sulaymī al-Baṣrī al-Warrāq (traditionist-stationer) (25 / 1, vol. 18, 156)

Abū ʿAmr Abdarraḥmān b. al-Aswad al-Hāshimī al-Baṣrī al-Warrāq, Hashimite client (traditionist-stationer) (25 / 2, vol. 18, 325–326)

al-Faḍl b. Abī Ḥassān al-Bukāʾī al-Warrāq, d. 249 (traditionist-stationer) (25 / 3, vol. 18, 392–393)

Abū ʿĪsā Muḥammad b. Hārūn al-Warrāq d. 247 (author-stationer) (25 / 4, vol. 18, 477)[15]

26TH GENERATION (death dates 251–260 A.H.)

Abū l-Azhar Ḥawthara b. Muḥammad al-Minqarī al-Baṣrī al-Warrāq (traditionist-stationer) (26 / 1, vol. 19, 128–129)

Abū l-Azhar Zāhir b. Khālid al-Samarqandī al-Warrāq, d. 256 (traditionist-stationer) (26 / 2, vol. 19, 137)

Abū ʿUthmān Saʿīd b. Nuṣayr al-Baghdādī al-Warrāq *nazīl* al-Thaghr wa-l-Raqqa, alive 250 (author-stationer) (26 / 3, vol. 19, 155–156)

Saʿīd b. Hāshim al-Samarqandī al-Kāghadī, d. 259 (traditionist-stationer) (26 / 4, vol. 19, 156)

Abū l-Ḥasan ʿAbd al-Wahhāb b. ʿAbd al-Ḥakam b. Nāfiʿ al-Warrāq al-Nasāʾī *l-aṣl* al-Baghdādī *al-ʿābid,* d. 251 (traditionist-stationer) (26 / 5, vol. 19, 200–201)

ʿUbayd b. Muḥammad b. al-Qāsim al-Naysabūrī al-Warrāq, d. 255 (traditionist-stationer) (26 / 6, vol. 19, 205)

Abū Jaʿfar Muḥammad b. ʿUthmān b. Karāma, d. 256 (stationer-disciple and scholar's stationer) (26 / 7, vol. 19, 303–304)

27TH GENERATION (death dates 261–270 A.H.)

Abū l-ʿAbbās Aḥmad b. Ibrāhīm al-Baghdādī al-Warrāq, d. 261–270 (scholar's stationer and author-stationer) (27 / 1, vol. 20, 39)

Abū Bakr Aḥmad b. ʿAbdallāh b. al-Qāsim al-Tamīmī al-Warrāq al-Ḥāfiẓ, d. 269 (traditionist-stationer) (27 / 2, vol. 20, 50–51)

Abū Bakr Aḥmad b. Muḥammad b. Abī Mūsā al-Warrāq, d. 268 (stationer-disciple) (27 / 3, vol. 20, 55)

28TH GENERATION (death dates 271–280 A.H.)

Abū Yaʿqūb Isḥāq b. Ḥanīfa al-Jurjānī *al-zāhid al-ʿābid* (stationer-disciple) (28 / 1, vol. 20, 300–301)

Jaʿfar b. Aḥmad b. Maʿbad al-Warrāq, Baghdādī, d. 280 (traditionist-stationer) (28 / 2, vol. 20, 323)

Jaʿfar b. Muḥammad al-Warrāq, d. 271 (traditionist-stationer) (28 / 3, vol. 20, 327)

Rajāʾ b. ʿAbdallāh al-Harawī al-Warrāq, d. 277 or 279 (book transmitter) (28 / 4, vol. 20, 349)

ʿAbdallāh b. ʿAmr b. Abī Saʿd al-Baghdādī al-Warrāq, d. 274 (author-stationer) (28 / 5, vol. 20, 377)

[Abū Mūsā] ʿĪsā b. Jaʿfar al-Baghdādī al-Warrāq, d. 2[7]2 (traditionist-stationer) (28 / 6, vol. 20, 410)[16]

Abū Bakr Muḥammd b. Idrīs b. ʿUmar al-Makkī al-Warrāq al-Ḥumaydī (scholar's stationer) (28 / 7, vol. 20, 436)

Abū Jaʿfar Muḥammad b. ʿAlī al-Baghdādī al-Ḥāfiẓ, known as Ḥamdān al-Warrāq, d. 272 (traditionist-stationer) (28 / 8, vol. 20, 455)[17]

al-Haytham b. Khālid al-Kūfī al-Washshāʾ al-Warrāq, d. 278 (scholar's stationer) (28 / 9, vol. 20, 487)

29TH GENERATION (death dates 281–290 A.H.)

Abū Jaʿfar Aḥmad b. ʿAmr al-Fārisī al-Warrāq al-Muqʿad, alive after 280 (traditionist-stationer) (29 / 1, vol. 21, 77)

Aḥmad b. Muḥammad b. Bakr al-Naysabūrī al-Warrāq al-Qaṣīr [the Bleacher], d. 284 (29 / 2, vol. 21, 83–84)

Saʿīd b. Yāsīn al-Balkhī al-Warrāq (traditionist-stationer) (29 / 3, vol. 21, 184)

Abū ʿAbdallāh Muḥammad b. ʿAbd al-Salām b. Bashshār al-Shaykh al-Naysabūrī al-Warrāq *al-zāhid,* d. 286 (scholar's stationer) (29 / 4, vol. 21, 271–272)

Abū l-Faḍl Muḥammad b. Abī Hārūn Mūsā al-Warrāq al-Baghdādī, known as Zurayq, d. 283 (traditionist-stationer) (29 / 5, vol., 21–291)

30TH GENERATION (death dates 291–300 A.H.)

ʿAbd al-Razzāq b. al-Ḥasan b. ʿAbd al-Razzāq al-Anṭākī al-Warrāq al-Muqriʾ (book transmitter) (30 / 1, vol. 22, 195–196)

al-Qāsim b. ʿAbd al-Wārith al-Warrāq, d. 2[9]4 (traditionist-stationer) (30 / 2, vol. 22, 230)

31ST GENERATION (death dates 301–310 A.H.)

Muḥammad b. Zakariyyāʾ b. Yaḥyā b. ʿAbdallāh b. Nāṣiḥ b. ʿAmr b. Dīnār [d. 126 / 743–744] (Qahramān Āl al-Zubayr) al-Dīnārī al-Bukhārī al-Warrāq, d. 302 (traditionist-stationer) (31 / 1, vol. 23, 98)[18]

Abū Yaʿqūb Isḥāq b. Ibrāhīm b. Yūnus, al-Manjanīqī al-Warrāq, Baghdādī, *ḥāfiẓ,* d. 304 (stationer-disciple) (31 / 2, vol. 23, 137–138)[19]

Abū Ḥafṣ ʿUmar b. Muḥammad b. Naṣr, al-Kāghadī al-Muqriʾ, Baghdādī, d. 305 (traditionist-stationer) (31 / 3, vol. 23, 165)

Abū Bakr Aḥmad b. Muḥammad b. Abd al-Khāliq, al-Baghdādī al-Warrāq, d. 309 (traditionist-stationer) (31 / 4, vol. 23, 249)

ʿĪsā b. Sulaymān b. ʿAbdalmalik al-Qurashī, al-Warrāq, d. 310 (scholar's stationer) (31 / 5, vol. 23, 273)

Abū Bishr Muḥammad b. Aḥmad b. Ḥammād b. Saʿīd b. Muslim al-Anṣārī al-Dūlābī al-Ḥāfiẓ al-Warrāq of Rayy, d. 310 (author-stationer) (31 / 6, vol. 23, 276)

32ND GENERATION (death dates 311–320 A.H.)

Abū Ḥafṣ ʿUmar b. Muḥammad b. Ḥafṣ al-Warrāq, Balkhī, d. 313 (traditionist-stationer?) (32 / 1, vol. 23, 458)

[Abū Yaʿqūb] Isḥāq b. Aḥmad al-Kāghadī, d. 315 (32 / 2, vol. 23, 490–491)[20]

ʿAbd al-Wahhāb b. ʿĪsā b. Abī Ḥayya al-Warrāq, d. 319 (scholar's stationer) (32 / 3, vol. 23, 585)

Abū l-Ṭayyib Muḥammad b. Aḥmad b. Ḥamdān al-Marwazī then al-Raʾsʿanī al-Warrāq (32 / 4, vol. 23, 637–638)

33RD GENERATION (death dates 321–330 A.H.)

Abū ʿAlī Ismāʿīl b. ʿAbbās b. ʿUmar b. Mihrān al-Warrāq, d. 323 (33 / 1, vol. 24, 127)

Abū l-Qāsim al-Ḥasan b. Saʿīd al-Baghdādī al-Warrāq, known as Ibn al-Harash, d. 323 (stationer-disciple) (33 / 2, vol. 24, 128)

ʿAbdalmalik b. Salmān al-Warrāq, d. 323 (traditionist-stationer) (33 / 3, vol. 24, 130)

Abū Bakr Muḥammad b. Zakariyyāʾ al-Kāghadī al-Muzakkī, d. 324 (traditionist-stationer) (33 / 4, vol. 24, 161)

Abū Muḥammad ʿAbdallāh b. al-ʿAbbās al-Shamʿī al-Warrāq al-Baghdādī, d. 326 (traditionist-stationer) (33 / 5, vol. 24, 193)

Abū l-Ḥusayn Aḥmad b. Muʿāwiya al-Kāghadī al-Rāzī, d. 328 (traditionist-stationer) (33 / 6, vol. 24, 224)

Abū Muḥammad ʿAbdallāh b. Sulaymān b. ʿĪsā al-Warrāq al-Fāmī [the Grocer], Baghdādī, d. 328 (traditionist-stationer) (33 / 7, vol. 24, 230)

Abū l-Ḥasan ʿAlī b. al-Ḥasan b. ʿAbd al-Warrāq, d. 328 (scholar's stationer and book transmitter) (33 / 8, vol. 24, 232)

Aḥmad b. Aḥayd b. Fārīnām al-Warrāq, d. 330 (traditionist-stationer) (33 / 9, vol. 24, 276)

Abū ʿAbdallāh Muḥammad b. ʿAbdallāh b. Qaran al-Farghānī al-Warrāq, known as Akhū Arghal, d. 330 (traditionist-stationer) (33 / 10, vol. 24, 290)

Abū Muḥammad ʿAbdallāh b. al-Faḍl b. Jaʿfar al-Warrāq (scholar's stationer) (33 / 11, vol. 24, 305)

ʿAlī b. Muḥammad b. Aḥmad b. Fūr al-Naysabūrī al-Warrāq, d. 320 or 324 (traditionist-stationer) (33 / 12, vol. 24, 308)

34TH GENERATION (death dates 331–340 A.H.)

[no stationer's entry]

35TH GENERATION (death dates 341–350 A.H.)

Abū Saʿīd ʿAmr b Muḥammad b. Yaḥyā al-Dīnawarī al-Warrāq, d. 341 (scholar's stationer) (35 / 1, vol. 25, 247)

Abū Aḥmad ʿAbd al-ʿAzīz b. Aḥmad al-Warrāq al-Naysābūrī, d. 342 (traditionist-stationer) (35 / 2, vol. 25, 264–265)

[Abū l-Ḥasan] Aḥmad b. ʿAbdallāh b. ʿAbdak al-Jurjānī al-ʿAdasī al-Warrāq, d. 344 (traditionist-stationer) (35 / 3, vol. 25, 290)

ʿAlī b. ʿĪsā al-Warrāq al-Harawī, d. 344 (author-stationer) (35 / 4, vol. 25, 301)

Abū l-ʿAbbās Muḥammad b. Yaʿqūb b. Yūsuf b. Maʿqil b. Sinān al-Umawī al-Naysābūrī al-Aṣamm, client of the Banū Umayya, d. 346 (stationer-disciple and book transmitter) (35 / 5, vol. 25, 362–69, called al-Warrāq on p. 367).

[Abū l-Ḥasan] Ibrāhīm b. ʿAbdallāh b. [Isḥāq] al-Warrāq, d. c. 341–350 (traditionist-stationer) (35 / 6, vol. 25, 463–464)[21]

36TH GENERATION (death dates 351–360 A.H.)

Abū l-Ḥusayn Aḥmad b. Qāj b. ʿAbdallāh al-Warrāq, d. 353 (traditionist-stationer) (36 / 1, vol. 26, 83–84)

Within the investigated period, al-Dahabī includes sixty-eight entries of persons who carried as part of their names the professional designation of *warrāq* or *kāghadī*. Many of these are merely short biographical notes: a third of them (twenty-four entries) contain no more than twenty-five words, which are mostly parts of names, and the shortest counts a mere six words: "Isḥāq b. Aḥmad the Stationer, [his death date is] by approximation" (*kutiba taqrīban;* 32 / 2). Only nine of the entries exceed five full lines of text in the printed edition, but a third of them (twenty-five entries) supply at least some description of stationery activities beyond the mere professional label.

STATIONERS IN BRIEF

Even these short entries nonetheless yield in their sum important information. This is because Arabic names contain many details besides an individual's profession, such as geographical provenance and place of activity, both of which are given as epithets to the name (*nisba*). As to the location, an epithet such as al-Baghdādī is ambiguous, because it may denote the place of either origin or activity, except in cases where a relocation is made explicit. Unsurprisingly, a great number of stationers are Baghdadis (twelve entries) and fewer are from Basra (six entries) and Kufa (three entries). Another large group hails from the eastern regions of the Arabic-Islamic world, namely from the city of Rayy (31 / 6, 33 / 6) in northern Iran; Naysabūr (Nishapur) and Marw (32 / 4) in Khurasan; the cities of Bukhara (31 / 1), Samarqand

(26 / 2, 26 / 4), and Farghana (33 / 10) in the region of Transoxania (with 33 / 9 assigned to the region as a whole); and the cities of Balkh (29 / 3, 32 / 1) and Herat (28 / 4, 35 / 4) in Afghanistan. This does not come as a surprise since papermaking had been introduced from the east, where the craft had a longer tradition (and where it had arrived, spreading along the Silk Road). The highest number in the east—namely, six stationers—are Naysabūrīs (26 / 6, 29 / 2, 29 / 4, 33 / 12, 35 / 2, 35 / 5), which may indicate that the hub of stationery, once located in Samarqand, had shifted to Naysabūr in the ninth century. Some of these moved elsewhere during their lifetimes. Potentially, craftspeople from the east had a well-recognized expertise that gave them an easy entry to the markets further west. But it is impossible to say in the single case whether such a move occurred in the pursuit of practicing stationery in a place with higher demand or in order to study with renowned authorities, since mobility was common among scholars of this period, and personal audition was valued more highly than the study of written notes or books for acquiring knowledge.

In terms of scholarly vocation, the great majority of the listed stationers are Ḥadīth transmitters, or traditionists (*muḥaddithūn*), and since in a biographical entry an individual's teachers and students are named, a short biography implies that the person heard Ḥadīth from only a few teachers and transmitted those to only a few students. In many cases, the activity of transmitting appears not to have been a major scholarly commitment but rather just sufficient to make the individual worthy of inclusion.

One might ask why in al-Dhahabī humongous Who's Who it was predominantly traditionists who were recorded as engaged in book production. Several factors may have influenced this preponderance. First, this coincidence may simply be a statistical phenomenon, since a majority of the lesser-known people included by al-Dhahabī are traditionists. Since Ḥadīth transmission was a pious and meritorious activity, and even a moderate involvement afforded a person scholarly status, it is not unlikely that a certain percentage of them simply happened to be stationers, a practicable and lucrative business for any literate person. Second, Ḥadīth transmission was a service to fellow Muslims and the passing on of the sacred tradition was not something that allowed for taking payment. Ḥadīth was, after all, the source of law and theology and an authoritative component in most types of compilations. Thus, more than any other scholars, full-time transmitters needed a second activity as a source of income, and stationery offered a logical and accessible option. In a few biographies, the craft of stationery is mentioned explicitly as a respectable means of subsistence for a pious person, who practiced it only when needed. Third, Ḥadīth were highly coveted texts even among barely literate Muslims, and accounts abound of thronged public lectures on Ḥadīth, in which even regular people took notes. These written Ḥadīth collections must have proved a sellable item (and they figure among the preserved codices of the ninth century).[22] Fourth, Ḥadīth studies came with its own kind of record keeping—to wit, noting down on a manuscript the names of the students who had audited it and, in a second step, compiling such auditing notes from the manuscripts studied with a teacher into the student's personal register (*thabat*). Over time, a massive number of records were assembled in the field of Ḥadīth studies, on which later authors of biographical dictionaries would rely.[23] Fifth, given that the writing of Ḥadīth had become largely accepted at the beginning of the ninth century, and written Ḥadīth were in demand, traditionists, who themselves were loath to gain from it (or uninterested in doing so), may have nonetheless desired a scholarly legacy and therefore ceded the financial gain to the persons ensuring it.[24] Given the frequent coincidence of the activities of traditionist and stationer, it is likely that pious and famous traditionists gladly included among their students such individuals who were apt at copying in order to ensure the survival of their own repertoire, even though these student-copyists may not have been promising scholars. This is manifested in the third type of stationer, the book transmitter. In the ninth century, a stationer still needed to be someone who also orally transmitted what he copied, not only as a function of scholarly convention but also because the reductive Arabic script was ambiguous to a reader uninitiated in a book's subject matter. Ergo, a stationer reproducing someone's books for sale was assumed to be his (direct or indirect) student in the subject of the book's discipline.

TYPES OF STATIONERS

Among al-Dhahabī's twenty-five biographies that shed some light on the exercised craft (beyond the mere professional designation), the context in which stationery was practiced falls into four types. The first, a traditionist, reproduced works he had audited with a teacher (hereafter: stationer-disciple). The second type was a stationer used by a notable scholar (hereafter: scholar's stationer). The third was a stationer who reproduced a specific corpus of books, of which he held the sole copies and as such became de facto these books' transmitter (hereafter: book transmitter). Such stewardship of a text is akin to that of a poet's transmitter, but here it takes on a written form. Fourth, some stationers wrote and sold their own books (hereafter: author-stationer). In all cases, the making of a book was still tied to familiarity with its contents. We are as yet far from anything like mere reproduction, as the English word *copyist* suggests. Rather, these were individuals deemed competent to transmit text in written form, because this competence was vouched for by study with, or work for, a scholar, or proven by their own capacity of independent compilation (*taṣnīf*). This applied foremost to scholarly books, especially Ḥadīth collections. On history, anecdotes, or unspecified other topics, which al-Dhahabī often simply summarizes as "compilations" (*taṣānīf*), he cites no comments or anecdotes that would reveal any disagreement about the stationers' competence to transmit these or the propriety of such a procedure.

The Stationer-Disciple

The first type, the stationer-disciple, is well documented by al-Dahabī (six cases). At times this was not practiced regularly but only on a per-demand basis for subsistence, as in the following descriptions: "He lived [*kāna ja' kulu*] from his stationery earnings" (28 / 1), and "Now and then he found himself in financial need and practiced stationery to live from its fees [*ujra*], since he was loath to take anything for Ḥadīth" (35 / 5).

These stationers reproduced the works of their own teachers, who were mostly Ḥadīth scholars. This is clear, for instance, in the case of Muḥammad b. ʿUthmān (d. 870, 26 / 7), who had come from Kufa to Baghdad to study with and reproduce the books of the respected Ḥadīth scholar ʿUbaydallāh b. Mūsā al-ʿAbsī, called al-Ḥāfiẓ al-Kūfī (d. 828), who figures as an important authority in the classic Ḥadīth compendium of al-Bukhārī.[25] The simultaneity of oral control and written production of knowledge is particularly vivid in the case of Isḥāq b. Ibrāhīm al-Manjanīqī (d. 916, 31 / 2), who had moved from Baghdad to Cairo and received his epithet from working next to a catapult (*manjanīq*) near the Friday mosque. He was a trusted transmitter whom even Aḥmad b. Shuʿayb al-Nasā'ī (d. 915) cites in his authoritative Ḥadīth compilation (*Sunan*). Insisting on his personally received written records, al-Manjanīqī once retorted to an inquiring student, "I transmit from all those whose Ḥadīth I wrote down" (*wa-ana fa-kullu man katabtu ʿanhu fa-innī uḥaddithu ʿanhu*). This group of stationers drew their status and probity from being (however minor) Ḥadīth scholars, and their authority over the content they reproduced was therefore beyond question.

Such individuals then gained from written copies (whether only of Ḥadīth or also of other texts is not specified) while orally parting with the Prophetic tradition for free. Payment for reproduced Ḥadīth compilations by students of Ḥadīth scholars who were scholars themselves seemed to be accepted. This is clear from recorded objections to the converse case, when a book was copied by someone outside the circle of disciples. Al-Dhahabī mentions one Aḥmad b. Muḥammad al-Baghdādī (d. 843, 23 / 1), who served the vizier al-Faḍl b. Yaḥyā from the powerful family of the Barmakids as a copyist (*nāsikh*), and who received the order to provide a copy of the *Maghāzī* (*The Campaigns*), as transmitted by the noted traditionist and judge of Baghdad, Ibrāhīm b. Saʿd (d. 798 or 799).[26] This third part of the Prophet's biography circulated independently and, like many books of the time, it had the makeup of a compilation of Ḥadīth and *akhbār*. The entry quotes several authorities listing Aḥmad as a student of Ibrāhīm b. Saʿd, next to one quote calling this claim a lie: "He was a pretender and did not study with Ibrāhīm b. Saʿd." Another quote confirms that Aḥmad was no Ḥadīth student at all but a stationer who had copied the *Maghāzī* for a Barmakid official who ordered him to have it proofread by Ibn Saʿd "and [Aḥmad] claimed that Ibrāhīm [b. Saʿd] had read it out to him and corrected it." A further authority is cited as having categorically forbidden Aḥmad to transmit any Ḥadīth from Ibn Saʿd.

The phenomenon of a vizier putting up his copyist to infiltrating a circle of Ḥadīth transmitters clearly violated scholarly etiquette. Usually a written work of Ḥadīth was assembled to be disseminated only among vetted students or colleagues. The fact that the vizier resorted to such subterfuge also shows that accessing a text from outside the scholarly circles was not easy, and officials who wanted to obtain a specific work needed to be inventive.

A similar case is reported in the literary sources about the work of the renowned philologist and polymath Abū ʿUbayda, whom we encountered in Chapter 1. Unlike al-Dhahabī's terse and dry entries, the following literary account was turned into a tale of suspense. It clearly shows traces of reworking, but the core issue is analogous. This case involved a stationer by the name of Abū l-Ḥasan ʿAlī b. al-Mughīra al-Athram (d. 844), who chose not to disclose to Abū ʿUbayda his own intentions of reproducing his works for an official. The event occurred in 804 C.E., when this scholar visited Baghdad.[27] Al-Athram was a skilled and thorough copyist and at the same time, familiar with his scholarly subject matter. Knowing what importance attached to his copies, he executed them with minute precision.[28]

The immediate impulse came from a secretary in the caliphal palace, Ismāʿīl b. Ṣubayḥ al-Ḥarrānī, who desired to have at his disposal the complete works of Abū ʿUbayda, whose high quality had become known in Baghdad.[29] The secretary had to reckon with two potential hurdles: first, the famously reticent scholar was unlikely to relinquish control over his knowledge by passing it on in written form to anyone other than his students; and second, any profit-conscious stationer might try to capitalize on the books' inaccessibility and demand an exorbitant price. It is uncertain which exact reason compelled the secretary to act as he did, but in any case, he circumvented the author and went to the person who was familiar with the books' content *and* able to reproduce them. He did not seek al-Athram's consent or negotiate a fee with him, but instead used his governmental authority to simply place him under arrest. This use of such a drastic measure to obtain books shows again how difficult access to scholarly books could be. Having placed the stationer behind lock and key in one of the palaces, the secretary gave him the books of Abū ʿUbayda and ordered him to copy them.[30]

Thus, Ibn Ṣubayḥ had a set of the books at his disposal, as he gave them to al-Athram, but the fact that he wanted them copied indicates that he did not own them. Perhaps these copies were autographs brought by the visiting scholar himself (whose book writing had pricked the ruling caliph's curiosity), with the intention of offering them to the caliph's library or taking them back to his hometown of Basra.

Confined to the palace and charged with more copying labor than he could handle, al-Athram appealed to his stationer colleagues and, to speed up the process, resorted to a system of having each book copied in distributed parts.[31] A more common procedure to accelerate copying was to dictate a book to several writers simultaneously.[32] This was not useful here, since the task was to reproduce single copies of a number of different books. One of the copyists involved, Abū Misḥal (a Bedouin who had moved to town) reported that he used to go with a group of colleagues to al-Athram, who passed them a book underneath the door, distributed its folios among them, gave them blank sheets, and asked them to complete the copying by a certain deadline. Abū Misḥal questioned this procedure, explaining that al-Athram was indeed Abū ʿUbayda's student, but the latter was "one of the stingiest people with his books" and, had he been aware, would have forbidden al-Athram's wholesale reproduction of them.[33] Again, Abū Misḥal's comment (similar to the criticism made of the interloping copyist Aḥmad al-Bagdādī, quoted by al-Dhahabī) brands such reproduction a violation of accepted customs and implies dishonesty on the part of the student. Profit was not involved here, neither for al-Athram nor for his colleagues, whose assistance he seems to have expected as a collegial favor. The fact that they did help him may point to a burgeoning self-awareness of the stationers as a professional group. The details of grounding the stationer and his way of seeking the aid of his colleagues may well be literary embellishment. What matters is that a student (a pretended student in the case of Aḥmad al-Baghdādī and a true student in the case of al-Athram) was used by an administrator to avail himself of high-quality reproductions of scholarly works: Aḥmad al-Baghdādī's copy was checked by the author, and in the case of al-Athram, his expertise was known and he copied from what was probably the author's autographs.

Who was al-Athram and what had brought him into this situation? His book production had followed from a combination of factors: the demand of the palace, his access to knowledge, and most importantly, his failure to produce his own scholarship. Minor scholars like him, who worked mainly as transmitters, were common and figure in the biographical dictionaries within the scholarly vitae of their more prominent colleagues, unless they had their own brief entries. The author of the earliest biographical dictionary on grammarians, Abū l-Ṭayyib al-Lughawī (d. 962), distinguishes explicitly between leading scholars (*aʾimma*) and transmitters. Al-Athram belonged to the latter, but unlike some of them who were true memory artists, his poor oral performance precluded success on the teaching circuit. His way to excel became book production, and the written scholarship he offered was attractive to two groups of people: scholars, who paid for copies of books, and courtiers, such as Ibn Ṣubayḥ, who did not. The new medium gave al-Athram the relevance that he had failed to gain as a scholar.

In the cases of both Aḥmad al-Baghdādī and al-Athram, scholarly etiquette was infringed on, but in slightly different ways. The Barmakid copyist Aḥmad was no scholar to begin with, and unqualified to copy Ḥadīth compilations. His posing as a student to obtain a scholar's proofreading of his own copy was regarded as dishonest. Al-Athram was a real student of Abū ʿUbayda and competent to produce accurate copies, but he skirted the scholar's likely refusal to have his writings disseminated outside the teaching circle, and he did so in secret, even if not by his own choosing. The recorded attitudes of contemporaries show two things: first, a stationer-disciple had to be competent to reproduce his teacher's works, and second, he had to have secured the permission do so.

The Scholar's Stationer

A second type of stationer was one who worked for a scholar and regularly reproduced one or several of his books. This type is even more amply documented (eleven cases). It was a service to the respective scholar in terms of spreading his work and bolstering his renown, even though the exact mode of payment in each case is uncertain; that is, it is uncertain whether the scholar paid the stationer directly, or the stationer received permission to reproduce the works and set a price independently, by license, so to speak. The mode of remuneration is thematized only when disagreements occurred. In two cases, prices demanded by stationers were questioned by the books' authors. In the case of al-Farrāʾ, discussed in the Chapter 1, his stationers were clearly independent entrepreneurs and set a price that the author deemed excessive. He had no say in the transaction, however, and was only able to prevent its going through by offering (orally) a more comprehensive version of his book for free. This forced the stationers to halve their fee. The historian Muḥammad b. Jarīr al-Ṭabarī (d. 923) had a similar encounter with his own profit-hungry assistants (*aṣḥāb*), which Yāqūt recounts as follows:

> *Al-Ṭabarī said to his assistants:* "Would you undertake [*tanshaṭūna li-*] a Qurʾān commentary?"
> *They said:* "What will be its size?"
> *He said:* "30,000 sheets."
> *They said:* "This takes lifetimes to complete." So he shortened it to circa 3,000 sheets. Thereafter he said: "Would you undertake a history of the world from Adam to our time?"
> *They said:* "What will be its size?" He responded roughly the same as about the commentary, and they responded with the same.
> *So al-Ṭabarī said:* "We belong to God, and aspirations die," and abridged it in the way he had abridged the commentary.[34]

A number of scholars of different disciplines are recorded by al-Dhahabī to have used their own stationers (listed in chronological order): the traditionist ʿUbaydallāh b. Mūsā (d. 819, 26/7), the Qurʾān reciter Khalaf b. Hishām al-Bazzāz (d. 844, 27/1), the traditionist Abū Bakr al-Ḥumaydī (d. 834, 28/7), the traditionist Abū Nuʿaym al-Faḍl Ibn Dhakwān (d. 834, 28/9), the traditionist Isḥāq Ibn Rāhawayh (d. 853, 29/4), the traditionist Dāwūd b. Rāshid [al-Khawārazmī] (d. 854, 31/5), the litterateur and essayist al-Jāḥiẓ (d. 868–869, 32/3), the traditionist and author of a *Sunan* work Abū Dāwūd Sulaymān b. al-Ashʿath al-Sijistānī (d. 889, 33/8), the traditionist [Abū Yaḥyā ʿAbd al-Karīm b. al-Haytham] al-Dayrʿaqūlī (d. 901, 33/11), and the historian al-Ṭabarī (d. 923, 35/1).[35] Some of the craftsmen assisting these scholars may have simultaneously been junior scholars, but they appear here in the function of disseminating the senior scholars' writings.

These stationers are given the label of "*warrāq* of So-and-so," but their study with the scholars whose books they copied (in five of the nine cases) is mentioned immediately thereafter.[36] "He was *warrāq* of So-and-so and audited So-and-so." The book production thus immediately receives a label of quality by specifying that the stationer was taught his material by the book's author. The exact repertoire of a stationer is reported only in one case: the *warrāq* of Ibn Rāhawayh (29/4) copied solely his *Exegesis* (*Tafsīr*) *of the Qurʾān* and not his *Musnad,* a Ḥadīth compilation organized by transmitter, which he had likewise studied with Ibn Rāhawayh. Neither did he reproduce the works of another scholar, Yaḥyā b. Yaḥyā (d. 848), which the stationer had likewise studied with the author.[37] This means that for his living, he specialized in one book, either because the demand for it was greatest or because he knew it best.

The stationer of al-Ṭabarī (35/1) taught orally in Damascus this scholar's *Exegesis* (*Tafsīr*) *of the Qurʾān*—probably the book that he also reproduced as a stationer, and about which the above-cited dispute took place (in which he may have been involved; Yāqūt does not identify the stationers). As in any market, entrepreneurs selected the merchandise that moved most quickly. With al-Ṭabarī it was not his *History,* for which he is famous today, but rather in the two known cases, works of Qurʾānic exegesis. Such books gave access to the holy scripture of Islam and were obviously of greatest concern to regular Muslim readers.

A single scholar's stationer, Aḥmad b. Ibrāhīm al-Baghdādī al-Warrāq (d. 875–883, 27/1), who was also noted for his skill as a Qurʾān reciter, is described as additionally compiling his own books on the number of verses in the Qur'ān. He thus overlaps with the fourth type, the author-stationer, discussed below.[38]

Whether this type of stationer was a transitional phenomenon of the ninth century, to be replaced by pure craftsmen once the reproduction of books by persons other than vetted scholars came to be accepted, remains to be investigated. The next two types of stationers, who appear still less frequently in al-Dhahabī's Who's Who of the ninth century, do suggest such a development.

The Book Transmitter, or Rāwī-*Stationer*

With the third type, we encounter the new phenomenon of a stationer who reproduced a certain repertoire of books in which he specialized, but for which he was not recorded as their author's student. Instead, he is referred to either as "in possession" of the books he reproduced or as *rāwī* of the same. The joint appearance of the terms *rāwī* and *warrāq* implies that such a stationer knew texts well enough to correctly reproduce them and that he also had the authority to do so.

This is the case, for instance, of Rajā' of Herat (d. 890 or 892, 28 / 4), described as one of the foremost traditionists of this city. "He held [*kāna ʿindahū*] the compilations [*muṣannafāt*] of Mālik b. Sulaymān al-Harawī and those of Saʿīd b. Manṣūr (d. 842)" and he also transmitted from a number of others scholars.[39] It is clear that his book making was based on written copies he held. The sentence describing this situation continues listing authorities whose work he disseminated, yet the word *rawā,* "to transmit," is indifferent to the medium in which this takes place. In pre-Islamic times a poet's *rāwī* certainly did so by relying on his memory. But already in Umayyad times *rāwīs* had begun to use notebooks. The poet Dhū l-Rumma in particular appreciated notebooks for giving the texts of his poems stability, and he dictated his poems to his *rāwī.*[40] In early Abbasid times, the *rāwī* of Muslim b. al-Walīd kept a notebook of collected poems of his master which he wanted him to correct (probably for later reuse), but the poet did not comply, whereas the poet ʿUmāra b. Aqīl valued (and remunerated) his *rāwī* for a written collection of his verse for his own reuse.[41] To return to Rajā', in his biographical entry, the conjunction *also* (*ayḍan*) between the two groups of transmitted works may be understood in the sense that his transmission of the second part followed the way of the first (i.e., that the *riwāya* here applied to both oral and written dissemination).

ʿAbd al-Razzāq of Antioch (d. 905–913, 30 / 1) was a teacher of Qurʾān recitation in addition to being a traditionist. The title of the book he was in charge of is combined with the same ambiguous verb: "He transmitted [*rawā*] *The* [*Book of*] *Letters* [*al-Ḥurūf*] from Ahmad b. Ḥabīb."[42] It is of course conceivable that he used a written copy to transmit the book orally, but his professional label of *warrāq* makes it likely that he also sold copies of the same. Nonetheless, the written copies did not make his teaching redundant, since the correct reading of an Arabic scholarly text (specifically, foreign names, rare words, and words that were ambiguous in the script) made audition necessary to prevent mistakes and eliminate polysemy. A specific type of book on *taṣḥīf* arose in this period precisely to remedy errors that occurred in the process of reading and copying scholarly texts.[43] At the end of the tenth century Abū Aḥmad al-ʿAskari (d. 993) still records in the preface of his so-titled book (*al-Taṣḥīf*) that traditionists and linguists had asked him to produce such books specific for either discipline.[44]

The third such biographical entry (33 / 8) again combines the verb "to transmit" (*rawā*) with a book and adds that the stationer had kept the company of the author, although he is not mentioned as a student: "ʿAlī b. al-Ḥasan al-Warrāq (d. 940) . . . was the companion [*ṣāḥib*] of Abū Dāwūd al-Sijistānī and the transmitter of his book [*rāwī kitābihī*]," which refers to his authoritative Ḥadīth collection (*Sunan*). What distinguishes ʿAlī from the two previous book transmitters is that he was not a scholar in any discipline; his function rested solely on his mastery of the contents of one book and his long familiarity with it, doubtless through many auditing sessions in which the author commented on readings of the book by his students. This is expressed in al-Dhahabī's description of him as the author's "companion."

All three stationers are treated as competent (to a certain degree) to transmit books. The entries on them focus on their quality in this respect and specify one or several books of which they are in charge. ʿAlī b. al-Ḥasan's competence, however, is strictly secondary and reproductive and unconnected to any independent scholarly pursuit of his own. In his case, the written dissemination (for pay) of one book seemed to be the sole skill of an individual who was not a noteworthy scholar himself. In this, he resembles another stationer who is depicted at greater length in the *akhbār,* precisely because such a circumscribed expertise limited to the contents of one book clashed with the reigning assumptions about teaching and learning.

That is al-Athram, who has already been encountered above as a stationer-disciple. He had audited eminent authorities in grammar of the generation preceding him and transmitted to those who would become the leaders of the Kufan and Basran schools of grammar—both located at this time in the Abbasid metropolis Baghdad—even though al-Athram was no great scholar himself. What he had achieved was to become a conveyor of knowledge from one generation to the next. In the vita of Ibn al-Sikkīt (d. 858), al-Athram is cited among his teachers, but he is not defined, like others, by a discipline, such as grammar or lexicon, but as a transmitter, passing on the books of al-Aṣmaʿī and Abū ʿUbayda to his own students.[45] This by itself was a common enough function, but the unusual part was that al-Athram had a poor memory. This handicap would have made the exercise of his profession impossible a generation earlier. But now technology came to his aid.

In a session of al-Athram (here called an assistant to al-Aṣmaʿī) held outside his home, he dictated the poetry of the Umayyad poet al-Rāʿī (d. c. 709), literally "the Herder," so nicknamed for his minutely drawn portraits of Bedouin life and desert travel in archaic vocabulary. The attending Thaʿlab (still a student at the time, long before he would become the leader of the Kufan school) described how, after the gathering was over, al-Athram laid aside the book from which he had dictated. Another student, young Ibn al-Sikkīt, wanted to ask al-Athram a question about the poetry. Thaʿlab inveighed that al-Athram, being only a book transmitter, might not know the answer and would be embarrassed before those gathered. But Ibn al-Sikkīt insisted and recited a verse chock-full of difficult vocabulary to al-Athram for comment, who indeed had no answer to give. Ibn al-Sikkīt cited another verse for comment and al-Athram remained silent, showing his displeasure. The situation escalated to mutual insults until the teacher terminated the gathering by disappearing into his house.[46]

Al-Athram did not store his knowledge in his mind, but held it in his hands in the form of the books of al-Aṣmaʿī and Abū ʿUbayda. He had taken the opportunity to benefit from an emerging technology in order to turn a weakness into an advantage. Al-Athram further maximized its potential by copying his teachers' books carefully, correcting and fully vocalizing them to guarantee an accurate phonetic reading.[47] This was not done regularly in the Arabic script at that time. In his case, it was necessary, "for he memorized nothing."[48] But more importantly, it constituted a further step in the process of making a book stand in for a person.

Al-Athram was also an entrepreneur. He took the initiative in offering copies of his books to scholars for purchase, instead of waiting to be asked.[49] As we have seen, Thaʿlab had accessed the teachings of Abū ʿUbayda solely through al-Athram's books. The stationer's presence in this was vital. Being both owner of and an expert on the books, he controlled their circulation. He exemplifies this new type of book scholar, limited to and specializing in a specific set of books.

Books were thus important for men who were experts but produced no scholarship themselves, for it permitted them a derivative intellectual ownership, or rather stewardship, within scholarly circles, with the additional option for material profit. In this sense, it was a logical consequence for the abovementioned al-Athram to become a stationer.

Given his particular weakness of memory, he optimized the book-making technology by executing his copies with precision and adding vowel markers, which were not necessarily required and often omitted in manuscripts. He thus moved the book closer to a medium that could replace the author—in a way the prolific essayist al-Jāḥiẓ once described thus: "A book does not forget, nor does it replace some words for others."[50]

A copy of *The Epistle (al-Risāla)* by al-Shāfiʿī from the ninth century (Dār al-Kutub MS 41 uṣūl fiqh) seems to confirm this kind of book transmitter. The manuscript was taken down from the author himself by the writer of the manuscript, al-Rabīʿ b. Sulaymān al-Murādī (d. 884), who identifies himself as the companion (*ṣāḥib*) of al-Shāfiʿī, and therefore it is very valuable. It also shows numerous corrections (see fig. 8a). In the same scribe's hand in shaky script, at about ninety years old in 879, he provides a general permission to transmit the book in the colophon (see fig. 8b).[51] Though the exact circumstances are uncertain, it seems that during his long life he had used it only himself, and he gave permission to copy from it once he was no longer able to do so, to preserve it for the future.

Books had given oral text a second life. The recited or dictated text of books, whose circulation was limited to the scholars and students involved with it, now received competition from multiple written copies. This competition was serious, because the written reproduction was held to meet scholarly standards—and it raised criticism in cases where this was not guaranteed. Once a written copy was for sale on the market (or obtained through other means by members of the administration), the material object passed out of scholarly control. The book transmitters created a point of bifurcation by making books accessible to two kinds of audiences: scholars of a book's discipline and any other scholars or amateur readers who could afford it.

Concomitant with the wider circulation of scholarly books came the realization that this was a labor worthy of remuneration. This gradual acceptance is depicted by al-Dhahabī in one longer entry devoted to a stationer who experienced this change over his own long lifetime. Muḥammad b. Yaʿqūb al-Umawī al-Naysābūrī (d. 957, 35/5) had himself practiced stationery occasionally for dislike of taking tuition for Ḥadīth teaching. His father, who accompanied him on his travels during his youth to study Ḥadīth, had reproduced his son's compilations presumably for free, because at the end of his nearly centenary life, Muḥammad objected to his own son and another stationer charging customers for copies of his works.

This "traditionist of his age" transmitted orally a large number of books, but did so for free. To survive, he practiced stationery himself. But he parted with his memorized materials without pay and objected to his son and his own stationer requesting payment from people. This time-honored transmitter seems to have been a throwback, mixing written and oral practices not unlike the grammarian al-Farrāʾ, discussed in Chapter 1. He heard and transmitted orally and memorized his material. But in his well-attended lectures he employed an assistant dictating the text (*mustamlī*); that is, his audience was supposed to write things down.[52] He also kept a "book" of his own, containing certain texts, and when other people's Ḥadīth were once inserted into his repertoire, he used a written format (*tawqīʿ*) to exclude from his record those Ḥadīth that he declared he had not transmitted himself, which had been falsely attributed to him.

Later in his life, his son and his stationer (as he used the services of one) must also have had written copies for reproduction, and one might wonder why Muḥammad b. Yaʿqūb retained a stationer's services but objected to his taking remuneration. By then the aged traditionist was behind the times. As a function of his long life, he had ended up in a period when the sale of written collections of Ḥadīth had become a sine qua non. But being advanced in years, he made only certain allowances, such letting others write his lectures down, but he was not willing to fully embrace the changed situation of books as merchandise.

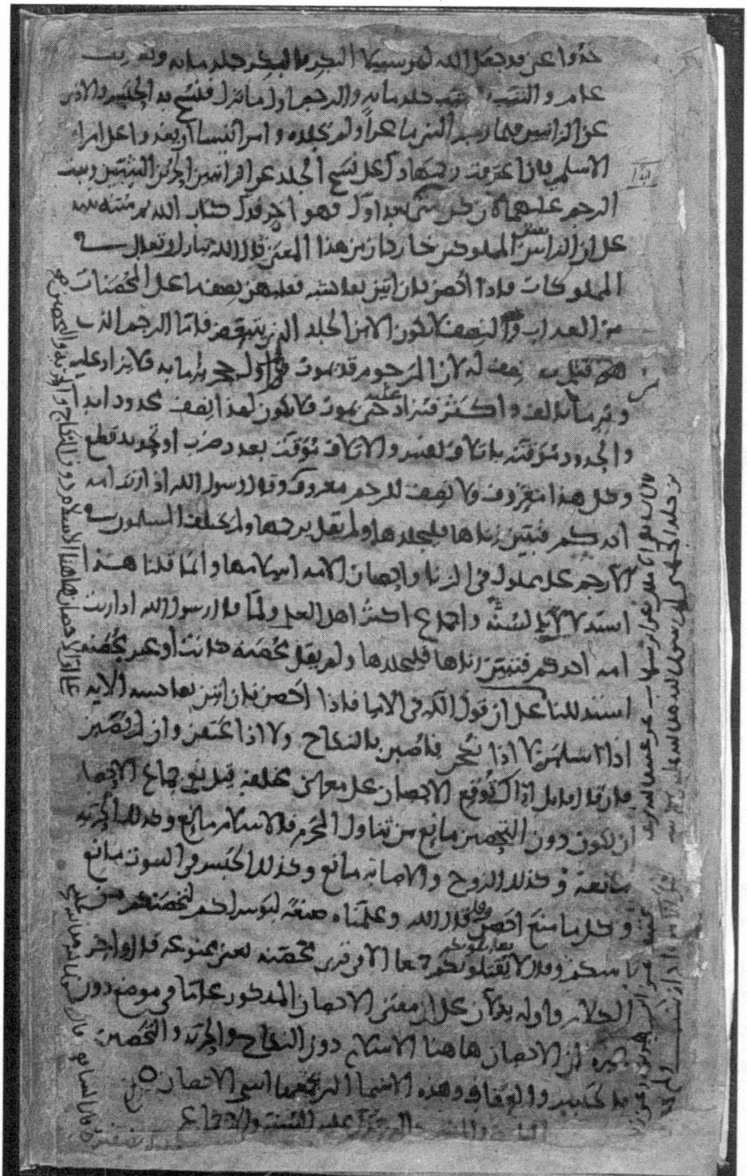

(*a*)

FIG. 8A. Al-Shāfiʿī, *The Epistle* (*al-Risāla*), with marginal corrections. (Cairo, Dār al-Kutub 41 uṣūl al-fiqh, fol. 19 verso.)

(*b*)

FIG. 8B. Al-Shāfiʿī, *The Epistle (al-Risāla)*, colophon with the aged scribe's general permission to transmit, dated 265/879: "Al-Rabīʿ b. Sulaymān, the Companion of al-Shāfiʿī, gave permission to copy *The Book of the Epistle*, being in three parts, in the month of Dhū l-Qaʿda of the year 265." (MS 41 uṣūl al-fiqh, fol. 75 recto, Egyptian National Library.)

Summarizing the preceding first three types of the stationer-disciple, the scholar's stationer, and the book transmitter, these may be seen as successive stages in the development of book production, whereas the fourth and last type, the author-stationer, constitutes a parallel phenomenon.[53]

The Author-Stationer

Stationers who were at the same time book authors occur seven times in the surveyed period of al-Dhahabī's lexicon. The earliest one, the poet Maḥmūd al-Warrāq (23 / 2) (died in the reign of al-Muʿtaṣim, 833–842), practiced in addition to poetry and stationery a third profession as a slave trader, which gave rise to *akhbār* in the literature. About his book production al-Dhahabī gives no details other than citing a couplet in which Maḥmūd, weary of court service in old age, describes stationery as a more convenient source of income:

> An old man is beyond *adab,* for an old man *adab* is toil.
> How much longer? Until when is this game going on?
>
> Gain [*rizq*], if you don't pursue it, comes to you by itself [*ʿafwan*] from books.
> When you rest, gain rests not but a cause sets it in motion.[54]

The books Maḥmūd copied may have contained his poetry, which focused on pious admonition (*mawāʿiẓ*) and wise sayings.

For some of the recorded author-stationers, al-Dhahabī mentions no titles of their books. Such is the case with Muḥammad b. Aḥmad al-Anṣārī al-Dūlābī of Rayy (d. 922, 31 / 6). He was a widely traveled Ḥadīth scholar who is said to have "made compilations" (*ṣannafa l-taṣānīf*). The same is true for ʿAlī b. ʿĪsā from Herat (d. 955, 35 / 4). In both cases, their compilations may have been Ḥadīth collections, since both stationers were also traditionists, and both were remarkably long-lived: they reached eighty-six and eighty-five years of age, respectively.

As for Aḥmad b. Ibrāhīm from Baghdad (27 / 1), who has been mentioned above as a scholar's stationer serving Khalaf b. Hishām al-Bazzāz, he composed a book on the number of verses contained in the Qurʾān. This fell within his expertise as a skilled Qurʾān reciter. For the Baghdadian Saʿīd b. Nuṣayr (d. after 864, 26 / 3), likewise a traditionist, the titles of his books are given as the *Book of Weeping* (*Kitāb al-Bukā'*), the *Book of the Devout* (*Kitāb al-ʿAwābid*), and "other such things" subsumed under the category of "soft-hearted [or God-fearing] matters" (*raqā'iq*)—that is, concerned with personal piety.

From another Baghdadian, Abū ʿĪsā Muḥammad b. Hārūn (d. 861, 25 / 4), a copious book production is mentioned; "He had many compilations" (*lahū taṣānīf kathīra*), which al-Dhahabī subsumes under the themes of theological causes (*al-ʿillāt*), the imamate (*al-imāma*), and theological speculation (*al-naẓar*).[55]

As for ʿAbdallāh b. ʿAmr (d. 887, 28 / 5), he is described as multifaceted—namely, a traditionist, an *akhbārī* (what later would become historians), and a "teller of jokes" (*ṣāḥib mulaḥ*); that is, he collected historical and entertaining accounts, which he probably kept in notebooks. It is not stated which of these corpora he reproduced as books; potentially, all three.

All in all, the author-stationers, with the exception of one poet, cover religious topics, ranging from personal piety to speculative theology, but most of their books are compilations that probably contained Ḥadīth. Al-Dhahabī seems not to be interested in (or informed about) the full lists of every individual's book titles. It is also not stated whether they sold only their own compositions or other books as well (or instead). This seems likely, however, since stationery was practiced as a means of income, and specifically by this new category of self-sustained authors, who thus financed their own book writing. To limit sales to one's own compositions would have curtailed potential profit. This was different, of course, for famous authors, such as al-Wāqidī or al-Jāḥiẓ, who needed to employ copyists to satisfy the demand for their books.[56]

However, apart from Muḥammad b. Hārūn (25 / 4), the author-stationers listed by al-Dhahabī were not prolific scholars, and they are given no voice in his brief biographical notes. But in the *akhbār* literature, in one similar instance, a *warrāq* of this type speaks out and testifies to a professional pride no less than that of the more highly regarded administrative secretaries. This illustrates the general demand that existed for this craft, a demand that made it lucrative—even if not prestigious.

ʿAllān b. al-Ḥasan al-Warrāq al-Shuʿūbī (d. after 813), from Fars in southwest Iran, was a transmitter of Arab genealogy and of rank disputes among Arab tribes. His major work, *The Arena on Vices of the Arabs*, was a collection of arguments for questioning and impugning the lineages of the blood-based

Arab aristocracy.[57] Demand for this kind of anti-Arab propaganda came from the growing leadership of non-Arabs, notably Iranians, who claimed cultural equality, if not superiority, to the Arabs and who looked back on a much longer history. ʿAllān and his patrons, the Barmakid family of statesmen, shared this attitude.[58] The new Abbasid rulers whom they served differed from the preceding Umayyad dynasty (661–750) in giving opportunities to Iranians and other non-Arab ethnic groups, some of whom had just recently converted to Islam. Pedigree was now matched by skill and by a new type of professional solidarity among government clerks.[59] ʿAllān also aired his pro-Iranian sentiment in poetry—in short, he was not silent about his convictions. The leniency of his caliphal employers, who cannot have been unaware of his attitude, is surprising, because it implied disparagement of the very Arabic genealogy on which the Abbasids' claim to legitimate rulership partly rested. ʿAllān's outspokenness was not confined to the Iranian cause, for he was an equally proud representative of the stationers' profession. His case is one of the rare instances in which the sources record a *warrāq* speaking for himself and even boasting of his profession.[60]

Aside from his copying work in a palace library (*bayt al-ḥikma*), ʿAllān kept a shop near the Syria Gate in Baghdad, where he sold and copied books with the assistance of a local youth.[61] Then he received an offer from the caliph's chief counselor Aḥmad b. Abī Khālid al-Aḥwal (d. 826–827) to become his copyist.[62] ʿAllān took up quarters in the counselor's palace and began his work. Once, however, he failed to rise in the presence of the counselor, who commented on this as the stationer's "poor breeding." ʿAllān responded, defending his education and his profession:

> How come poor breeding [*sūʾ al-adab*] is attributed to me, when the literary arts [*ādāb*] are learnt from me, and I am their source? What did you want me to rise for? I did not come to beg for gifts, nor did I want you or seek anything from you. *It was you who wanted me to come* and write in your palace, and I came to you out of the need to receive a salary, even though I deserve better from you than that.[63]

The incident concludes with ʿAllān vowing never again to serve in any one's house as a personal copyist. ʿAllān al-Shuʿūbī prides himself both on his education and on his importance as producer of much-needed books; this was justified in his case, as he was also a noted author.

Reviewing the book repertoire of stationers listed by al-Dhahabī, the dearth of those from among the literati (*udabāʾ*) is at first surprising, because works of *adab* and collected works of poets (*dawāwīn*) certainly circulated, as seen in Chapters 1 and 2. There are two possible reasons for this. *Udabāʾ*, who were the prime audience for such works, were educated and connected to the courtly circles, where they had access to the literature en vogue in the ninth century, which was especially modern poetry, and they kept collections in their own handwriting. Since much of the practice of poetry was conducted orally, the *udabāʾ* had to be able to cite ad hoc apposite verse and have select passages memorized, which was best achieved through one's own copying. When a poem was long or unavailable, a colleague could be asked to dictate it. Such requests among *udabāʾ* for dictation were frequent.[64] A refusal of dictation was rare, but there is recorded one instance that occurred because the poem, a panegyric, had not yet been presented to its dedicatee, and the poet, ʿUmāra b. ʿAqīl, wished to secure his reward, citing an earlier instance of fraud, when an unpublished poem he had shared by dictation had been stolen and presented by another to the addressee and he lost his prize.[65] For a poem that had been presented (and rewarded) and for poems of any other genres, no such risk existed, and dictation could be freely dispensed.

Such personal records of poetry took the shape of notebooks or fascicles (*ajzāʾ*), which individuals made for themselves or exchanged. In this format, poetry is most often described as being consulted. The secretary al-Ḥasan b. Wahb, for instance, had the poems of Abū Tammām thus at his disposal, having prepared citable abridgments for recitation.[66] Newcomers to the courtly circles needed such writings to prepare themselves, thus the grammarian Thaʿlab approached a family of secretaries, the Banū Nawbakht, to produce for him a selection of Abū Tammām's verse.[67] These notebooks did not yet have the form of redacted books, nor did they circulate on the market, and their presence in shops of stationers must have been limited.[68] Most book authors on literary subjects made fair copies of their own books and produced copies to dedicate them to patrons. Poets shared some of their poems with colleagues. *Adab* and modern verse thus reached educated audiences either through oral exchange or informal copying, while it was of lesser relevance to the upper middle classes, among whom collections of Ḥadīth held a higher priority.

The fact that modern poetry circulated effectively (even though stationers had no large share in it) is confirmed by Ibn al-Muʿtazz in his biographical dictionary of modern poets (*Ṭabaqāt al-shuʿarāʾ*), in which he cites longer passages only from lesser-known poets. He assumes that the major poems by the famous ones were all known and available to his audience. For Abū Tammām, for instance, he limits himself to quoting the incipits of the famous *qaṣīda*s so as not to bore his readers. Elsewhere he states, "Whoever wants people's complete poetry [*ʿalā l-wajh,* i.e., the complete poems], their collected works [*dawāwīn*], especially those of the famous poets, are owned by most people. As for those whose poetry is owned only by the elite, we include a fair share in our book."[69] The oral life of contemporary verse in educated circles and the copies made by their members for their own use may have delayed poetic *dīwān*s in becoming a regular item for booksellers. They did become widespread a century later, when Ibn al-Nadīm cites numerous *dīwān* titles in his *Catalogue*, and al-Ṣūlī boasts that his redaction of the *dīwān* of Abū Nuwās had become so prevalent that it made the price of an earlier and inferior redaction drop to "a couple of *dirham*s, whereas previously it had sold for the same number of *dīnār*s."[70]

One must also keep in mind that paper in the ninth and early tenth centuries, even though copiously extant and less expensive than papyrus, was still not cheap, and a book purchase was a serious investment.[71] Al-Dhahabī mentions the case of one Aḥmad b. al-Qāj (d. 964, 36 / 1), who was one of the most studious auditors of Ḥadīth in Baghdad, notably from al-Ṭabarī. When fortune had him inherit 700 *dīnār*s, he spent it all at once on paper (*kāghad*) and then used that up to copy down all the Ḥadīth he had memorized. This "accidental stationer" obviously would have had no funds to purchase enough paper otherwise.

Unrecorded Stationers

As most of the early stationers were included in their capacity as traditionists, one must assume an unrecorded number of stationers who did not receive mention, being solely craftsmen, because they were not deemed fit to figure in such an encyclopedia of noteworthy people. This is corroborated by some cases in which the student status of a stationer is called into question, or he is disparaged for his profession: "He did not belong to the traditionists. No one knew him as a student. He was just a stationer [*innamā kāna warrāqan*]" (23 / 1); and "He was a craftsman [*min ahl al-ṣanʿa*], and he was weak [as a transmitter]" (31 / 6).

It is risky to propose a percentage for this missing share of members of the stationery trade, yet one assumes that an unknown number has simply left no traces in the written sources. However, the *akhbār* preserve one case of such a stationer from Basra, who aroused the displeasure of a scholar, which earned him inclusion in the sources. For stationers like him did more than replicate books; they intruded on the territory of scholarship by evaluating books and recommending them to customers. This was the case with the Basran stationer who pronounced on a book's quality. We do not know his name, as the sources simply refer to him as "one of the *warrāqūn*."[72] Neither do we know the selection of books he (and others) offered to their customers in Basra's book market. But considering the number of books from the first quarter of the ninth century that the later *Catalogue* lists, there must have been a rich selection.[73]

The anonymous but astute member of the stationer profession recommended to his buyers a reference work on words that looked alike in writing but could be pronounced in different ways, which in many cases changed their meaning (this work is of the same type as the lexicon by Abū l-ʿAmaythal; see fig. 4). This polysemy is a feature of the Arabic alphabet type, an *abjad,* which does not denote short vowels in the basic script (*rasm*).[74] Though these could be marked by small additional signs above and below the line, invented in the eighth century, these were little used in early manuscripts. The result was that many words looked alike in the script but sounded different when read aloud. With the increased use of the written medium, these visual homonyms became a source of error, they were identified as a problem, and they were collected as a book's subject under the title "Solecisms of the Commoners" (*laḥn al-ʿāmma*). Actually, this has to be understood as solecisms of educated people, for it was they who cared to avoid lapses in the *ʿarabiyya*.[75] This type of book served the growing number of people who owned and read books but had not received oral instruction on how to fill in the blanks left by the Arabic script (which was far easier to write than to read aloud).

The book in question happened to be penned by the abovementioned precocious Ibn al-Sikkīt.[76] He had become a respected lexicographer of the Kufan philological school, which was at this time losing ground to the upcoming Basran school, whose superior grammatical system would dominate the field.[77] The contentious book, titled *The Rectification of Speech* (*Iṣlāḥ al-manṭiq*), pointed out the pitfalls to avoid in reading and speaking and was topical on two accounts.[78] First, Ibn al-Sikkīt had skillfully composed it, ensuring that the information it contained was accurate and easy to locate. He was appreciated as a good writer, better, for instance, than the school's leader Thaʿlab.[79] The awareness was growing that the organization and visual presentation of information in books was a skill in itself. Second, the book was of practical benefit for educated people who wanted to speak flawless *ʿarabiyya*. The genre was much in demand. Nearly every philologist authored a book on the subject, but Ibn al-Sikkīt's rendition is among the earliest, and it did survive.[80] It is also a testimony of a new kind of readership who had not necessarily acquired their knowledge in scholarly circles.

Ibn al-Sikkīt was not the inventor of the genre, however. The lexicographer Quṭrub (d. 821) had earlier inaugurated a book genre on a subtype—namely, words with three possible readings, or "triplets" (*muthallathāt*).[81] But Ibn al-Sikkīt had reservations about this pioneer. He took an entire book chest (*qimaṭr*) full of notes from him before he judged him to be unreliable and discarded his notes.[82] He decided to do a better job and indeed, he succeeded.

During his lifetime, Ibn al-Sikkīt promoted his own book with dictation sessions, for which he hired a professional assistant (*mustamlī*) who would continue to transmit the book after the author's death in 858.[83] The work was well known, but soon only available for purchase and no longer through teaching. The anonymous bookseller thus favored a popular and user-friendly but hard-to-obtain resource. But his advocacy caused a stir. The Basran grammarian Ibn Durayd reports the following event:

> I saw one of the stationers in Basra prefer the *Book of [the Rectification of] Speech* [*Kitāb* (*Iṣlāḥ*) *al-Manṭiq*] by Yaʿqūb b. al-Sikkīt and favor the Kufan [philologists]. Al-Riyāshī, who was sitting among the stationers, was told this and he said: "We were the ones who took the lexicon from none but hunters of lizards and eaters of jerboas [that is, true Bedouins] but these [Kufan lexicographers] took the lexicon from farmers who collect truffles and eat sour milk," or something along those lines [*innamā akhadhnā l-lughata ʿan ḥarashati l-ḍubāb wa-akalati l-yarābīʿ wa-hāʾulāʾi akhadhū l-lughata ʿan ahli l-Sawādi aṣḥābi l-kawāmīkhi wa-akalati l-shawārīzi*].[84]

Al-Riyāshī (d. 871), the grammarian who challenged the bookseller, was in several respects a man in-between.[85] Belonging to the Basran school, he bridged the gap between the generation of the triumvirate of al-Aṣmaʿī, Abū

ʿUbayda, and Abū Zayd al-Anṣārī and that of the towering al-Mubarrad.[86] Al-Riyāshī was generally respected, but his colleague Abū Ḥātim al-Sijistānī seems to have been of two minds about him. Once he deplored that the times had nothing better to offer than al-Riyāshī, concluding that "knowledge will pass from the hands and books will vanish."[87] It is understandable that a contemporary scholar still thought of books as perishable. What he meant was that works not put into circulation and taught in a scholarly fashion risked getting lost, and cases of "book-stingy" scholars, who died without sharing their writings, confirm this.[88]

In terms of his method, al-Riyāshī emphasized his school's direct oral access to the most authentic language—that is, that of the Bedouins. He wrote few books himself but had read either half or the whole of the *Kitāb Sībawayhi* with the grammarian al-Māzinī, and his teacher conceded that al-Riyāshī understood the book better than he did himself.[89] Al-Riyāshī also borrowed the recently deceased al-Jumaḥī's *Classes of Great Poets,* on poetic criticism, fascicle by fascicle as it was being edited by his nephew and transmitter.[90] Al-Riyāshī clearly appreciated books as a backup if their author was no longer alive. But if possible, he preferred person-to-person teaching, and he deplored, for instance, that he could not have heard al-Jumaḥī in addition to reading his book.

Al-Riyāshī still memorized books. He read the books of his teacher Abū Zayd al-Anṣārī under his tutelage until he knew them by heart. With his other teacher, al-Aṣmaʿī, he simply audited his works until he memorized them—though he admitted that reading the material with Abū Zayd had sped up the process.[91]

Oral debate remained the means to establish status. When he discovered that a student of his also studied with another teacher, al-Riyāshī challenged the rival to a debate to put him in his place.[92] In a couplet he emphasizes the importance of asking questions in the learning process:

> A good question cures blindness,
> but keeping silent in ignorance prolongs blindness instead.
>
> Be a questioner about what troubles you,
> you were created with reason in order to ask questions.[93]

Al-Riyāshī thus navigated between oral and written types of information and their combination, accepting scholarly books as necessary and unavoidable, but convinced that they needed an oral existence to survive intact. He is on record for once requesting clarification about the example verses in Sībawayhi's grammar. In a session with the philologist Abū ʿUbayda, who was the best authority on this book, he asked a lot of questions apparently about the host's own work, but the scholar wised up to his true purpose and refused to give any further information about "the book by that Khūzistānī."[94]

In confronting the nameless stationer in the Basran book market, al-Riyāshī took offense not only at a book from the rival school but also at its promotion by someone who was not a trained scholar. In his eyes, the craftsman had overstepped his competency. And he took the challenge seriously by counteradvertising his own school's superior method instead of attacking or insulting the merchant. He argued this in succinct, ornate prose joining erudition to eloquence, coining a slogan that was easy to remember. Al-Riyāshī obviously felt the necessity to oppose an opinion from outside the scholarly circuit. The bookseller had launched a competition. But this was taking place not in a closed scholarly gathering but in the city's open market. A book promotion by a merchant and craftsman stood against the pronouncement of a scholar, and the buying public was to judge.

However, this scholar's protestations proved futile, and the subsequent reception of the book would vindicate the merchant. An unnamed colleague opined: "No book on lexicon like the *Rectification of Speech* has crossed the bridge to Baghdad." Further praise came from the great philologist al-Mubarrad, who conceded the book's excellence and admitted that his own school had nothing to match it.[95] Al-Mubarrad did not always show himself to be this generous. He had even criticized a book of his own school, Sībawayhi's *Kitāb,* before endorsing it as the foundational work of Arabic grammar.[96] During al-Riyāshī's time, the *Kitāb Sībawayhi* was attaining the status of a classic. A century later, in al-Sīrāfī's biographical dictionary of Basran grammarians, it is the book mentioned most often as having been read in any class.[97] The Basran school had become a book-centered tradition. Basrans respected knowledge that came in book form and the absence of a match to Ibn al-Sikkīt's *Rectification* must have been a sore point.

This was only the beginning of the *Rectification's* triumph. But before considering another, albeit unacknowledged tribute, the book itself deserves a closer look. Its opening chapters help address the most pressing problem any user of the Arabic script faces: because of the unwritten short vowels, simple nouns (those lacking any long vowels, prefixes, or suffixes that would indicate the morphological form and its vowel sequence) can be pronounced in a number of ways. Some variants are synonymous, but often a different reading alters the meaning; for instance, *<k-b-r>* can be realized as *kibr, kibar, or kubr,* signifying "pride," "old age," or "large size," respectively. A simple noun consisting of three radicals without any affixes offers theoretically up to nine ways of reading, though, of course, not all of these constitute real words in a given root.[98] Such simple word types, whose various phonetic realizations were not made explicit in the script of codices, invited mispronunciation and confusion with their visual cognates. Their correct rendition was no mere matter of style, but important to avoid misunderstandings, as the alteration of a single vowel could turn one word into another.

Ibn al-Sikkīt collected and arranged these words based on their unvocalized written form. He laid out his book of 114 chapters along clear and logical principles, placing the simple before the complex and making it usable for quick reference. His selection was furthermore problem-oriented, as he devoted special chapters to letters and symbols whose orthography posed particular difficulties, namely the *hamza* for the glottal stop and the semivowels *w* and *y,* whose double duty as consonants and long vowels made them ambiguous. For its time, the book's arrangement was pioneering.

As a reference, the *Rectification* offered practical advantages to the general reader: it was a handy book, assembling much information in little space. The same anonymous scholar quoted above states: "There is no doubt that it is one of those useful and engaging books that comprise a great deal of vocabulary. In this size [*ḥajm*] we know of nothing like it of its kind."[99] Furthermore, it was applied knowledge, limited to words that people actually used, and a handy book for specialists and generalists, the latter of whom might well be the potential customers in the market the anonymous stationer had targeted.[100]

Ibn al-Sikkīt also received praise (but not acknowledgment) in written form. Much of his material was lifted and reused for the most famous exemplar of the genre. Its author was the man of letters Ibn Qutayba, one of the two most prolific book writers of the late ninth century. In essence, he retooled Ibn al-Sikkīt's *Rectification* for a new kind audience emerging at his time, "a burgeoning political and cultural group to the creation of which he [i.e., Ibn Qutayba] was central, one in need of texts to define and vindicate it, and, on the strength of them, to be able to prove to other competing religio-political and cultural groups that it merited its hegemonic place in the community," as James Montgomery puts it.[101] For this, Ibn Qutayba picked the best available precursor and recycled much of his material as well as his organizational principles.[102] The unacknowledged dependence on the *Rectification* by a work that would become the standard desk reference for scribes earns Ibn al-Sikkīt implicit acclaim as the perfect model. The borrowing by the popularizing author proves to be the highest compliment for Ibn al-Sikkīt.

In terms of distribution, the case of the later Ibn Qutayba resembles the situation of Ibn al-Sikkīt in that a book was promoted outside the circle of scholarship and beyond earshot of its author. But Ibn Qutayba had intended this, while in Ibn al-Sikkīt's generation, the second quarter of the ninth century, the "unheard" reception of a book was still unusual and hesitantly accepted. Only few recognized the book's potential to lead an independent life, and stationers were just becoming a new conduit for book distribution and for helping (or compelling) authors to transcend their limited dissemination through teaching.

The *Rectification* would be read and debated avidly for the next four centuries.[103] The Ottoman historian and bibliographer Ḥajjī Khalīfa (d. 1675) lists no fewer than eleven scholars who revised it, commented on it, enlarged or abridged it, or wrote *responsae* from the tenth to the thirteenth centuries. Nearly 300 years after its composition, the book was still judged important enough by al-Tibrīzī (d. 1109) to receive a revision.[104]

The unnamed stationer had proven his foresight and good judgment. Perhaps he had observed customers' repeatedly choosing Ibn al-Sikkīt's handy and useful volume over others of its kind that had less to offer and were more cumbersome to use (there were many, though few survive). He was proven right over the rival philologist al-Riyāshī by the leader of that very school, al-Mubarrad, by the implicit praise of emulation by the "prime craftsman of Arabic literary prose," Ibn Qutayba, and by four centuries of subsequent philologists—no small feat for a merchant and craftsman.[105]

CONCLUSION

The wealth and variety of Arabic sources affords various perspectives on identical groups of people, so that the little-esteemed profession of the stationers received treatment from different angles in the systematic and sober compilation of al-Dhahabi and in literary *akhbār* of the *adab* tradition. It is striking that these different kinds of sources yield analogous types of stationers, confirming each other with regard to the development of the stationers' various professional profiles, and they both highlight moments of friction between established conventions in the dissemination of scholarship and new ways available through the rapid production and spreading of manuscript codices. Particularly in cases where stationers' actions and ambitions collided with those of scholars or administrators, supplying a good plot for the story, this is fleshed out in the *akhbār* literature.

If author-stationers who produced their own books did so from the beginning without raising eyebrows, those stationers who produced others' works took some time to be accepted as professionals in their own right. The access to, and reliability of, the scholarly material they transmitted often were subject to criticism. In the interlocking oral and written procedure of passing on scholarship in the ninth century, a mere craftsperson had no place. Scholarship was not deemed to be safe in the hands of amateurs. Manuals on secretaryship that discuss the copying procedure elaborate on the knowledge required by copyists of scholarly books. This included, besides careful revision, things such as subdividing a text logically and correcting misspelt foreign names and technical terminology, which required linguistic expertise and familiarity with a book's subject.[106]

The fact that *warraqūn* eventually occupied a firm place in the transmission and dissemination of knowledge also meant that the typical representative of the profession was more than what the name implied; not a mere copyist, a stationer had to have a basic understanding of the content of the books he reproduced. The way to acquire such knowledge was still unregulated at the beginning of the ninth century, but in its course, the autodidact and the independent scholar, operating outside of the teaching circuit, came to acquire a secure position in the changing cosmos of knowledge to which the rapidly increasing availability of books had contributed.

CHAPTER FOUR

BOOK OWNERS AND READERS

In the previous chapters, events involving single books, the scholars and poets writing them, and the craftsmen producing them have been reviewed, showing how individuals interacted with and profited from the new Arabic manuscript codex. This final chapter is devoted to how the books were used in further ways and what they meant to their owners and readers. Regarding ownership, physical books as collections became a new institution: the library, which developed its own dynamic. In a broader sense, owned books and private notebooks were even supposed to reveal something of their owners' convictions and beliefs, and they were adduced in a number of court cases, discussed below. As for the readers, and this includes readers who were themselves book writers, their concept of what constituted a book, beyond the physical object, will receive attention, and their responses to a specific book show what they expected from this new medium.

LIBRARIES

A salient phenomenon of the ninth century was that the readers (those who could afford the cost and the time) very quickly began to collect books, to maximize the amount and variety of written data at their disposal. Among the elite, rulers (who had been among the first to commission books on subjects on which none yet existed, such as Ḥadīth and history) now amassed the largest libraries. Not infrequently they employed notable scholars to assemble and curate these or to copy books in their libraries. Thus, ʿAllān al-Shuʿūbī copied (*nasakha*) in the palace library called *bayt al-ḥikma* for both caliphs al-Rashīd and al-Maʾmūn.[1] For people outside the educated elite, the sprouting book markets in every larger city were the best places to supply themselves with books. The ubiquity of copyists (whether solely craftsmen, or simultaneously students or minor scholars, or major scholars who practiced it as a sideline) made book reproduction fast and easy.

Scholars also had to rely on markets for books they had not acquired through the teaching circuit. They very soon followed suit as owners of libraries (despite some scholars' public protestations to the contrary), though they themselves tended to copy many of their books. On scholars' deaths their libraries often ended up again in one of the many book markets and were fought over by potential buyers. Thus the books of the *akhbārī* ʿUmar b. Shabba (d. c. 877) were sold after his death by his son to the secretary ʿAlī b. Yaḥyā al-Munajjim (d. 888), who in turn assembled a library for the vizier al-Fatḥ b. Khāqān.[2] Libraries created a competing venue to the oral method of disseminating (or rather, channeling) knowledge in teachers' circles, precisely because they gave access to competitors, scholars from other disciplines, and literate amateurs. Ibn al-Nadīm describes the libraries of the authors he lists, such the one of the transmitter, litterateur, and judge Abū l-Ḥassān al-Ḥasan b. ʿUthmān al-Ziyādī (d. 857). Besides owning a large and beautiful collection (*khizāna ḥasana kabīra*), al-Ziyādī also both produced and commissioned books (*yaʿamalu l-kutuba wa-tuʿmalu lahū*). One library Ibn al-Nadīm praises particularly is the abovementioned one belonging to the vizier al-Fatḥ; "Nothing of its size and beauty has been seen," he writes, and adds that the vizier hosted scholars and eloquent Bedouins, probably in the library itself.[3]

It is difficult to obtain a precise impression of the size, composition, and monetary value of such libraries.[4] Details on libraries in the ninth century are scarce, and any figures supplied may not be taken at face value. Nonetheless, the few cited numbers, assembled by Houari Touati, carry rhetorical value and show that scholars' libraries in particular were prized acquisitions. The size of a library became a particular subject of interest when it was transported for sale upon the owner's death. The library of the deceased traditionist Yaḥyā b. Maʿīn filled one hundred boxes and four large clay jars. Much larger was that of the historian al-Wāqidī, which required 600 boxes, or 120 mule loads, to be transported by his heirs to the market, where it was sold for 2,000 *dīnār*s. At other times, only the total price is mentioned without any indication of the number of books. Thus, the judge Yaḥyā b. Aktham (alive first half ninth century) considered purchasing a bequest library, but could not afford the 200 *dīnār*s it was assessed at. A multiple of that, 3,000 *dīnār*s, was paid by an unnamed customer for the library of the deceased philosopher Yaḥyā b. ʿAdī (d. 973). Finally, 10,000 or 14,000 *dirham*s (equivalent to about 400 or 560 *dīnār*s) was spent by the Ṣaffārid condottiere Yaʿqūb b. Layth (r. 861–879) for the library of an unnamed deceased grammarian.[5]

These few cases contrast scholars, who assembled libraries over their lifetimes, potentially copying many notebooks and books with their own hands, with wealthy individuals who could afford the wholesale purchase of what others had painstakingly collected. This was only possible for the well-to-do—in one case a general, in the other an anonymous buyer. The shouldering of a considerable expense for a library, by individuals who may have limited time to actually read the acquired books, demonstrates that owning scholarly books had become a matter of collectors' pride. For members of the elite, libraries served as a new status symbol, and these owners strove variously for quality (by having autographs copied and collated), completeness, or luxury (commissioning fancy copies written in beautiful hand by renowned copyists).

Books as Prestige Objects

Indeed, for some individuals who owned libraries, they were as much a matter of prestige as a source of information. Bound books could be large and cumbersome. This might be useful for display, but impractical for use, for which unbound loose sheets or separate fascicles were more practical. Al-Jāḥiẓ, for instance, in his praise of books in the preface of his book *Animals* (*al-Ḥayawān*), belittles books' material value as objects.[6] In a section about how Manichaeans (*zindīqs*) took care to beautify their writings, he reports that Manichaeans prized white paper—they apparently used only the best, perhaps the Samarqand type of paper still made with the original ingredient of mulberry bast, which was resistant to bookworms—and they preferred glossy black ink and beautiful writing.[7] But al-Jāḥiẓ opines that all such efforts were wasted, because the Manichaeans restricted themselves to non-Islamic religious books (which he compared to Christian crosses and church ornamentation and Magian fire temples), and they did not spend any effort on wisdom sayings, philosophy (*falsala*), analogies (*maqāyīs*), laws (*sunan*), clarity of expression (*al-tabayyun wa-l-tabyīn*), crafts (*ṣināʿāt*), gain and commerce (*al-takassub wa-l-tijārāt*), seeking help (*irtifāqāt*), self-improvement (*riyāḍāt*), or other educational (*ādāb*) or intelligent (*fiṭan*) things.[8] In the view of al-Jāḥiẓ, content trumped any fancy physical form. To his mind, books were meant for serious subjects, not entertainment. That this was not the prevailing opinion is shown by the large final section in Ibn al-Nadīm's tenth-century *Catalogue,* devoted to popular books, both Arabic and foreign, with the latter subdivided into tales of Indian, Iranian, and Greek provenance. A few of these titles are preserved from later times, and we are uncertain of the exact makeup of popular readings from the ninth century, other than the numerous tantalizing titles (see also fig. 5).

Paper was copious but not yet as cheap as it would become in subsequent centuries, and scholarly books still constituted a serious financial investment. Al-Jāḥiẓ thus criticized a man for trying to come by knowledge cheaply. In a section devoted to scholars' opinions on the excellence of the book, the *akhbār*-transmitter Muḥammad b. ʿUbaydallāh [or ʿAbdallāh] al-ʿUtbī (d. 842) told Ibn al-Jahm (probably the amateur philosopher Muḥammad b. al-Jahm al-Barmakī, alive 833–842) that one day he saw a man with a slave girl who belonged to the erudite Salmawayh (d. 840), the physician of Caliph al-Muʿtaṣim, reading together Euclid's book on geometry. She, being a fast reader, finished it, while he was still struggling with the first section (*maqāla*), although, as the narrator emphasizes, "He was a free nobleman and she a servant living in seclusion," and apparently he "cared more about reading than the physician [Salmawayh cared] about teaching slave girls."

Ibn al-Jahm retorts that he believed the man did not understand a single problem (or geometrical shape; *shakl*), not to mention the entire first *maqāla.* Al-ʿUtbī found this hard to believe, as the individual—who was probably well known but is not identified—was "eloquent and educated" (*dhū lisānin wa-adabin*). But Ibn al-Jahm inveighed that he heard that man ask his son how much he had paid for the book by Euclid, and on learning its high price, he disapproved of the whole enterprise of assembling a scholarly library. He commented, “I was interested in knowledge because I thought I could gain a lot by spending little, but when I started to spend a lot, all I got was promises. I don’t care about knowledge any longer.”[9] He had hoped to gain knowledge cheaply in the form of books, and when this calculation did not work out, he lost interest. This was the case of a potential library owner for the sake of prestige, not scholarship, and a little effort and expense discouraged him. Al-Jāḥiẓ as a writer and compiler is known to have relished controversy and enjoyed taking polemical positions opposite to what readers expected. His portrait of the failed book collector embarrassed by a smart slave girl displays certainly satirical notes, yet it captures a social type whose existence among the group of new library owners seems credible.

(In)complete Libraries

A more successful a book collector appears in an account related by the poet ʿUmāra b. ʿAqīl. He was sitting with Caliph al-Maʾmūn when a voice behind him suddenly called out a satirical quatrain, insulting the poet as a cowardly deserter from battle. The poet ʿUmāra recognized the author immediately: “This was the poetry of Farwa b. Ḥumayḍa about me, and God knows what this made me feel like.” He was amazed at how the satire, presumably delivered orally outside in the city, had made it behind the walls of the caliphal palace. Later he spotted General ʿAlī b. Hishām (executed 832) leaving the assembly laughing, and the poet understood that he had been the culprit and confronted him thereafter in the caliph’s presence.[10] The following dialogue is related in his words:

> “Abū l-Ḥasan, is this what you are doing to me, though you are my friend?”
> “This doesn’t hurt you.”
> “How did Farwa’s poetry fall into your hands?”
> “Is there any book [*kitāb*] that I do not possess?”
> “Commander of the Faithful,” I said, turning to al-Maʾmūn, “Shall I be satirized in your palace? Give me satisfaction!”
> “Leave that,” the caliph responded, “and tell me the story of this man and of what happened between you and him.”

This is followed by the account of ʿUmāra's recent satire match with the poet Farwa.[11] The account shows that a general (and not a scholar) prided himself on owning every new book known—not only scholarship but also satire, a genre some despised and did not touch, but also a genre that was potentially very powerful. Not only that, but it is the latest satire to appear, against a major court poet and the only one al-Ma'mūn patronized. The general's library thus was an up-to-date database on salon and street culture. This was certainly useful as a repertoire to cut a good figure in literary gatherings, but it was also politically expedient, and in this case, it gave him ammunition against an important personality at court.

Most importantly, libraries exerted an influence on the circulation of ideas. They allowed for the boundaries of disciplines to be crossed, and scholarly control over the once closely delimited spheres of erudition could be circumvented. Moreover, foreign knowledge in the form of Iranian statecraft and Greek science had been added to the cosmos of knowledge since the early Abbasid times and generated new categories of books a library needed to contain. As such, libraries were the spaces in which the acceleration and cosmopolitan gamut of knowledge that characterized this period became physically manifest, and this occurred to the greatest extent in the libraries of the caliphs, who were, since al-Maʿmūn, active sponsors of the translation movement.[12]

The following incident of a missing and restored book tells much about al-Ma'mūn's approach to his library. The book in question received its expanded final form a century later in the hands of the historian and ethical philosopher Miskawayh (d. 1030), who relates his own discovery of it in the preface:

> I read in my youth a book by Abū ʿUthmān al-Jāḥiẓ entitled *Furthering Understanding* [*Istiṭālat al-fahm*], in which he mentioned a book entitled *Jāvīdān khirad* ["Eternal wisdom"] and quoted a few pithy sayings [*kalimāt*] from it, then he praised it beyond his usual measure. I avidly searched for it in the regions I passed though and found it in Fars [in southwest Iran] with the Zoroastrian high priest [*mūbadh al-mūbadhān*].[13]

Miskawayh then retraces the book's history to the moment when Caliph al-Ma'mūn first became aware of this work as a collector's item. This occurred in a conversation with his vizier al-Ḥasan b. Sahl (d. 850), whom the caliph quizzed about the best types of books.[14] The vizier relates it in his own words:

"Which are the best and noblest books of the Arabs?" al-Ma'mūn asked me one day. I began to enumerate books about the early Muslim campaigns and annalistic chronicles [*kutub al-maghāzī wa-l-tawārīkh*] and so forth until I reached the exegetical works of the Qur'an.

"The Word of God Most High, is beyond par," the caliph said.

"Which are the most splendid books of the Persians?" he then continued. So I mentioned a great number of them and finally said: "*Jāvīdān khirad,* Commander of the Faithful." He had the list of his books [*fihrist kutubihī*] brought and began to leaf through its pages, but found no trace or mention of the book.

"Why is the mention of this book missing in the list?"

"It is Dhūbān's book, Commander of the Faithful, I happened to write down part of it."

"Bring it to me at once!"[15]

The caliph covers a wide scholarly spectrum with his two questions, and at the same time, his separate queries for the books of Arabs and (pre-Islamic) Persians imply their different fields of scholarly endeavor: Arab scholars initiated Qur'ān scholarship and historiography (to be sure, including also Persian converts to Islam among the authors), whereas Persian authors of Sasanian times had produced works on statecraft and advice to rulers (*andarz*), which were translated into Arabic, even before the Graeco-Arabic translation movement would take off with al-Ma'mūn.

The caliph's questions pursue two goals. One is to test his vizier's knowledge and the other is to verify the completeness of his library. His silence in reponse to the answer about the first group of titles implies that he knew and owned all of them. The same is true with the Persian books, until al-Ḥasan referred to one title that the caliph did not recognize. To verify, he consulted the catalogue of his library. This is a rare mention of such a record, and no library catalogue of that early period has survived.[16] One must assume that caliphs or other wealthy patrons who employed a curator occasionally had such catalogues prepared. The first large surviving catalogue of Ibn al-Nadīm, a century later, is instead a bookseller's record of all books he had found extant, but he mentions a least one earlier catalogue he used as a basis for his own.[17] The caliph is displeased at this lacuna that reveals his library's incompleteness and wants it remedied immediately. The secretary's account continues as follows:

> I had [the book] fetched, and the messenger arrived with it just as the caliph had risen for prayer. When he saw him approach with the book, he turned away from the *qibla* and started reading. Every time he completed a section he exclaimed, "There is no God but He!" As this went on I said, "Commander of the Faithful, you are missing [the time of] the prayer, and the book will still be here."
>
> "You are right. But I am afraid to commit a mistake in my prayer, because my heart is occupied with [the book]." Then he prayed and went back to his reading.
>
> "Where is the rest?" he then asked.
>
> "Dhūbān did not give it to me," I said.
>
> "If a promise were not a band whose one end is in the hand of God and the other in mine, I would take it from him. By God, *this* is wisdom [*ḥikma*], not what we move our tongues with between our teeth."[18]

What the vizier had given the caliph was indeed only part of the book, and the caliph had once before laid eyes on it, though he was unable at the time to claim it for himself. Miskawayh reproduces the events based on al-Jāḥiẓ via the historian al-Wāqidī, who in turn quotes the vizier al-Faḍl b. Sahl (d. 818), brother and predecessor in the vizierate of al-Ḥasan.[19] To wit, at the installation of al-Maʾmūn as caliph in Khurasan in 812, the king of Kābulistān had sent him a wise man by the name of Dhūbān, describing his knowledge as the best possible present for the caliph.[20] Before retaking Iraq from his brother al-Amīn in the brothers' civil war, the caliph consulted the sage, who called the venture auspicious, and he was proven true. Al-Jāḥiẓ further reports on the authority of Dhūbān himself that this sage mastered the rhymed prose in which pre-Islamic soothsayers would utter their predictions, and he was correct in everything he foretold to al-Maʾmūn. As news of the victory over Iraq arrived, the caliph offered to the sage a reward of 100,000 *dirhams*. But the sage desired something different: "I will accept from you something that is worth all this money and more. It is a book that exists in Iraq and contains the noble virtues [*makārim al-akhlāq*] and universal knowledge [*ʿulūm al-āfāq*] from the books of the Great Persian. It lies [buried] among the treasures beneath the Arch [*īwān*] in Ktesiphon."[21] The motif of a buried book is frequent in pseudepigraphy, notably in hermetical texts, and likewise, it emphasizes here the value of the book as a source of secret knowledge. Its subject, described as wisdom and ethics (*akhlāq*), places it among the Persian writings on advice that were of particular importance to rulers. On al-Ma'mūn's arrival in Baghdad and the establishment of his reign, he fulfilled his promise and wrote to the sage requesting a precise description of the book's location in order to have it retrieved, and indeed a small locked box made of dark glass was unearthed at the designated place. The remainder of Miskawayh's account is again based on al-Jāḥiẓ, here quoting al-Ḥasan b. Sahl.

The caliph handed the sage the box and told him to take it and leave, restraining his own curiosity with effort. The sage, however, opened it in his presence, took out a bundle of one hundred folios wrapped in brocade, which he kept, and donated the box to the caliph's treasury. Al-Ḥasan proposed to the caliph that they ask about the book's content, but the caliph forbade him to do so, in observance of his own promise. The secretary, however, not being bound by the caliph's promise, was not too shy to ask the sage about the book on a later occasion:

> After the sage left, I visited him in his home and inquired about the book.
>
> "This is the book *Jāvīdān khirad.* Kanjūr, the vizier of the King of Iran redacted [*akhraja*] it, based on ancient wisdom," the sage said.
>
> "Give me one of the folios, so I can look at it," I said. He did and I looked it over, trying my best to understand it, but the more I tried the less I understood. So I summoned al-Khiḍr (or Khaḍir) b. ʿAlī. This was early morning, and before noon he had deciphered it all by himself. Then he began to translate, and I wrote down his translation. After this I returned the sheet to the sage and took another one, while al-Khiḍr was still with me. He started reading while I wrote [his oral translation] and so forth until I had taken circa 30 sheets. Then I had to leave for that day. Later I visited the sage again and asked him:
>
> "Is there anything better in the world than this kind of knowledge [*ʿilm*]?"
>
> "If one shouldn't keep knowledge to oneself—and this is the way of the Here and the Hereafter—I would give you the whole book. But I cannot give you more than what you already took."
>
> The folios I had taken were obviously not in the original order of composition, because there were things one could not figure out [*lā yumkinu ikhrājuhā*].[22]

The book had obviously been composed in an Iranian language, most likely Middle Persian, and the process of dual translation depicted here must have been current when the translator was not bilingual himself. That had been the case with Ibn al-Muqaffaʿ, a Zoroastrian convert and the first major translator of Middle Persian writings at the transition from the Umayyad to the Abbasid dynasty. In turn, al-Ḥasan, likewise of Zoroastrian background, did not have full command of Middle Persian, even though his initial attempt to decipher it himself indicates that he had at least some familiarity with it.

The account also highlights the secret nature of the writing, as the sage parts with only scattered pages making up less than a third of the book. Here Miskawayh ends his account. Active in the early eleventh century, he found another complete copy in Fars and was able to reproduce it in its entirety. He identified the book as the testament of Hūshang (Ūshahanj), a mythical Iranian king and first lawgiver, said to have lived shortly after the Deluge, whose vita (*sīra*) and lore (*adab*) were regarded as the earliest surviving of any individual. Miskawayh likened its content to the wisdom sayings of the Arabs and preceding nations (Persians, Indians, and Greeks; *rūm*), copied it, and combined it in his book with selected texts of advice (*waṣāyā*, literally "testaments") and adages (*ādāb*) of these four peoples to produce his own book on the subject, giving it the same title, *Jāwīdān khirad*.[23] After concluding his preface with a statement of his purpose—to educate the young (*li-yartāḍa bihā l-aḥdāth*) in wisdom sayings (*ḥikam*) and scholarly disciplines (*ʿulūm*), to improve his own and later readers' moral education (*taqwīm al-nafs*), and to gain God's reward—he places the recuperated testament at his book's beginning. It is a collection of brief wisdom sayings of ethical-religious and antimaterialist character, which emphasize the interdependence of knowledge (*ʿilm*) and action (*ʿamal*).[24] The testament concludes with the exhortation to "read books" (*qirāʾat al-kutub*), because they constitute "culture and knowledge [*al-adab wa-l-ʿilm*] fixed in writing by the ancients and bound to increase one's intellect [*ʿaql*]."

Miskawayh had been able to restore this source of foreign wisdom in all completeness. This had been possible in part because of the earlier tandem-translated excerpts of a vizier, which found their way into a caliphal library, according to the account, thanks to a library catalogue of Caliph al-Maʾmūn, which had permitted him to identify and close a lacuna in his otherwise comprehensive collection.

Libraries as institutions thus gave owners the possibility to have the totality of assembled knowledge, ancient and contemporary, conveniently at their fingertips, even if only few individuals had the means and connections to carry this out. This was the best possible goal to which books might be devoted. Yet, knowledge placed in physical objects was open to a host of other possible uses.

BOOKS IN ESTATES AND COURT TRIALS

Another new potential books offered was the ability to probe them for the secret thoughts of their owners if they had fallen foul of the authorities. To begin with, books did not by their mere existence guarantee the dissemination of their content, as a book could remain a unique copy in the possession of its author or his student. In this way, a book held by only one person would ensure his income through teaching and his status as the guardian of the knowledge it contained. This is the stationer type of the book transmitter, as described in Chapter 3. But objects, however well guarded, tend to circulate eventually, and scholars and poets in the early ninth century would often gain access to one another's writings (through other people who owned them or students who carried them to class) with the sole intention of finding points for criticism.[25]

A more drastic application of this idea was the investigation by authorities of the religious beliefs of individuals who had come under suspicion of heresy, by requisitioning their books. In one such case, a falling out between the philologist Abū ʿUbayda and the poet Abān al-Lāḥiqī (d. c. 815), the scholar accused the poet of being a bad Muslim based on his possession of Torahs: "The authorities have neglected everything to the point of failing to take poll tax from Abān al-Lāḥiqī and his kin, and these houses of theirs contains scrolls [*asfār*] of the Torah but no Qur'ān codex [*muṣḥaf*]." The poet retorted with a couplet, calling this a denunciation. Abū ʿUbayda's attack was certainly polemical, but Abān was known to have versified many foreign works that had been translated into Arabic, such as Aristotle's *Logic* and *Kalīla wa-Dimna,* a widespread wisdom text that came into Arabic from Sanskrit via a Middle Persian redaction in the mid-eighth century. At the same time, Abān was patronized by the Barmakid family of viziers, who had a more diversified view of culture, and furthermore, his neighbors' attestations of his regular nocturnal Qur'ān recitation were juxtaposed by the compiler with his vita to counteract the attack on his orthodoxy and place it in context.[26] In this case, the attack remained a threatening joke without follow-up.

A Poet's Personal Effects

The obverse occurred in the case of the Basran poet Bashshār b. Burd (d. c. 784). The event in question was in this case posthumous, because a vizier had taken the initiative to rush to Basra himself and inflict a fatal punishment on the poet for his heresy (*zandaqa*), in order to prevent the caliph al-Mahdī from seeing Bashshār and perhaps allowing him to redeem himself.[27] The caliph found the swift execution suspicious and decided to investigate the matter in person. The following account is given by the princely poet and critic Ibn al-Muʿtazz in his book on contemporary poets: "It is related that when al-Mahdī had Bashshār executed he regretted his deed and wanted to find some [evidence] to hold onto [*yataʿallaqu bihī*]. So he sent for his books. He had them brought and ordered their investigation [*taftīsh*] with the desire to find in them something of what had vexed him regarding the poet, but he found nothing." The account continues with details about the poet's personal effects. One sealed papyrus (*ṭūmār makhtūm*) is found, which on opening is revealed to be a note in which the poet admitted having been tempted to satirize a clan of the Abbasid family, but then refrained from this out of reverence for their parentage of the Prophet. Instead, he contented himself with two verses of satire about their stinginess. The caliph, distraught, commented, "Now, by God, I truly feel regret."[28]

The poet had in fact stirred up controversy. His graphic *ghazal* had upset several theologians of Basra and offended public morality by encouraging, for instance, adulterous love, and the caliph had forbidden the poet to compose any further *ghazal*. Bashshār's satires were feared, and the people of Basra allegedly danced at the news of his death. In fact, the more likely cause for the public lashing that had led to his death was his satire of the above-mentioned vizier.[29] The charge of heresy, however, was an easier one make and more effective for the purpose at hand, and the caliph could be quickly persuaded. The investigation of the poet's effects had proven the miscarriage of justice too late.

High Treason on Trial

On another occasion, a defendant's books were adduced as evidence in order to achieve a verdict. This was the case of high treason made against the Sogdian general al-Afshīn. His full name was Khaydar b. Kāwūs and his epithet is the royal title given to him as ruler of the region of Ushrūsana, a Sogdian principality located in Transoxania between the Jaxartes River (today's Amu Darya) and the Hissar Mountains. Al-Afshīn looked back on an illustrious career, having quelled the revolt of the Khurramite rebel Bābak, which had been celebrated in a famous ode by the poet Abū Tammām.[30] But later he colluded with another rebel, Māziyār, the ruler (*Ispahbadh*) of Ṭabaristān (located in northwestern Iran on the southern border of the Caspian Sea), to overthrow the Abbasids. This plot was foiled with the help of his rival ʿAbdallāh b. Ṭāhir, governor of Khurasan, and al-Afshīn was taken prisoner in the Jawsaq palace in Samarra to await trial for high treason. The trial was conducted in 841 in the audience hall in the presence of the supreme judge Ibn Abī Du'ād (d. 854), the Ṭāhirid governor Isḥāq b. Ibrāhīm b. Muṣʿab (d. 849–850), and the secretary Muḥammad b. ʿAbdalmalik b. al-Zayyāt (d. 847), who served as prosecutor. Members of the Abbasid family were present, but all courtiers had to leave the audience hall. The Zoroastrian high priest, another Sogdian monarch and Sogdian nobles, and the rebel Māziyār were called as witnesses. Among the questions posed to al-Afshīn was the following:

> "What is this book you own, which you embellished with gold, precious stones, and brocade? Does it contain any unbelief?"
>
> "This is a book I inherited from my father. It contains lore [*adab*] of the Persians. Regarding the unbelief that you mention, I enjoyed the book for its education and ignored the rest. I found it illuminated [*muḥallan*] as it is, and there was no pressing need to remove the illumination [*ḥilya*], so I left it intact. Just like the book of *Kalīla wa-Dimna* and the *Kitāb Marwak* in *your* house. I did not think this to be un-Islamic."[31]

Thus the accused launched a counterattack on the prosecutor. Far from constituting a proof of heresy, the book in question belonged to the type of works the prosecutor himself owned—namely, wisdom literature. Indeed, Iranian books of wisdom and Greek works of science were fashionable among secretaries; half a century later, the prolific proponent of Arabic lore Ibn Qutayba chastises the secretaries as a group for busying themselves with superficialities such as beautiful handwriting, love poetry, astrology, and logic, while neglecting their own cultural heritage and the Islamic religious sciences.[32] The prosecutor, himself a parvenu from the middle classes (his father had been an oil merchant, as his epithet *al-Zayyāt* still showed), shared the predilection of his new professional class.

As for the description of the book, it is ambiguous. *Ḥilya,* "decoration, adornment," and its epithet *muḥallan,* "decorated, adorned," can be understood either as illumination (i.e., colored or gilded titles, frames or medallions) or as illustration (i.e., actual images). Both appear in, for instance, *Kalīla wa-Dimna,* the very book the prosecutor is revealed to own himself. In fact, *Kalīla wa-Dimna* is one of the most frequently illustrated manuscripts in Arabic literature (together with the *Maqāmāt* of al-Harīrī, d. 1122). Its manuscripts that display such adornment are admittedly no older than the thirteenth century, and the same is true for a passage in the book that explicitly refers to its images as a source of gain for book illustrators. However, an early illustrated fragment from the Cairo Geniza survives that can be dated, based on the paper, between 950 and 1250, whereas the script assigns it to the earlier portion of this period (see fig. 9).[33] However, the argument in the trial about the work as illustrated confirms that images appeared in early copies. The same is true of a Sasanian history of kings, *Kitāb al-Ṣuwar,* described by the historian al-Masʿūdī (d. 956) as containing portraits of twenty-five male and two female Sasanian rulers.[34]

The question about the adorned book was one of many posed to the accused on that day. Among the other facts he was confronted with were the public lashings he had ordered for two Muslim men after they had built a mosque on the site of a fire temple in his home state of Ushrūsana. Al-Afshīn explained that this had violated his local orders against converting houses of worship from one religion to another, a law designated to safeguard free coexistence of all religions in his region. Other petty accusations involved his apparent consumption of meat that had not been ritually slaughtered and his failure to have himself circumcised on his conversion to Islam. The crowning witness, however, was his fellow conspirer Māziyār, who cooperated with the authorities here, but in the end that was not enough to save his own life.

It is clear that the procedure was a show trial; whatever arguments the general put forth in his defense, the outcome had already been decided. For the Abbasid caliph al-Muʿtaṣim, the act of high treason was beyond doubt. After the examination, al-Afshīn was sent back to the prison that had been built for him in the center of the palace, where he was left to starve to death.

No ownership of any heretical books had been proven. On the contrary, the question had exposed the prosecutor as disingenuous. Nonetheless, this and the previous case show that a person's books were taken to reveal his

FIG. 9. Geniza fragment of *Kalīla wa-Dimna,* datable between 950 and 1250 C.E. The passage derives from the chapter of the Ringdove, and the image (painted in dark blue, red, yellow, and green colors) depicts the raven carrying the rat in his beak from the city to the countryside, to his friend the turtle. (Geniza Collection, T-S Ar. 40.9 verso, Cambridge University Library.)

true religious attitudes. This practical depository of information not only afforded endless possibilities for study and entertainment but also posed a hazard when its contents offended or violated reigning moral conventions and religious tenets. As in other cases of new media, use and abuse were a matter of the purpose to which books were put, and in a trial situation, confiscated books offered the possibility of reading their owners' minds in a way memorized knowledge had not made possible. Yet, it was not the books that redeemed or condemned their owners; rather, these neutral objects were liable to fall into the hands of those who exploited them for their own agendas. In the case of al-Afshīn, the book ownership had been a minor detail in his verdict, and not an effective one at that. But the requisitioning of books owned by suspicious or disliked persons had become a new investigative practice of the authorities. It hinged on the fact that books lent themselves both to disseminate knowledge and to keep it to oneself, and people collected books on both publicly held and secret attitudes, and as such, these constituted a new potential as much as a personal hazard.

A BOOK THAT FAILED

In spite of the general appreciation for books by the first quarter of the ninth century (including even such phenomena as book addiction) and the avid production, transmission, trade, readership, and collection of books, not every extant written text of some length was automatically accepted as a book.[35] Neither did the physical existence of a book (*kitāb*) suffice to guarantee its circulation and transmission in one piece. A book was defined as much by its physical form as by its format and content. To review, as far as book formats are concerned, several types existed side by side in the ninth century: first there was the transcript of oral events, presided over by an author, host, or patron and often titled "Gatherings of So-and-so" (*majālis*) or "Dictations of So-end-so" (*amālī*); second, the compilation of extant texts on a certain topic (*taṣnīf*); third, the epistle (*risāla*) addressed to a real or fictive person; and finally, the translated book (from a Greek or Middle Persian source), including works that claimed to be translations but were in fact pseudepigraphical.[36] The Qur'ān was of course sui generis and not a model for imitation, but its formulae pervaded Arabic literature, and its associative order of topics and the recurrence of smaller themes is reflected in the composition of many books.

The following details the case of an early book that entered Arabic literature through translation and came with the features of a "redacted book" (as Gregor Schoeler defines it); namely, a preface, subdivision into chapters, and internal cross-references. In comparison, the contemporary book types listed above displayed these elements only partly or not at all. The first type, the transcript of oral events, lacked all three. Instead, each of the included text pieces began with its own chain of transmission, and often without any arrangement or introduction to the series as a whole. The second type, the compilation, contained chapters organized by theme but not necessarily a preface. The third type, the epistle, had a preface but often lacked chapter division.

The book in question, *Kalīla wa-Dimna* (which played a role in the abovementioned court case), not only counted a number of prefaces and chapters but also displayed an intricate structure consisting of intercalated narrative frames with subtales and strewn-in wisdom sayings. Nonetheless, this book was not preserved as a whole but picked apart in the transmission of the ninth and tenth centuries. The failure of its ever-so-sophisticated format to keep the work intact raises the question of why this alone did not suffice.

Kalīla wa-Dimna is a book of advice for rulers in the form of parables with human and animal characters, and it reunited diverse elements, among them two older Indian works, the *Pañcatantra* and the *Mahābhārata*. The redaction of these Indian elements had been accomplished in the sixth century in Middle Persian with the addition of further chapters, and this version was then translated into Arabic and redacted by the already mentioned Persian-born secretary Ibn al-Muqaffaʿ shortly before his death in 757. He was a prolific translator of Middle Persian works, and perhaps also Greek (namely, the *Logic* of Aristotle, though its translator may have been his son), and he also composed epistles addressed to the Abbasid caliph and the members of his court.[37] His literary fame rested on his creation of a new kind of elegant and limpid prose. This made his works popular among secretaries who regarded his style as exemplary and a model for imitation. The book and its author are well attested in the literary sources since the eighth century, and at least one versification was commissioned as an aid for memorization. Curiously, the work as a whole disappeared from circulation in the next five centuries. Full manuscripts resurface beginning in the thirteenth century, though translations into Syriac, Persian, Greek, Hebrew, and Latin had already been made in the preceding two centuries (from the eleventh to the thirteenth century).

Not so with the pieces of the book. Quotations from it were ubiquitous from the ninth century, notably in the *adab* literature, aimed at both edifying and entertaining its readers. The book's modular structure, comprised of subtales, analogical images, und wisdom sayings, made it easy to detach pithy parts and reuse them in different contexts. This was also done also with Arabic verses, but the entire poems these were taken from (if the poets were of some importance) were transmitted simultaneously in collected works (*dawāwīn*) available for consultation. In the case of *Kalīla wa-Dimna,* there seems to have been little desire or need for the book as a whole.

Kalīla wa-Dimna must have been available as a book, because the historian al-Yaʿqūbī narrates the history of its composition and presents a table of contents including synopses of each chapter. He does so in his *Geography,* in the section on the kings of India, and he attributes the book's authorship to the sage Baydabāʾ, a fictional character in it. What al-Yaʿqūbī actually describes is the *Arabic* version, since he includes chapters that Ibn al-Muqaffāʿ added, and he lists the chapters in a sequence found in later Arabic manuscripts, which differs from that of the Middle Persian redaction (which is lost, but most likely resembled its preserved older Syriac translation, dated to the end of the sixth century).[38] Al-Yaʿqūbī omits mention of the Arabic translator-redactor Ibn al-Muqaffaʿ here, as also in his *History,* when giving the date of the Arabic translation under Caliph al-Manṣūr; elsewhere, he mentions only Ibn al-Muqaffaʿ's death by torture. In his description of *Kalīla wa-Dimna,* al-Yaʿqūbī notes "its form of parables [*amthāl*] which the intelligent reflect on, penetrate, and coach themselves with" (*yaʿtabiru bihā wa-yatafahhamuhā dhawū l-ʿuqūl wa-yataʾaddabūna bihā*). His summaries of each chapter skip the actual plots and extract instead each parable's political meaning, followed by the citation of the original title, as follows:

> The eighth chapter is the chapter of the ruler's knowing his aides, relatives and intimates; how he should render well-affected those whom his harshness may have harmed and how he should obtain their assistance; how he should seek help in his affairs from people of modesty and affection; how he should examine the state of his aides and entourage and reward those who do good and punish those who do evil for their wickedness. It is the chapter of the Lion and the Jackal.[39]

Al-Yaʿqūbī's presentation shows that he regarded the chapter titles as unhelpful for finding the desired content, and he also performed the "decoding" of the parables for his readers. Thus, he saved them having to read each chapter and find out its purpose for themselves. While offering a shortcut, he still remains the only source of the ninth century to treat the chapters of *Kalīla wa-Dimna* as entities. Ibn al-Nadīm's *Catalogue* of the tenth century likewise gives the number of chapters as "seventeen or eighteen" (without titles) but mentions that two more chapters occasionally were added.[40] The original form of *Kalīla wa-Dimna* as a book was therefore not in question.

The book is mentioned, for instance, by the essayist and man of letters al-Jāḥiẓ, in his polemical essay about secretaries, in which he chastises them for holding an unjustifiably high opinion of their own importance and for preferring *Kalīla wa-Dimna* and other works translated from Greek and Middle Persian to the Qurʾān and Islamic scholarship. In the following quote he shows what they mistake for knowledge and then goes on to contrast this with the full spectrum of Arabic-Islamic culture at the time. In this context he enumerates the kind of works the typical secretary admired, to wit: "He memorizes chiseled speech and niceties of knowledge, transmits the *Parables* [*amthāl*] of Buzurgmihr, the *Testament* of Ardashīr, the epistles of ʿAbd al-Ḥamīd, the *Great Book* [*of Culture*] [*al-Adab* (*al-kabīr*)] of Ibn al-Muqaffaʿ, has made the *Book of Mazdak* the mine of his knowledge and [his] notebook [*daftar*] of *Kalīla wa-Dimna* the treasure of his wisdom."[41] A slightly different list of works by *kuttāb* "on whose excellence everyone agreed" is supplied in Ibn al-Nadīm's *Catalogue,* where Ibn al-Muqaffaʿ and his *Kalīla wa-Dimna* also figure.[42] The last three works of al-Jāḥiẓ's list are from the pen of Ibn al-Muqaffaʿ, and as to *Kalīla wa-Dimna,* al-Jāḥiẓ notes that the typical secretary recorded it in his "notebook." Since the work itself is voluminous, this implies that secretaries culled from it passages for their own use, disregarding the book's compositional entity. This is also confirmed by Ibn al-Nadīm, who reports that a number of Abbasid scribes made collections and extracts (*jawāmiʿ wa-ntizāʿāt*) from the work.[43]

In contrast to this, the work speaks about itself at length as a book, and it might even be compared to the Qurʾān it this insistent self-referentiality. In the latter case, however, the definition of the holy scripture as a *kitāb* eased its transformation from an oral recitation to a written codex, which remained parallel to its oral existence (*qirāʾa*). The latter became in fact the subject of a scholarly discipline *(qirāʾāt),* devoted to the various acceptable readings of the consonantal text.[44] At first, the Qurʾān's oral delivery was even more trusted than the written form, since the Qur'ān reciters (*qurrā'*) were scholars trained in memorization, whereas the written medium relied on a script that was still far from being phonetic.[45]

As to *Kalīla wa-Dimna,* its book character is the theme of three of its prefaces. (I leave aside a fourth, later preface, as well as incipits and tables of contents from manuscripts postdating the twelfth century.) One preface that goes back to the Middle Persian version tells about the book's importation from India to Persia. It exists in two versions, of which the older and shorter one has recently been rediscovered in Middle Persian.[46] Here the book is the subject of an allegory; the knowledge it imparts is represented as a life-giving herb. Its importation is a mission ordered by the Sasanian king Khosroe (r. 531–579 C.E.). In the longer version of this preface, the book character is declared from the beginning, and the mission's cost and danger and the Indian episode are elaborated in more detail. The high cost the Persian king is willing to pay and the public audience at which it is presented after its retrieval from India and translation into Persian showcase the book's value. The early existence of such prefaces is confirmed by Ibn al-Nadīm: "One says the Indians composed it, the account is in the preface of the book [*ṣadr al-kitāb*]."[47] Another preface, probably also derived from a Middle Persian source, is devoted to the hero of this scholarly mission, the physician Burzoy, who may or may not be historical.

Most to the point is the third preface added by the Arabic translator-redactor Ibn al-Muqaffaʿ. Its surviving later versions vary in focus, but they agree in explaining *Kalīla wa-Dimna* as a book that has to be read conscientiously as a whole and its content reflected on. This is epitomized in the subtale of the "yellow sheet," in which a person attempts to learn the rules of the Arabic language by memorization without trying to understand them, and he embarrasses himself in front of scholars at a gathering (see fig. 10). The subtale can be taken as a manifesto for critical reflection based on written text as opposed to unthinking rote learning, and it may well be a veiled criticism by Ibn al-Muqaffaʿ of prevailing modes of teaching and transmission in his lifetime, half a century before the book revolution took off. His entire preface emphasizes critical thinking, the vetting of received information, and learning from one's own and others' experience.

That being said, the surviving manuscripts of the thirteenth and subsequent centuries emphasize either the analogous decoding of the fables or the importance of in-depth reading and fact-checking before acting on received information. But even though the details of the original formulation must

FIG. 10. A rare illustration from the subtale of the "yellow sheet" about a man who memorizes text without understanding it and then embarrasses himself in front of scholars. From the preface to *Kalīla wa-Dimna* by the translator-redactor Ibn al-Muqaffaʿ. (MS Pococke 400, fol. 21 verso, Bodleian Library, dated 755/1354.)

remain unknown, the general thrust is to present *Kalīla wa-Dimna* as a book that as to be read entirely and which requires a sort of cogitation specific to the written medium.

Readers nonetheless ignored such preaching over the course of the ninth century. The book is often referred to as *The Book of the Indians* (*Kitāb al-Hind*), de-emphasizing the agency of its translator-redactor, and later Arabic manuscripts and early translations credited the fictional philosopher Baydabāʾ as the book's author (as al-Yaʿqūbī, did). Writers of the ninth century started to pick and choose from the book and ignore the rest. In quoted passages, the mention of animals was usually elided (except in those quotes al-Jāḥiẓ used in his book on animals). Two authors in particular, Ibn Qutayba and Ibn ʿAbdrabbih (d. 940), selected numerous microtexts about ethics and political strategy and placed these in the thematically arranged chapters of their own anthologies, notably their chapters on government. There are a few quotations of small subtales, such as one about an ascetic who allows his imagination to run away and thereby accidentally destroys the basis of the wealth from which his daydream had taken off. One rare narrative portion concerns a chapter of Buddhist provenance in which a queen and a vizier who share a mutual understanding are caught by their king, and each improvises a strategy to cover it up.[48] The differing formulations of the quotes show that the text, within a century of its Arabic translation-redaction, already varied too much to be reduced to a single version. The variation continued to grow, and fragments of the book preserved among the older Geniza documents (to be dated c. 950–1250) and which antedate the full manuscripts show rewritten passages that have not so far been found in any of the later manuscripts. This means that copyists very soon began to interfere with the text to an extent that is unusual for classical Arabic literature.[49]

Why did a text that declared itself so strenuously as a book, and displayed a sophisticated book structure, fall apart so soon in the written transmission? Other works by Ibn al-Muqaffaʿ survive as books, notably his *Great Book of Culture* (*al-Adab al-kabīr*) and his *Epistle on the Retinue* (*al-Risāla fī l-Ṣaḥāba*). Further works he translated from Middle Persian, mostly of an historical nature, are lost. The most plausible explanation is that parables—even if they might translate into political strategy—were not accepted as worthy content for serious books. The parable genre was not on the list of topics found fit for serious books (i.e., scholarship, trade, and professional crafts), nor was it at home in Arabic-Islamic culture. Popular epics and stories existed, as we know from titles and a few fragments, but they circulated among the uneducated public. *Kalīla wa-Dimna,* however, was a book authored by a secretary in a high literary style and intended for circulation among the educated. But Ibn al-Muqaffaʿ's role in it had been overtly as a translator, so his authorial share (in redacting the text and adding new chapters) was soon ascribed to named or unnamed Indian characters.

An indication is a counterwriting from the tenth century by the grammarian al-Yamanī (d. c. 1009). In his preface he deplores people's "addiction" (*idmān*) to reading and memorizing *Kalīla wa-Dimna,* and he claims that the kernels of its parables had been anticipated in Arabic poetry long before. He then demonstrates this with citations of classical Arabic poetry matched with quoted passages from *Kalīla wa-Dimna*—165 quotes in total, ranging from one to eleven lines, mostly *ḥikam,* some of which are rather long and conclude with analogical images. Al-Yamanī scathingly declares the parables (*amthāl*) themselves to be dispensable "stuffing" (*ḥashw*) and "fluff" (*zabad*), and states that the entire book could be cut to about ten pages.[50] Though polemical in tone, he may have pronounced what a majority of readers felt. To him (as had been the case with those ninth-century authors who quoted from the book), the wisdom sayings constituted the book's true value. In them, ethical advice and useful precepts were condensed in shortest form. The lengthy tales in which they were embedded with great narrative skill did not find favor with him or the abovementioned anthologists. Whether his poetic selections actually matched the quotes remains to be investigated, but his project demonstrates a lack of appreciation for parables in book form.

This is not to say that fiction per se played no part in the literature of the ninth century. Yet, as far as scholarly books were concerned, fictionality came in the guise of historical verisimilitude, whether this occurred in *adab,* historical writing, or the Prophetic tradition.[51] Overtly fantastic tales belonged to popular books, which scholars frowned on. These abounded, to judge from the plethora of preserved titles, but they addressed a different public and their written form probably served as an aide-mémoire for storytellers rather than silent reading. Contents fit for scholarly books were instead scriptures (the Qurʾān and the Bible), Prophetic tradition, law, theology, and linguistic scholarship—all topics documented in surviving codices of this century.

These and other topics are enumerated by al-Jāḥiẓ in the introduction to his book on *Animals* (*al-Ḥayawān*). To his abovementioned critique of sumptuously illuminated Manichaean scriptures, he appends a further list of useful topics those books lacked: famous proverbs (*mathal sāʾir*), novel accounts (*khabar ṭarīf*), fine literature (*ṣanʿatu adabin*), foreign wisdom (*ḥikma gharība*), philosophy, theological questions (*masʾala kalāmiyya*), crafts, the invention of tools (*istikhrāju ālatin*), agriculture (*filāḥa*), war strategy (*tadbīru ḥarbin*), and the defense of a creed (*al-muqāraʿa ʿan dīnin wa-l-munāḍala ʿan niḥlatin*). Also acceptable are topics he cites a few lines later: beautiful exhortation (*mawʿiẓa ḥasana*), elegant discourse (*ḥadīth mūniq*), ways of managing one's livelihood (*tadbīru maʿāshin*), general government (*siyāsa*

ʿāmma), and organization of the elite *(tadbīru khāṣṣatin).*[52] These, according to him, were topics to which authors should devote books, because the theoretical and practical knowledge contained therein benefitted people.[53]

In a subsequent section, about a debate between partisans of books and partisans of poetry, he goes into further detail in describing a book's manifold contents—namely, science (including medicine, logic, geometry, and music), crafts (including accounting, agriculture, and commerce), material life (such as knowledge of dyes, perfumes, foods, and tools), and so forth.[54] Among the many aspects of books al-Jāḥiẓ discusses his idiosyncratic magnum opus, *al-Ḥayawān,* he foregrounds their improving and educational purpose and values the social cohesion and intellectual benefits they bring to society, as James Montgomery has shown.[55]

Kalīla wa-Dimna certainly contained much useful information on strategies of government and the conduct of courtiers and humans in general, which would have fitted some of al-Jāḥiẓ's categories, but this was coded in the literary device of the fable, which caused the book, based on its outer appearance, to be classified among entertainment literature, where Ibn al-Nadīm places it, right next to *The Thousand Nights* (*Alf layla*).[56] The book's high literary style could be reused by partial quotation, to which its detachable wisdom sayings lent themselves; there was no need to keep the entire fables intact.

Finally, the book's uncertain origin between India and Persia, which already puzzled Ibn al-Nadīm, separated it from Ibn al-Muqaffaʿ, who on the face of it was only its latest translator. This combined lack of an accepted scholarly discipline or practical expertise it could be assigned to and an author it could be reliaby attributed to left it unprotected in the written transmission of the ninth century. The surviving later manuscripts show the interference of anonymous redactors in content and language, the extant versions differ to the degree that they are irreducible to one text, and Middle Arabic features proliferate. The case of this book demonstrates most clearly that in the preservation of a book, its intrinsic shape was a less powerful determinant than the community of scholars transmitting it. While its perfect structure did not prevent radical change, other books without such structure developed inversely from simple oral teaching into redacted books, because they were part of a succession of scholars within a well-defined field. The fate of *Kalīla wa-Dimna* proves (as a negative case) that to remain intact, a book in the ninth century still needed to be embedded in a scholarly network or to serve established areas of expertise.

CONCLUSION

The present book has shown the quick adaption of the book as a new medium, its quickly diversifying production, and its various uses. The Arabic book revolution had occurred so incredibly rapidly; within less than three decades of the incipient ninth century, any controversy about the book per se was moot. This is similar in span to the more recent triumph of the internet, which has mesmerized, distracted, and occupied us since the 1990s. The book was quick to gain acceptance and popularity. The initial debate about writing down Ḥadīth, in particular, had calmed down and the last remnants subsided at the end of the eighth century.[1] Some resistance and reservation still lingered among philologists in the first quarter of the ninth century, as illustrated in the encounter discussed in Chapter 1 between the memory artist al-Aṣmaʿī and the book scholar and polymath Abū ʿUbayda, in which each demonstrated the advantages of his medium, memory versus manuscript codex. But in the world of literature, written information quickly gained evidentiary status next to oral performance; in fact, the two systems would coexist for at least another two centuries.

In the middle of the ninth century, the poet and critic Diʿbil tried to prove a case of plagiarism by the great Abū Tammām with a written notebook that apparently contained the poet's true source. This has been seen in Chapter 2. The counterproof was also presented in the form of a notebook, but one fabricated specifically for the purpose of defense. That is, the written form by itself had gained traction. A notebook was evidence.

Paper had been manufactured since the end of the eighth century and was available in unlimited quantity, and the ubiquity of copyists made reproduction fast and easy. Unfortunately, reconstructing the genesis of the profession and social group of the stationers in Abbasid society is fraught with difficulties, because of the disdain of Arabic historical and literary sources for people of the crafts. These sources are generally of little help, revealing their social biases. Although they are uncommonly copious on many subjects in comparison to written records from medieval Europe, they are nearly silent with regard to crafts and their practitioners. Nonetheless, terse records of those stationers who were also minor scholars have left some traces that allow us to establish at least four subtypes of this profession over the course of the ninth century, and at times, when their practice raised controversy, more detailed portraits emerge in the literary sources that have helped flesh out some of these types, as demonstrated in Chapter 3.

In their mass, books came to constitute a status symbol in the form of libraries owned mainly by members of the elite (in addition to scholars). In a broader sense, owned books and private notebooks of individuals could now be adduced to reveal something about their owners' convictions and beliefs, and they figure in a number of court cases. Finally, the writers and readers of books show through their usage what they expected a book to be, and they did not accept as such any item that merely displayed a book's formal features, as shown in Chapter 4.

Notably, books as circulating ideas not only made the growth of many disciplines and the independent author possible, but also removed book authors' control and exposed them to criticism, and made the lives of book owners less safe by their use as evidence in prosecutions. Also at the beginning of the ninth century, books were often still used by some to attempt to retain control, but those doing so were not the authors but the books' transmitters, out of motives of gain and personal furtherance, and the battle for control soon turned out to be a losing proposition.

Book writing started out as a multistep process, emerging within a tradition of oral literature; their conception was often collaborative and the result of oral situations. A book took many steps to be "finished," and the roles in engaging and developing a book were numerous, from the first author of its elements to the last copyist and included at times reorganization and rewriting. Many versions of early books that are attributed to different people testify to this process.

In the same century the existence of a book prompted learners and critics to avail themselves of easily accessible information and new or contrarian ideas; the speed and amount of their production, thanks to paper, a vibrant community of scholars, and the aid of stationers, resulted in a plethora of books about books in which individuals engaged in restless productivity and formed over centuries what Muhsin al-Musawi has called the "Islamic republic of letters." Focusing on the thirteenth to fifteenth centuries, he places at center stage the book as the very medium through which Arabic-Islamic society communicated and assembled and reorganized its repertoire, notably through lists of books in prefaces; the book type of the encyclopedic compendium, which itself became a microcosmos of the knowledge society, and whose readership broadened increasingly over this time period; and finally through the way books received commentaries, abridgments, and rewritings in a dialogical process. This was a society, or rather, societies, in which the constant reuse and reproduction, reorganization, and digestion of a vast body of information created a textual coherence across a spatial and temporal distance, surviving changing systems of rule, unrest, war, and natural catastrophes.

Some aspects could only be touched upon and deserve their own in-depth studies, among them the role of Arabic script as an open system that was controlled through interpersonal transmission of knowledge in some fields, but that allowed, in the absence of such control, creative rereading and rewriting, especially in later centuries, from which multiple copies of manuscripts are extant for comparison. This moves the copyists into focus as individuals who could more or less interfere in a text and gain something akin to silent coauthorship.

What also remains to be done is a systematic study of surviving artifacts of the ninth century with the material practices documented in the literature, including analysis of scripts, book layout, and so forth, which cannot be done without a digital component. This also will require a closer look at the purpose for which individuals produced copies of books, whether as a product of the teaching circle or as copies for personal use.

Such endeavors will greatly benefit from an integration of recent thorough investigations of early Christian Arabic codices, especially on three points. First, regarding study of scripts, both Christina and Muslim corpora have to be looked at jointly. A second avenue is the study of the mixing of *Vorlagen* observed in early Gospels and designated as "eclectic copies" by Hikmet Kashouh.[2] In the case of eclectic Gospels, these had no known reception, whereas similar products of cross-copying on manuscripts of *Kalīla wa-Dimna* (by then treated as popular literature) were among those most frequently recopied.[3] A third domain where a comprehensive approach is desirable is the study of Middle Arabic, which experienced a far more widespread use of Arabic than commonly realized, since the purview of scholars of Arabic is often skewed by the greater focus on the classical texts situated at the higher end of the literary spectrum (and by the practice of older editions to silently smooth out traces of nonstandard language). What has been said here about the ninth century will have to be pursued through the tenth century to trace the development of the phenomena here identified, but due to the far more copious extant codices, this will require a separate study.

Other subsequent projects might focus on the conceptual and theoretical level. To be developed and compared with practices of other cultures is the concept, first defined by Gregor Schoeler, of a complementary (written and oral) transmission of knowledge in the realm of Arabic scholarship. As unique as this might appear against the background of the general assumption that orality ultimately yields to the written word, the long coexistence of both in Arabic-Islamic culture certainly has parallels, for instance in medieval Europe.[4]

Another matter is that in the ninth century, communication was not an "absent concept," as John Guillory diagnoses it for early modernity. He finds the first definition of the term *communication* in the words of John Wilkins (1668), who understood writing as a technology for overcoming distance, both spatial and temporal.[5] Such an investigation would be equally rewarding if applied to in the ninth and subsequent centuries, because writers such as al-Jāḥiẓ and Isḥāq b. Ibrāhīm Ibn Wahb al-Kātib (d. early tenth century) already conceptualized ways of human communication.[6] In the field of language this led to a standard theory of language, and in the sciences to various overall classifications across the disciplines.[7] Yet more overarching research remains to be done to explore the Arabic-Islamic cosmos of knowledge and its theories from the vantage of those participating in it.

I have tried to place at the disposal of historians of media some of the particular traits of Arabic-Islamic book culture, not only for its own sake, to fill the gap of knowledge on the early Arabic book, but also to allow discovery of comparable aspects with other book cultures of the premodern world. Too often, media histories are conceived from a European perspective, or begin with the printing press as the first media revolution. John Guillory makes remediation a condition of media awareness, and the age of internet confronts us permanently with this phenomenon, so we are attuned to the dynamic process we are part of today. But the future of the internet as a still largely unregulated space of exchange is uncertain, and as with other technological innovations, the initial openness may increasingly be curtailed by governmental and commercial control. Paper is used far less today, but it is not about to completely disappear. And it is there to remind us that this time-honored medium owes its persistence also to the fact that it is today still regulated by noncommercial standards.

ABBREVIATIONS

A.H.	*Anno hegirae* ("in the year of the Hijra"), the year according to the Islamic calendar, beginning 622 C.E.
BJMES	*British Journal of Middle Eastern Studies*
EI2	*Encyclopaedia of Islam,* 2nd ed.
EI3	*Encyclopaedia of Islam,* 3rd ed.
EQ	*Encyclopaedia of the Qur'ān*
GAL	*Geschichte der arabischen Litteratur*
GAS	*Geschichte des arabischen Schrifttums*
HdO	Handbuch der Orientalistik
JAL	*Journal of Arabic Literature*
JAOS	*Journal of the American Oriental Society*
MEL	*Middle Eastern Languages*
REI	*Revue des études islamiques*
RSO	*Rivista degli studi orientali*
ZDMG	*Zeitschrift der Deutschen Morgenländischen Gesellschaft*

NOTES

INTRODUCTION

1. See John Maynard Smith and Eörs Szathmáry, *The Origins of Life: From the Birth of Life to the Origins of Language* (Oxford: Oxford University Press, 1999), 149–170.

2. See Stanislas Dehaene, *Reading in the Brain: The New Science of How We Read* (New York: Penguin Books, 2009), 121–193.

3. The French codicologist François Déroche was the first to characterize this phase as "une véritable révolution du livre"; see his *Le livre manuscrit arabe: Préludes à une histoire* (Paris: Bibliothèque nationale de France, 2004), 44.

4. See Jonathan Bloom, "How Paper Changed the Literary and Visual Culture of the Islamic Lands," in *By the Pen and What They Write: Writing in Islamic Art and Culture,* ed. Sheila Blair and Jonathan Bloom (New Haven, CT: Yale University Press, 2017), 107–127, esp. 116; and Geoffrey Roper, "The History of the Book in the Muslim World," in *The Oxford Companion to the Book,* ed. Michael F. Suarez, S. J. Woudhuysen, and H. R. Woudhuysen (Oxford: Oxford University Press, 2010), 527.

5. Dates are primarily given in the Common Era date, but may include the Islamic calendar A.H. (beginning 622 C.E.) and the Common Era, separated by a

slash, in captions and notes. On the awareness of the codex by Arabs since the first / seventh century, see Roper, "History of the Book in the Muslim World," 524–552, esp. 524.

6. Werner Faulstich, *Das Medium als Kult: Von den Anfängen bis zur Spätantike (8. Jahrhundert)* (Göttingen, Germany: Vandenhoeck and Ruprecht, 1997), 57–58; Herbert Hunger, *Schreiben und Lesen in Byzanz: Die byzantinische Buchkultur* (Munich: Beck, 1989), 25–26.

7. Al-Sīrāfī, *Akhbār al-naḥwiyyīn al-baṣriyyīn,* ed. Ṭāhā M. al-Zaynī and Muḥammad ʿAbdalmunʿim al-Khafājī (Cairo: Muṣṭafā al-Bābī al-Ḥalabī, 1374 / 1955), 37, 39.

8. See Michael Carter, *Sībawayhi* (Oxford: Tauris, 2004); Ramzi Baalbaki, *The Legacy of the Kitāb: Sībawayhi's Analytical Methods within the Context of the Arabic Grammatical Theory* (Leiden, Netherlands: Brill, 2008), 33–38; and Amal E. Marogy, *Kitāb Sībawayhi: Syntax and Pragmatics* (Leiden, Netherlands: Brill, 2010).

9. For the uses of the term *stationer,* see Chapter 1, section "Intellectual Property versus Entrepreneurship."

10. Ibn al-Nadīm, *Fihrist,* ed. Riḍā Tajaddud (Amman: Dār al-Masīra, 1408 / 1988; rpt. of Tehran, 1350 / 1971) / ed. Ayman Fu'ād Sayyid, 2 pts. in 4 vols. (London: al-Furqan Islamic Heritage Foundation, 1430 / 2009); both editions are cited hereafter in this order, separated by a slash. On the author, see Devin Stewart, "Abū l-Faraj Muḥammmad ibn Isḥāq Ibn al-Nadīm," in *Essays in Arabic Literary Biography 925–1350,* ed. Terri De Young and Mary St. Germain (Wiesbaden, Germany: Harrassowitz, 2011), 129–142.

11. For the lower figure, see Hugh Kennedy, "Baghdad as a Center of Learning and Book Production," in Blair and Bloom, *By the Pen and What They Write,* 89–103, esp. 95; and for the higher figure, Bloom, "How Paper Changed the Literary and Visual Culture," 108.

12. Abū ʿUbayda, *Ayyām al-ʿarab qabla l-Islām li-Abī ʿUbayda: Multaqaṭāt min al-kutub wa-l-makhṭūṭāt,* ed. ʿĀdil Jāsim al-Bayātī (Baghdad: Dār al-Jāḥiẓ li-l-Ṭibāʿa wa-l-Nashr, 1976).

13. Stefan Leder, "Grenzen der Rekonstruktion alten Schrifttums nach den Angaben im Fihrist," in *Ibn an-Nadîm und die mittelalterliche arabische Literatur. Beiträge zum 1. Johann Wilhelm Fück–Kolloquium Halle 1987* (Wiesbaden, Germany: Harrassowitz, 1996), 21–31.

14. On the importance of a shared language, see also Kennedy, "Baghdad as a Center of Learning," 97. Kennedy further cites widespread literacy and the growing demand for books. Bloom does not mention this factor, but adds as further factors (besides paper) the reverence for the written word, the dissemination by books through dictation, the general prestige of writing, and the Qur'ān as a book model; see Bloom, "How Paper Changed the Literary and Visual Culture."

15. The translation of the administration to Arabic is called *naql* or *taḥwīl.* Egypt will follow in 87 / 705 and Khurasan in 124 / 742. The mint had been converted to

Arabic in 76 / 674–675. See al-Ṭabarī, *Taʾrīkh al-rusul wa-l-mulūk,* ed. Muḥammad Abū l-Faḍl Ibrāhīm (Cairo: Dār al-Maʿārif, 1960–1968), 4:256; Abū Bakr al-Ṣūlī, *Adab al-kuttāb,* ed. Muḥammad Bahjat al-Atharī (Cairo: al-Maṭbaʿa al-Salafiyya 1341 / 1922–1923), 192–193 / ed. Aḥmad Ḥ. Basaj (Beirut: Dār al-Kutub al-ʿIlmiyya, 1415 / 1994), 200–201 (both editions are cited hereafter in this order, separated by a slash); Abū ʿAbdallāh Muḥammad b. ʿAbdūs al-Jahshiyārī, *al-Wuzarāʾ,* ed. Hans von Mžik [based on unicate MS Vienna Cod. mixt. 916, dated 546 / 1151] (Leipzig: Harrassowitz, 1926–1928), 33, 35, 64–65 / ed. Ibrāhīm Ṣāliḥ (Abu Dhabi: National Library Cultural Foundation, 1430 / 2009), 79, 81, 115–116 (both editions are cited hereafter in this order, separated by a slash); Abdalʿaziz Duri [al-Dūrī], "*Dīwān* i. The Caliphate," in *EI2,* 2:323–327, esp. 324a.

16. On literary patronage in Baghdad, see Hugh Kennedy, *When Baghdad Ruled the Muslim World: The Rise and Fall of Islam's Greatest Dynasty* (Philadelphia: Da Capo Press, 2004), 243–260.

17. Kennedy, "Baghdad as a Center of Learning," 103.

18. Abū ʿAlī Bakr b. Khārija al-Warrāq from Kufa was a client of the Banū Asad. See Abū l-Faraj al-Iṣbahānī, *al-Aghānī,* ed. Muḥammad Qumayḥa (Beirut: Dār al-Thaqāfa, 1374 / 1955; rpt., 1401 / 1981), 23:66–70; al-Shābushtī, *Kitāb al-Diyārat,* ed. Kūrkīs ʿAwwād (Baghdad: Maṭbaʿat al-Maʿārif, 1951), 156; and al-Ṣafadī, *al-Wāfī bi-l-wafayāt* [*Das biographische Lexikon des Ṣalāḥaddīn Ḫalīl ibn Aibak aṣ-Ṣafadī*], ed. Helmut Ritter et al. (Istanbul: Deutsche Morgenländische Gesellschaft / Franz Steiner Verlag, 1931–2013), 10:204–205.

19. See Shawkat Toorawa, *Ibn Abī Ṭāhir Ṭayfūr and Arabic Writerly Culture: A Ninth-Century Bookman in Baghdad* (London: RoutledgeCurzon, 2005), 31–34.

20. In the following, I distinguish between the body of Ḥadīth (capitalized and romanized), i.e., the corpus of the Prophet's recorded deeds and sayings that constitute the Sunna, and a single *ḥadīth* (lowercase and italicized).

21. See Gregor Schoeler, *The Oral and the Written in Early Islam,* trans. Uwe Vagelpohl, preface by James E. Montgomery (New York: Routledge, 2006), 28–44, Engl. trans. of Schoeler, "Mündliche Thora und Ḥadīṯ: Überlieferung, Schreibverbot, Redaktion," *Der Islam* 66 (1989): 213–241; and Michael Cook, "The Opponents of the Writing of Tradition in Early Islam," *Arabica* 44 (1997): 437–530.

22. See Ronald Egan, "To Count Grains of Sand on the Ocean Floor: Changing Perceptions of Books and Learning in the Song Dynasty," in *Knowledge and Text Production in An Age of Print: China, 900–1400,* ed. Lucille Chia and Hilde De Weerdt (Leiden, Netherlands: Brill, 2011), 33–62, esp. 42.

23. Michael Zwettler, *The Oral Tradition of Classical Arabic Poetry: Its Character and Implications* (Columbus: Ohio State University Press, 1978).

24. Some Bedouins, such as Muḥammad b. Ziyād al-Kilābī (d. end second / eighth century) and Abū Misḥal (d. mid-third / mid-ninth century), had moved to the cities (because of droughts, for instance) and could be consulted more easily.

25. On ʿUmāra, see Chapter 1, section "Intellectual Property versus Entrepreneurship," and on Dhū l-Rumma, see Chapter 3, section "The Book Transmitter, or *Rāwī*-Stationer."

26. See Abū Bakr al-Ṣūlī, *The Life and Times of Abū Tammām by Abū Bakr Muḥammad ibn Yaḥyā al-Ṣūlī, Preceded by al-Ṣūlī's Epistle to Abū l-Layth Muzāḥim ibn Fātik,* ed. and trans. Beatrice Gruendler (New York: New York University Press, 2015) §86.3 (the paragraph number refers to both Arabic edition and English translation on facing pages) / *Akhbār Abī Tammām,* ed. Khalīl Muḥammad ʿAsākir, Muḥammad ʿAbduh ʿAzzām, and Naẓīr al-Islām al-Hindī (Cairo: Lajnat al-Taʾlīf wa-l-Tarjama wa-l-Nashr, 1937; rpt., Beirut: Dār al-Āfāq al-Jadīda, 1400/1980), 173 (both editions are cited hereafter in this order, separated by a slash).

27. See Dimitri Gutas, *Greek Thought, Arabic Culture: The Graeco-Arabic Translation Movement in Baghdad and Early ʿAbbāsid Society (2nd–4th/8th–10th Centuries)* (London: Routledge, 1989); George Saliba [Jūrj Ṣalībā], *al-Fikr al-ʿilmī al-ʿarabī: Nashʾatuhū wa-taṭawwuruhū* (Tripoli: Markaz al-Dirāsāt al-Masīḥiyya al-Islāmiyya, Jāmiʿat al-Balimand, 1998).

28. Other translations were done or commissioned by scholars. See Gutas, *Greek Thought, Arabic Culture,* 133–143.

29. See Miklós Maróth, *The Correspondence between Aristotle and Alexander the Great: An Anonymous Greek Novel in Letters in Arabic Translation* (Piliscaba, Hungary: Avicenna Institute of Middle East Studies, 2006); and the review article by Dimitri Gutas, "On Graeco-Arabic Epistolary 'Novels,'" *MEL* 12 (2009): 59–70.

30. See François de Blois, *Burzoy's Voyage to India and the Origin of the Book of* Kalilah wa-Dimnah (London: Royal Asiatic Society, 1990); and Chapter 4, section "A Book that Failed."

31. Historiography was another scholarly discipline that took shape during the late second/eighth and early third/ninth century. See Chase Robinson, *Islamic Historiography* (Cambridge: Cambridge University Press, 2003), 18–38.

32. *School* is to be understood not as an institution but rather as a pedigree of scholars who built on each other's work. In the late third/ninth century students already occasionally sat in gatherings of the rival school, and when both groups relocated to Baghdad the distinction became blurred, as many studied with teachers from either school. The concept survived, however, as a convenient way to arrange biographical dictionaries and a literary model for books on grammar disputations.

33. On Qurʾāns in Ḥijāzī script, see François Déroche, *Qurʾāns of the Umayyads: A First Overview* (Leiden, Netherlands: Brill, 2014) and *The Abbasid Tradition: Qurʾans of the 8th to the 10th Centuries AD* (London: Nour Foundation, 1992), 27–33; and online, Corpus Coranicum, https://corpuscoranicum.de/.

34. Some reports make variants in the recitation the immediate cause for the edition of a master copy by the order of Caliph ʿUthmān (r. 23–35/644–656). There is vast literature on the redaction of the Qurʾān. See Frederik Leemhuis, "Codices

of the Qur'ān," in *EQ,* 1:347–351 and John Burton, "Collection of the Qur'ān," in *EQ* 1:351–361. On the self-referentiality of the Qur'ān, see Stefan Wild, ed., *Self-Referentiality in the Qur'ān* (Wiesbaden, Germany: Harrassowitz, 2006).

35. On him, see *GAS,* 1:634.

36. See, e.g., the report about the grammarian al-Mubarrad being called to the capital to settle a dispute over a correct Qur'ān reading and managing to do so without offending the caliph who was mistaken, in al-Zubaydī, *Ṭabaqāt al-naḥwiyyīn wa-l-lughawiyyīn,* ed. M. Abū l-Faḍl Ibrāhīm (Cairo: Dār al-Maʿārif, 1392/1973; rpt., 1984), 101–103; Ibn al-Qifṭī, *Inbāh al-ruwāt ʿalā anbāh al-nuḥāt,* ed. Muḥammad Abū l-Faḍl Ibrāhīm (Cairo: Maṭbaʿat Dār al-Kutub, 1369/1950–1393/1974), 3:243–244. The recitation of the Qur'ān in various versions *(qirā'āt)* became a scholarly discipline. The verb *qara'a* means both "to read" and "to recite" and here both meanings apply, since a reciter knew the Qur'ān by heart and could also read aloud the written text, which was in early codices the mere consonantal outline *(rasm)* without diacritics and vowel marks. See Anna M. Gade, "Recitation of the Qur'ān," in *EQ,* 4:367–385.

37. Conversely, in high literature the elliptic denotation served as a threshold. See Samer Ali, *Arabic Literary Salons in the Islamic Middle Ages: Poetry, Public Performance, and the Presentation of the Past* (Notre Dame, IN: University of Notre Dame Press, 2010), 52–53.

38. On the format of the sheets (*ṣaḥīfa*), see Beatrice Gruendler, "Sheets," in *EQ,* 4:587–589.

39. Schoeler, *The Oral and the Written,* 111–141; Schoeler, "Mündliche Thora und Ḥadīṯ"; Talya Fishman, "Guarding Oral Transmission: Within and between Cultures," in "Oral Tradition in Judaism, Christianity and Islam," ed. Werner H. Kelber and Paula Sanders, special issue, *Oral Tradition* 25, no. 1 (2010): 41–56.

40. See Schoeler, *The Oral and the Written,* 28–44; Schoeler, "Mündliche Thora und Ḥadīṯ"; and Cook, "Opponents of Writing," 447–450, 489–491, for an alternate opinion.

41. See Ali, *Arabic Literary Salons,* 41–42.

42. Aḥmad b. ʿAlī al-Khaṭīb al-Baghdādī, *Ta'rīkh Baghdād,* ed. Bashshār ʿAwwār Maʿrūf (Beirut: Dār al-Gharb al-Islāmī, 1422/2001), 3:45.

43. Ibn al-Nadīm, *Fihrist,* 73/pt. 1, 199.

44. Gregor Schoeler, *The Genesis of Literature in Islam: From the Aural to the Read* (Edinburgh: Edinburgh University Press, 2009), English trans. of Schoeler, *Écrire et transmettre dans les débuts de l'Islam* (Paris: Presses Universitaires de France, 2002).

45. See Schoeler, *Genesis of Literature in Islam,* 60–63.

46. See Robinson, *Islamic Historiography,* 24–38.

47. On the invention and spread of paper to the Islamic lands, see Jonathan Bloom, *Paper before Print: The History and Impact of Paper in the Islamic World* (New Haven, CT: Yale University Press, 2001), 32–45. On the production techniques,

see Bloom, "Papermaking: The Historical Diffusion of an Ancient Technique," in *Mobilities of Knowledge,* ed. Heike Jöns, Peter Mensburger and Michael Hefferman (Cham, Switzerland: Springer, 2017), 51–66. See, further, François Déroche et al., *Islamic Codicology: An Introduction to the Study of Manuscripts in Arabic Script,* trans. Deke Dusinberre, and David Razinowicz (London: al-Furqan Islamic Heritage Foundation, 2015), 49–52; Johannes Pedersen, *The Arabic Book,* trans. G. French (Princeton, NJ: Princeton University Press, 1984), 60–62; and Clément Huart and Adolf Grohmann, "Kāghad," in *EI2,* 4:419–420. Still useful are the older studies by Helen Loveday, *Islamic Paper: A Study of an Ancient Craft* (London: Don Baker Memorial Fund, 2001), 20; and Joseph von Karabacek, *Arab Paper,* trans. D. Baker and S. Dittmar (London: Islington Books, 2001), 27, after Ibn al-Athīr, *al-Kāmil fī l-taʾrīkh,* ed. C. J. Tornberg (Leiden, Netherlands: Brill 1851–1876; rpt., Beirut: Dār Ṣādir, 1965–1967), 4:96, 100, 101. The sources give the dates of al-Faḍl's governorship but remain silent on any actual paper manufacture in Baghdad.

48. See Jahshiyārī, *Wuzarāʾ,* 158 / 211–212.

49. See also Bloom, "How Paper Changed the Literary and Visual Culture," 115.

50. See also the chronological chart in Beatrice Gruendler, "Aspects of Craft the Arabic Book Revolution," in *Globalization of Knowledge in the Post-antique Mediterranean, 700–1500,* ed. Jürgen Renn and Sonja Bentjes (London: Routledge, 2016), 31–66, esp. 66.

51. François Déroche, "Les manuscrits arabes datés du IIIe / IXe siècle," *REI* 55–57 (1987–1989): 343–379.

52. Edited and translated by Raif G. Khoury, *Wahb b. Munabbih, Der Heidelberger Papyrus PSR Heid Arab 23, pt. 1: Leben und Werk des Dichters, pt. 2: Faksimiletafeln* (Wiesbaden, Germany: Harrassowitz, 1972).

53. See the publication and plates by Jean David-Weill, *Le Djâmiʿ d'Ibn Wahb,* 2 vols. (Cairo: Institut Français d'Archéologie Orientale, 1939–1941).

54. MS Cairo, Dār al-Kutub 41 uṣūl fiqh, discussed in Chapter 3, section "The Book Transmitter, or *Rāwī*-Stationer."

55. A traditionist and student of Ibn Wahb, he died 104 / 819; see *GAS,* 1:466.

56. A traditionist and jurisconsult who died 234 / 848; see *GAS,* 1:468.

57. A renowned Malikite jurisconsult and judge of Qayrawān, he died 213 / 828; see *GAS,* 1:467.

58. A minor traditionist, disciple of al-Awzāʿī, and fighter at the Islamic frontier in Maṣṣīṣa, he died 188 / 805. His book treats *jihād* from a legal perspective in the form of *responsae;* see Nasser Rabbat, "Ribāṭ," in *EI2,* 8:493–506, esp. 498b.

59. On Abu ʿUbayd and his works, see Chapter 1, section "Book Production and fig. 6."

60. Abū l-ʿAmaythal, a poet from Rayy and sponsored by the Ṭāhirids, authored a book on poetic motifs and another on famous verses (see *GAS,* 1:59, 90) in addition to three lexicographical treatises (see *GAS,* 8:189–190); only the dictionary on polysemic words survives. For an edition, see Abū l-ʿAmaythal ʿAbdallāh b.

Khulayd, *Kitāb al-Ma'thūr fīmā ttafaqa lafẓuhū wa-khtalafa ma'nāhu*, published as *Kitāb al-Ma'thūr: Das Buch der Wörter mit gleichem Laut und verschiedener Bedeutung*, ed. Fritz Krenkow (London: Probsthain, 1925).

61. On no. 29, Mt. Sinai, Codex Sinaiticus Ar. 72, see Samir Arbache, *L'Évangile arabe selon Saint Luc: Texte du VIII siècle, copié en 897. Édition et traduction* (Paris: Éditions Safran, 2012).

62. See Sara Schulthess, "Les manuscrits arabes des lettres de Paul: La reprise d'un champ de recherche négligé" (PhD diss., l'Université de Lausanne / Radboud Universiteit Nijmegen, 2016), 124–125, based on Frances C. Burkitt and Georg Graff. Schulthess's study of Vat. Ar. 13 includes a commented diplomatic and standardized edition of Paul's letter to the Corinthians, and an online component shows the manuscript: https://digi.vatlib.it/view/MSS_Vat.ar.13.

63. See Schulthess, "Manuscrits arabes des lettres de Paul," 105–106, based Sidney H. Griffith, "The Gospel in Arabic: An Inquiry into Its Appearance in the First Abbasid Century," *Oriens Christianus* 67 (1983): 126–167, esp. 162.

64. For a detailed description, see Déroche, "Manuscrits arabes datés," 356–360. For the script of a Gospel specimen, Codex Vatican, Ar. 13, see Hikmat Kashouh, *The Arabic Versions of the Gospels: The Manuscripts and Their Families* (Berlin: De Gruyter, 2012), 145–147.

65. See Khoury, *Wahb b. Munabbih*, pt. 1, 76–81 (edition and translation), and pt. 2, GD 17–18 (facsimile).

66. M. J. De Goeje, "Beschreibung einer alten Handschrift von Abû 'Obaid's Ġarîb-al-ḥadîṯ," *ZDMG* 18 (1864): 781–807, gives a description of the manuscript, with a tentative translation of the *ḥadīth* and its commentary. For a discussion of the transmission, philological, and gender aspects of this *ḥadīth*, see Franz Rosenthal, "Muslim Social Values and Literary Criticism: Reflections on the Ḥadīth of Umm Zarʿ," *Oriens* 34 (1994), 31–56, reprinted in Rosenthal, *Man versus Society in Medieval Islam*, ed. Dimitri Gutas (Leiden, Netherlands: Brill, 2015), 909–940. In the Leiden codex, the *ḥadīth* occupies fols. 12v–17r. For the printed edition, see Abū ʿUbayd, *Gharīb al-ḥadīth*, ed. Ḥusayn Muḥammad M. Sharaf, 6 pts. (Cairo: Majmaʿ al-Lugha al-ʿArabiyya, 1419 / 1999), pt. 2, 157–200, no. 188. The *ḥadīth* proper ends on p. 162 with the Prophet's saying to his wife ʿĀ'isha, "I am to you what Abū Zarʿ was to Umm Zarʿ" (*kuntu laki ka-Abī Zarʿ li-Umm Zarʿ*), i.e., extremely generous and caring. Then follows the *isnād* (p. 163) and Abū ʿUbayd's statement that he relied on a number of previous authorities in his following explanation, which takes up pp. 164–200, i.e., forty-three pages compared to five folios in the manuscript. Explaining this highly eloquent but terse literary text was not always easy, and Abū ʿUbayd, who is the first author to record it, once comments with desperation: "I do not think that any of these words come from the speech of the Arabs—I do not know what this is" (188).

67. See, in general, Franz Rosenthal, "The Technique and Approach of Muslim Scholarship," *Analecta Orientalia* 24 (1947): 1–74. For a glossary of technical terms

in English translation, see Adam Gacek, *Arabic Manuscripts: A Vademecum for Readers* (Leiden, Netherlands: Brill, 2012); and for a listing by the Arabic designations, Gacek, *The Arabic Manuscript Tradition: A Glossary of Technical Terms* (Leiden, Netherlands: Brill, 2001, supp. 2008).

68. On papyri, the foundational works by Adolf Grohmann can be consulted, as well as recent studies by Geoffrey Khan, Werner Diem, Petra Sijpesteijn, and Andras Kaplony, and online, the Arabic Papyrology Database, https://www.apd.gwi.uni-muenchen.de/apd/project.jsp.

69. For a third / ninth century example, see the Qurʾān of Amājūr. Déroche, "Manuscrits arabes datés," 346, no. 9.

70. On Manichaean books, see Chapter 4, section "Books as Prestige Objects"; on bound books, al-Jāḥiẓ, *"al-Risāla fī l-jidd wa-l-hazl,"* in *Rasāʾil al-Jāḥiẓ,* ed. ʿAbdassalām M. Hārūn (Beirut: Dār al-Jīl, 1991), 1:225–278, esp. 248–254.

71. See Jonathan Bloom, "Literary and Oral Cultures," in *The New Cambridge History of Islam,* vol. 4: *Islamic Cultures and Societies to the End of the Eighteenth Century,* ed. Robert Irwin (Cambridge: Cambridge University Press, 2011), 668–681, esp. 673, and Beatrice Gruendler, "Stability and Change in Arabic Script," in *The Shape of Script: How and Why Writing Systems Change,* ed. Stephen D. Houston (Santa Fe, NM: Publications of the School of Advanced Research, 2012), 93–111.

72. On the various explanations of *aḥruf* in exegesis and the fact that the interpretation as "readings," based on a *ḥadīth* promulgated by al-Zuhrī (d. 124 / 742) was not undisputed among scholars, see Shady Hekmat Nasser. *The Transmission of the Variant Readings of the Qurʾān: The Problem of Tawātur and the Emergence of Shawādhdh* (Leiden, Netherlands: Brill, 2013), 15–34.

73. On the growth of compendia in general, see Robinson, *Islamic Historiography,* 32–35; and in the field of lexicography, see Ramzi Baalbaki, *The Arabic Lexicographical Tradition: From the 2nd / 8th to the 12th / 18th Century* (Leiden, Netherlands: Brill, 2014).

74. See Gutas, *Greek Thought, Arabic Culture.*

75. On *ammā baʿdu,* see Gacek, *Arabic Manuscripts,* 200–203. On the letter to the secretaries, see Wadad al-Qadi, "Early Islamic State Letters: The Question of Authenticity," in *The Byzantine and Early Islamic Near East,* vol. 1: *Problems in Literary Source Material,* ed. Averil Cameron and Lawrence I. Conrad (Princeton, NJ: Darwin Press, 1992), 215–275, esp. 248–260.

76. On the biographical dictionary, see Michael Cooperson, *Classical Arabic Biography* (Cambridge: Cambridge University Press, 2000) and literature cited there.

77. See Robinson, *Islamic Historiography,* 5–6, 15–24; and Fred Donner, *Narratives of Islamic Origins: The Beginnings of Islamic Historical Writing* (Princeton, NJ: Darwin Press, 1998).

78. See Stefan Leder, "Conventions of Fictional Narration in Learned Literature," in *Story-Telling in the Framework of Non-fictional Arabic Literature,* ed. Stefan Leder (Wiesbaden, Germany: Harassowitz, 1998), 34–60.

79. See Isabel Toral, “Erzählen im arabischen *adab:* Zwischen Fiktionalität und Faktualität,” in *Faktuales und Fiktionales Erzählen: Interdisziplinäre Perspektiven,* ed. Monika Fludernik, Nicole Falkenhayer, and Julia Steiner (Würzburg, Germany: Ergon Verlag, 2018), 59–76.

80. For the sources of compilations, see Walter Werkmeister, *Quellenuntersuchungen zum Kitāb al-ʿIqd al-farīd des Andalusiers Ibn ʿAbdrabbih (246/860–328/940)* (Berlin: Schwarz, 1983); Manfred Fleischhammer, *Die Quellen des Kitāb al-Aghānī* (Wiesbaden, Germany: Harrassowitz, 2004); and Sebastian Günther, *Quellenuntersuchungen zu den „Maqātil al-Ṭālibiyyīn“ des Abū l-Faraj al-Isfahānī (gest. 356/967)* (Hildesheim, Germany: Georg Olms, 1991). The latter two provide useful glossaries of early authors whose works have not survived independently. For the functions of individuals in *isnāds*, see Sebastian Günther, “Assessing the Sources of Classical Arabic Compilations: The Issue of Categories and Methodologies,” *BJMES* 32 (2005): 75–98.

81. See Henrik Skov Nielsen, James Phelan, and Richard Walsh, “Ten Theses about Fictionality,” *Narrative* 23, no. 1 (January 2015): 61–73 and the literature cited therein.

82. For a survey of the positions, see Gregor Schoeler, *Charakter und Authentie der muslimischen Überlieferung über das Leben Mohammeds* (Berlin: Walter de Gruyter, 1996).

83. For an example of this approach, see Beatrice Gruendler, “Verse and Taxes: The Function of Poetry in Selected Literary *Akhbār* of the Third/Ninth Century,” in *On Fiction and Adab in Medieval Arabic Literature,* ed. Philip F. Kennedy (Wiesbaden, Germany: Harrassowitz, 2005), 85–124.

84. See Gruendler, “Verse and Taxes,” and Beatrice Gruendler, “Meeting the Patron: An *Akhbār* Type and Its Implications for *Muḥdath* Poetry,” in *Ideas, Images, Methods of Portrayal: Insights into Arabic Literature and Islam,* ed. Sebastian Günther (Wiesbaden, Germany: Harrassowitz, 2005), 59–88.

85. For an example of this approach, see Beatrice Gruendler, “Abbasid Poets and the Qur'ān,” in *The Qur'an and Adab: The Shaping of Literary Traditions in Classical Islam,* ed. Nuha Alsha'ar (Oxford: Oxford University Press, 2017), 137–169; and Beatrice Gruendler, “Farewell to Ghazal: Convention and Danger of the Arabic Love Lyric,” in *Poetry and History: The Value of Poetry in Reconstructing Arab History,* ed. Ramzi Baalbaki, Saleh Said Agha, and Tarif Khalidi (Beirut: American University of Beirut, 2011), 137–172.

86. On the literary reworking of *akhbār,* see Stefan Leder, “The Literary Use of Khabar: A Basic Form of Historical Writing,” in *The Byzantine and Early Islamic Near East,* vol. 1: *Problems in Literary Source Material,* ed. Averil Cameron and Lawrence I. Conrad (Princeton, NJ: Darwin Press, 1992), 277–315.

87. For the presystematic period, see translator's preface in al-Ṣūlī, *Life and Times of Abū Tammām;* and on the standard theory, see Thomas Bauer, “Arabische Kultur,” in *Rhetorik: Begriff–Geschichte–Internationalität,* ed. Gert Ueding (Tübingen, Germany: Max Niemeyer, 2005), 283–300.

88. Letter writing is a plot device for instance in a *khabar* about the poet ʿIṣāba al-Jarjarāʾī (alive 218–227 / 833–842). See Gruendler, "Meeting the Patron," 67–68.

89. See Toral, "Erzählen im arabischen *adab*"; and Robinson, *Islamic Historiography*, 12.

1. SCHOLARS

1. Other famous clashes between different types of scholars are those reported between Ḥammād al-Rāwiya (d. 155 / 772) and al-Mufaḍḍal al-Ḍabbī—on which, see Rina Drory, "The Abbasid Construction of the *Jāhiliyya:* Cultural Authority in the Making," *Studia Islamica* 83 (1996): 33–49—and between al-Kisāʾī (d. 189 / 805) and Sībawayhi, also referred to *masʾalat al-zunbūr*—on which, see Zubaydī, *Ṭabaqāt al-naḥwiyyīn,* 68–70, and Carter, *Sībawayhi,* 13–14.

2. For his biobibliography, see Abū l-Ṭayyib ʿAbd al-Wāḥid b. ʿAlī al-Lughawī, *Marātib al-naḥwiyyīn,* ed. Muḥammad Abū l-Faḍl Ibrāhīm (Cairo: Maṭbaʿat Nahḍat Miṣr, 1954), 46–65; Sīrāfī, *Akhbār al-naḥwiyyīn,* 45–52; Zubaydī, *Ṭabaqāt al-naḥwiyyīn,* 167–174, no. 91; Abū ʿUbaydallāh Muḥammad b. ʿImrān al-Marzubānī, *Nūr al-qabas al-mukhtaṣar min al-Muqtabas fī akhbār al-nuḥāt wa-l-udabāʾ wa-l-shuʿarāʾ wa-l-ʿulamāʾ,* recension of Yūsuf b. Aḥmad al-Yaghmurī, ed. Rudolf Sellheim (Wiesbaden, Germany: Steiner, 1964), 125–170, no. 31; Ibn al-Nadīm, *Fihrist,* 6–7 / pt. 1, 155–157; al-Khaṭīb al-Baghdādī, *Taʾrīkh Baghdād,* 12:157–169, no. 5529; Abū l-Barakāt Ibn al-Anbārī, *Nuzhat al-alibbāʾ,* ed. Ibrāhīm al-Sāmarrāʾī (Baghdad: Maṭbaʿat al-Maʿārif, 1959), 74–85 / ed. Muḥammad Abū l-Faḍl Ibrāhīm (Cairo: Dār Nahḍat Miṣr li-l-Ṭabʿ wa-l-Nashr, 1386 / 1967), 112–124, no. 33 (both editions are cited hereafter in this order, divided by a slash); Ibn al-Qifṭī, *Inbāh al-ruwāt,* 4:197–205, no. 408; Ibn Khallikān, *Wafayāt al-aʿyān,* ed. Iḥsān ʿAbbās (Beirut: Dār Ṣādir, 1398 / 1977; rpt., Beirut: Dār al-Thaqāfa, n.d.) 3:170–176, no. 379; *GAS,* 8:71–76, 9:66–67; and Bernard Lewis, "al-Aṣmaʿī," in *EI2,* 1:717–719.

3. Ibn Khallikān, *Wafayāt al-aʿyān,* 6:177.

4. On classical Arabic poetry, see A. F. L. Beeston, T. M. Johnston, R. B. Serjeant, and G. R. Smith, eds., *Arabic Literature to the End of the Umayyad Period* (Cambridge: Cambridge University Press, 1983), and on the preservation of the case endings in the *ʿarabiyya,* see Zwettler, *Oral Tradition of Classical Arabic Poetry,* 97–188.

5. Lughawī, *Marātib al-naḥwiyyīn,* 5. On the development of classical Arabic, see Kees Versteegh, *The Arabic Language* (Edinburgh: Edinburgh University Press), 1997, 53–73.

6. Al-Khaṭīb al-Baghdādī, *Taʾrīkh Baghdād,* 16:228–229; Ibn Khallikān, *Wafayāt al-aʿyān,* 6:177–178, 181.

7. The redress of injustices (*maẓālim*) was an institutionalized form of secular justice that the Abbasid caliphs in particular used as a way of self-representation.

Their pithy verdicts were collected as models of eloquence. Beatrice Gruendler, "*Tawqīʿ* (Apostille): Verbal Economy in Verdicts of Tort Redress," in *The Weaving of Words: Approaches to Classical Arabic Literature,* ed. Lale Behzadi and Vahid Behmardi (Beirut: Ergon, 2009), 101–129.

8. Al-Khaṭīb al-Baghdādī, *Taʾrīkh Baghdād,* 12:162–163.

9. Zubaydī, *Ṭabaqāt al-naḥwiyyīn,* 171; al-Khaṭīb al-Baghdādī, *Taʾrīkh Baghdād,* 12:158. *Rajaz* stands both for a meter and the verse composed in it. The *rajaz* meter is very flexible, allowing several versions of its metrical foot: — — v —; — v v —; v — v —; and v v v — (— stands for a long syllable, and v for a short syllable). The *rajaz* verse is a half verse and rhymes at the end of each hemistich, as opposed to long verse (*qarīḍ*), which comprises two hemistichs separated by a caesura and rhymes at the end of the full verse. Later *rajaz* poems *(urjūza)* on scholarly topics, composed for memorizing purposes, change the rhyme after each couplet.

10. Sīrāfī, *Akhbār al-naḥwiyyīn,* 45.

11. Lughawī, *Marātib al-naḥwiyyīn,* 53–54.

12. Ibid., 52–53.

13. Marzubānī, *Muqtabas,* 162.

14. The last hemistich follows al-ʿAbbās b. al-Aḥnaf, *Dīwān,* ed. M. Ṭarrād (Beirut: Dār al-Kitāb al-ʿArabī, 1417/1997), 65, no. 94:3–4. The *Dīwān*'s first line lacks the paronomasia.

15. Lughawī, *Marātib al-naḥwiyyīn,* 59–60.

16. Marzubānī, *Muqtabas,* 129–132.

17. Lughawī, *Marātib al-naḥwiyyīn,* 54–55.

18. Ibid., 48; al-Khaṭīb al-Baghdādī, *Taʾrīkh Baghdād,* 12:166.

19. Sīrāfī, *Akhbār al-naḥwiyyīn,* 54; Zubaydī, *Ṭabaqāt al-naḥwiyyīn,* 175; Marzubānī, *Muqtabas,* 116. The timing of this event tallies with Abū ʿUbayda's coming to the city only in 188/804, the year following the Barmakid fall.

20. Sīrāfī, *Akhbār al-naḥwiyyīn,* 49; Marzubānī, *Muqtabas,* 142.

21. Sīrāfī, *Akhbār al-naḥwiyyīn,* 50–51, and a variant in Zubaydī, *Ṭabaqāt al-naḥwiyyīn,* 168–169. The verse implies that the Barmakids thought of themselves as indispensable due to their administrative power. The fall of the Barmakids became a paradigm in Arabic historiography; see Tayeb El-Hibri, *Reinterpreting Islamic Historiography: Hārūn al-Rashīd and the Narrative of the ʿAbbāsid Caliphate* (New York: Cambridge University Press, 1999).

22. Al-Khaṭīb al-Baghdādī, *Taʾrīkh Baghdād,* 12:165.

23. Abū ʿAbdallāh Muḥammad b. Dawūd Ibn al-Jarrāḥ, *al-Waraqa,* ed. ʿAbdalwahhāb ʿAzzām and ʿAbdassattār A. Farrāj (Cairo: Dār al-Maʿārif, 1372/1953), 32–33; Lughawī, *Marātib al-naḥwiyyīn,* 56–57; Marzubānī, *Muqtabas,* 166. In the third variant, it is al-Aṣmaʿī, rather than the poet, who pockets the reward.

24. Al-Khaṭīb al-Baghdādī, *Taʾrīkh Baghdād,* 15:343; Yāqūt, *Muʿjam al-udabāʾ,* ed. D. S. Margoliouth (London: Luzac, 1923–1931; rpt., Baghdad, 1964; rpt., Beirut: Dār Iḥyāʾ al-Turāth al-ʿArabī, n.d.), 19:160.

25. Al-Khaṭīb al-Baghdādī, *Ta'rīkh Baghdād,* 15:344. For the biobibliography of Abū ʿUbayda, see Ibn ʿAbdrabbih, *al-ʿIqd al-farīd,* ed. M. Saʿīd al-ʿAryān (Cairo: Dār al-Fikr, 1359 / 1940), 6:138–144; Lughawī, *Marātib al-naḥwiyyīn,* 44–46; Sīrāfī, *Akhbār al-naḥwiyyīn,* 52–55; Zubaydī, *Ṭabaqāt al-naḥwiyyīn,* 175–178, no. 92; Marzubānī, *Muqtabas,* 109–24, no. 30; Ibn al-Nadīm, *Fihrist,* 58–60 / pt. 1, 149–152; al-Khaṭīb al-Baghdādī, *Ta'rīkh Baghdād,* 15:338–346, no. 7162; Ibn al-Anbārī, *Nuzha,* 68–74 / 104–111; Yāqūt, *Muʿjam al-udabā',* 19:154–162; Ibn al-Qifṭī, *Inbāh al-ruwāt,* 2:276–87, no. 759; Ibn Khallikān, *Wafayāt al-aʿyān,* 5:235–543, no. 731; *GAS,* 8:67–71, 9:65–66; H. A. R. Gibb, "Abū ʿUbayda," in *EI2,* 1:158.

26. Further accounts treat his bad table manners, love of boys, and questionable religious beliefs.

27. Lughawī, *Marātib al-naḥwiyyīn,* 45.

28. Ibid., 44.

29. Zubaydī, *Ṭabaqāt al-naḥwiyyīn,* 170–171.

30. Ibid., 177.

31. On the Arabic meanings of *dīwān,* see Duri, "*Dīwān,*" and Wolfhart Heinrichs, "Prosimetrical Genres in Classical Arabic Literature," in *Prosimetrum: Crosscultural Perspectives on Narrative in Prose and Verse,* ed. Joseph Harris and Karl Reichl (Cambridge: D. S. Brewer, 1997), 249–275.

32. For his book on proverbs, see Zubaydī, *Ṭabaqāt al-naḥwiyyīn,* 177, and for his book on battles, see al- Sīrāfī, *Akhbār al-naḥwiyyīn,* 53.

33. Ella Almagor translates *ʿalā qadri* as "in the manner of"; see Almagor, "The Early Meaning of *Majāz* and the Nature of Abū ʿUbayda's Exegesis," in *Studia Orientalia Memoriae D. H. Baneth Dedicata,* ed. Joshua Blau et al. (Jerusalem: Magnes Press, 1979), 307–326.

34. Al-Khaṭīb al-Baghdādī, *Ta'rīkh Baghdād,* 15:341–342. The term *majāz* can mean both the paraphrase and the passage paraphrased, usually a lexically or syntactically difficult or idiomatic passage. See Wolfhart Heinrichs, "On the Genesis of the *Ḥaqīqa-Majāz* Dichotomy," *Studia Islamica* 59 (1984): 111–140, and Heinrichs, "Contacts between Scriptural Hermeneutics and Literary Theory in Islam: The Case of Majāz," *Zeitschrift für Geschichte der Arabisch-Islamischen Wissenschaften* 7 (1991): 253–284. For a monograph on the exegetical work in which Abū ʿUbayda applies this dictum, see Nora Schmidt, *Philologische Kommentarkulturen: Abū ʿUbaidas Maǧāz al-Qur'ān im Licht spätantiken Exegesewissens* (Wiesbaden, Germany: Harrassowitz, 2016).

35. See Schoeler, *Genesis of Literature in Islam,* 54–67.

36. Ibn al-Nadīm, *Fihrist* 58–60 / pt. 1, 149–152; Yāqūt, *Muʿjam al-udabā',* 19:160–162; *GAS,* 8: 67–71, 9:65–66.

37. Abū ʿUbayda, *Majāz al-Qur'ān,* ed. Fuat Sezgin, 2 vols. (Cairo: al-Khānjī, 1954–1962) / facs. ed. Fuat Sezgin (Frankfurt: Institute for the History of Arabic-Islamic Science at the Johann Wolfgang Goethe University, 2010).

38. Abū ʿUbayda, *Ayyām al-ʿarab,* reconstructed based on citations assembled from later classical sources. In the preface to this edition, the editor ʿĀdil Jāsim al-Bayātī notes that a third of all *ayyām* material is credited to Abū ʿUbayda.

39. On Arab brigands, see Peter Webb, *al-Maqrīzī's al-Khabar ʿan al-bashar,* vol. 5, sections 1–2: *The Arab Thieves: Critical Edition, Annotated Translation and Study* (Leiden, Netherlands: Brill, 2019), 17–64.

40. Abū ʿUbayda, *Naqāʾiḍ Jarīr wa-l-Farazdaq,* ed. A. A. Bevan (Leiden, Netherlands, 1905–1912; rpt., Baghdad, n.d.) / ed. M. I. ʿA al-Ṣāwī, 2 vols. (Cairo, 1935). Abū ʿUbayda's recension was transmitted by Ibn Ḥabīb with commentary by al-Sukkarī; *GAS,* 2:363.

41. Abū ʿUbayda, *al-Khayl,* ed. Fritz Krenkow (Hyderabad, India, 1358; rpt., 1402 / 1981), based on manuscript Medina dated A.H. 353.

42. Because the early Arabic lexicon, recorded by al-Asmaʿī and others, derives in great part from Arab Bedouin desert life, the numerous terms for utensils to draw and transport water figure prominently.

43. Thomas Bauer calls these simple transcriptions *konzeptlose Bücher;* see Bauer, *Das Pflanzenbuch des Ḥanīfa ad-Dīnawarī: Inhalt, Aufbau, Quellen* (Wiesbaden, Germany: Harrassowitz, 1988), 137.

44. Al-Khaṭīb al-Baghdādī, *Taʾrīkh Baghdād,* 15:343; Ibn al-Anbārī, *Nuzha,* 72 / 109. The version at Yāqūt, *Muʿjam al-udabāʾ,* 19:160, has the following (italicized) variants: What will you do with *the book; bring my* horse; [missing:] *a horse was brought;* Whatever he was right in is something *we know* (*shayʾun naʿlamuhū*). The last is probably the more correct reading, as both scholars used their own transmitters, and it is implausible that Abū ʿUbayda would claim that al-Aṣmaʿī depended on him.

45. Zubaydī, *Ṭabaqāt al-naḥwiyyīn,* 177, Yāqūt, *Muʿjam al-udabāʾ,* 19:160.

46. An exception is al-Dīnawarī's (d. 282 / 895) *Book of Plants,* which combines semantic and alphabetic order in its two parts; see Bauer, *Pflanzenbuch.* On the organization of lexica, see also Ramzi Baalbaki, *Arabic Lexicographical Tradition.*

47. This applies to *qarīḍ* poetry and *rajaz* poetry, both of which have a monorhyme, except that it occurs in *rajaz* poetry at every half verse and in *qarīḍ* poetry, composed of two hemistichs, at the end of the second.

48. Abū Bishr al-Yamān b. Abī al-Yamān al-Bandanījī, *al-Taqfiya fī l-lugha,* ed. Khalīl Ibrāhīm al-ʿAṭiyya (Baghdad: al-Jumhūriyya al-ʿIrāqiyya, Wizārat al-Awqāf, 1976), 36; Bauer, *Pflanzenbuch,* 69.

49. Al-Khaṭīb al-Baghdādī, *Taʾrīkh Baghdād,* 12:162, and a variant in Ibn al-Anbārī, *Nuzha,* 81–82 /120, and Ibn al-Qifṭī, *Inbāh al-ruwāt,* 4:202.

50. On the relation between changing media and reality, see, e.g., Ludwig Jaeger and Georg Stanitzek, eds., *Transkribieren: Medien, Lektüre* (Munich: Fink, 2002).

51. Ibn al-Anbārī, *Nuzha,* 74 / 112.

52. Likewise, al-Tibrīzī explains the varying versions of al-Aṣmaʿī's *The Human Body* as the result of his dictating it fifteen times. See also Ramaḍān ʿAbdattawwāb,

Das Kitāb al-Gharīb al-muṣannaf von Abū ʿUbaid und seine Bedeutung für die nationalarabische Lexikographie (Heppenheim, Germany: Wolf, 1962), 133n3.

53. ʿAbdalmalik b. Qurayb al-Aṣmaʿī, *al-Khayl,* ed. August Haffner (Sitzungsberichte der Kaiserlichen Akademie der Wissenschaften in Wien, Philosophisch-Historische Classe, 132, 10, Vienna: Tempsky, 1895) / ed. Nūrī Ḥammūdī al-Qaysī (Baghdad: Maṭbaʿat al-Ḥukūma, 1970), 27.

54. Ibn al-Qifṭī, *Inbāh al-ruwāt,* 4:198.

55. On the difficult performance of the *ʿarabiyya,* see Ibn Khallikān, *Wafayāt al-aʿyān,* 6:177.

56. On al-Aṣmaʿī's book-borrowing, see Sīrāfī, *Akhbār al-naḥwiyyīn,* 45, and on the scribe's book reproduction, see al-Khaṭīb al-Baghdādī, *Taʾrīkh Baghdād,* 13:594–595 and Chapter 3, section "The Stationer-Disciple."

57. Marzubānī, *Muqtabas,* 109.

58. Ibid.

59. On *rasama,* see Lughawī, *Marātib al-naḥwiyyīn,* 8. This shade of meaning is close to logicians' use of the term for formulating a nearly perfect definition (Lane s.v. *rasama*). On *ʿamila,* see p. 42.

60. For the separate listing of al-Madāʾinī's compilations and compositions, see Ibn al-Nadīm, *Fihrist,* 116,4 / pt. 1, 321, and for someone's compilation (or transmission) turned by a subsequent author into composition, see in the same source, 111,3 / pt. 1, 310 and 120,3 / pt. 1, 330.

61. Ibn al-Nadīm, *Fihrist,* 129–155 (*maqāla* 3.2) / pt. 1, 357–434. Ibn al-Nadīm distinguished between the first type, found mainly among third- / ninth-century secretaries and called variously *Rasāʾil majmūʿa* or variants of this formulation—*Kitāb Rasāʾil* (132,6 / pt. 1, 370), *Kitāb Murāsalāt* (131,1 / pt. 1, 363)—and their authors, *kuttāb mutarassilūn mimman duwwinat rasāʾiluhum* (135,ult. / pt. 1, 378); and the second type, dominant in the fourth / tenth century, described as *Kitāb Dīwān rasāʾil* (149,4 / pt. 1, 416), *Kitāb Rasāʾilihī l-majmūʿa fī kulli fannin min ṣanʿatihī* (149,2 / pt. 1, 415), *Kitāb Jāmiʿ rasāʾil* (*Fihrist,* 151,4 / pt. 1, 423 in eight fascicles); *Dīwān rasāʾil kabīr* (152,4 / pt. 1, 426 in 10 vols.).

62. See Abū ʿUbayda, *Ayyām al-ʿarab,* editor's preface, as well as the caveats of Stefan Leder against reconstructing books from the indirect transmission; Leder, "Grenzen der Rekonstruktion."

63. John Wansbrough translates it as "periphrastic exegesis"; see Wansbrough, "*Majāz al-Qurʾān:* Periphrastic Exegesis," *Bulletin of the School of Oriental and African Studies* 33 (1970): 247–266. See also Almagor, "Early Meaning of *Majāz,*" and Heinrichs, "On the Genesis" and "Contacts."

64. On al-Farrāʾ, see al-Khaṭīb al-Baghdādī, *Taʾrīkh Baghdād,* 15:342; on al-Sijistānī, see Zubaydī, *Ṭabaqāt al-naḥwiyyīn,* 176.

65. Regional differences in the resistance to the writing of Ḥadīth and its longest survival in Basra have been established by Cook, "Opponents of Writing," 447–450, 489–491.

66. Zubaydī, *Ṭabaqāt al-naḥwiyyīn,* 176.

67. At this early stage, the term *majāz* applies to linguistic phenomena (ellipsis, pleonasm, hysteron proteron, lack of grammatical agreement, and obscure words, often homonyms; cf. Heinrichs "On the Genesis," 122–123). It still seldom includes figurative expression, for which *majāz* would become a technical term in Qur'ānic hermeneutics in the fourth / tenth century and be paired with a literal counterpart (*ḥaqīqa*); see Heinrichs, "On the Genesis" and "Contacts." On Abū ʿUbayda's method as a commentator, see Schmidt, *Philologische Kommentarkulturen.*

68. For Abū ʿUbayda's word explanation, see his *Majāz,* 1:29; for al-Aṣmaʿī's, see Sīrāfī, *Akhbār al-naḥwiyyīn,* 48.

69. Zubaydī, *Ṭabaqāt al-naḥwiyyīn,* 176.

70. Abū ʿUbayda, *Majāz,* 1:8–9. See also Heinrichs, "On the Genesis," 129.

71. Al-Khaṭīb al-Baghdādī, *Ta'rīkh Baghdād,* 15:342–343.

72. See the criticism by Muḥammad b. Sallām al-Jumaḥī, *Ṭabaqāt fuḥūl al-shuʿarā',* ed. Maḥmūd M. Shākir (Cairo: Maṭbaʿat al-Madanī, n.d.), 1:7–8. Poetic criticism became its own discipline only a century later.

73. Beatrice Gruendler, "Pre-modern Arabic Philologists: Poets' Friends or Foes?," *Geschichte der Germanistik* 39 / 40 (2011): 7–21, esp. 7–8.

74. See *GAS,* 8:68.

75. Lughawī, *Marātib al-naḥwiyyīn,* 49–50.

76. Marzubānī, *Muqtabas,* 144.

77. Sīrāfī, *Akhbār al-naḥwiyyīn,* 45. For *naẓara fī* as a technical term, see section "The Incident of the Horse," above.

78. Zubaydī, *Ṭabaqāt al-naḥwiyyīn,* 167–168.

79. On *laḥn al-ʿāmma,* see Ramaḍān ʿAbdattawwāb, *Laḥn al-ʿāmma wa-l-taṭawwur al-lughawī* (Cairo: Dār al-Maʿārif, 1967), and on its sociocultural relevance, see James E. Montgomery, "al-Jāḥiẓ's Kitāb al-Bayān wa-l-tabyīn," in *Writing and Representation in Medieval Islam,* ed. Julia Bray (London: Routledge, 2006), 91–152.

80. Marzubānī, *Muqtabas,* 121; see also Lughawī, *Marātib al-naḥwiyyīn,* 52. Though Bedouins were effectively those whose transmission was recorded in poetic *dīwāns*, the more generic meaning of *register* is meant here. On *dīwān,* see Duri, "*Dīwān,*" and Heinrichs, "Prosimetrical Genres."

81. Manfred Ullmann, *Aufs Wasser schreiben* (Munich: Verlag der Bayerischen Akademie der Wissenschaften and Beck, 1989).

82. Al-Khaṭīb al-Baghdādī, *Ta'rīkh Baghdād,* 12:158–161; Ibn al-Anbārī, *Nuzha* 78 / 71–74. See also the variant in Ibn al-Qifṭī, *Inbāh al-ruwāt,* 4:199–201. For a fast-reading slave girl of al-Muʿtaṣim's physician Salmawayh (d. 225 / 840) who quickly finished Euclid's book, see al-Jāḥiẓ, *al-Ḥayawān,* ed. ʿAbdassalām M. Hārūn (Beirut: Dār Iḥyā' al-Turāth al-ʿArabī, 1357 / 1938; rpt., 1388 / 1969), 1:54, discussed in chapter 4, section "Books as Prestige Objects."

83. Al-Aṣmaʿī, *Fuḥūlat al-shuʿarā',* ed. and trans. Charles Torrey, *ZDMG* 65 (1911): 487–516 (rpt., Beirut: Dār al-Kitāb al-Jadīd, 1389 / 1971 / as *Su'ālāt Abī Ḥātim*

al-Sijistānī li-l-Aṣmaʿī wa-radduhū ʿalayhi Fuḥūlat al-shuʿarāʾ, ed. Muḥammad ʿA. Salāma (Cairo: Maktabat al-Thaqāfa al-Dīniyya, 1414 / 1994). The vultures in the couplet are a metonymy for a victorious battle, after which the slain enemies' corpses attract the birds.

84. Yāqūt, *Muʿjam al-udabāʾ*, 18:136–138. See also Ibn Khallikān, *Wafayāt al-aʿyān*, 4:323

85. Al-Khaṭīb al-Baghdādī, *Taʾrīkh Baghdād*, 16:225; Ibn Khallikān, *Wafayāt al-aʿyān*, 6:177–178. Ibn al-Nadīm, *Fihrist*, 73 / pt. 1, 199 gives an alternate genesis.

86. Schoeler, *The Oral and the Written*, 120–124; Schoeler, "Mündliche Thora und Ḥadīṯ," 230. For an alternate view on caliphal book commissions, see Cook, "Opponents of Writing," 460–461, 474–475, 486.

87. Ibn al-Nadīm, *Fihrist*, 73 / pt. 1, 198–199; Zubaydī, *Ṭabaqāt al-naḥwiyyīn*, 132; Ibn Khallikān, *Wafayāt al-aʿyān*, 6:178. Al-Ḥasan b. Sahl (d. 236 / 850) was secretary and, later, vizier to al-Maʾmūn.

88. Al-Khaṭīb al-Baghdādī, *Taʾrīkh Baghdād*, 16:228–229; Ibn Khallikān, *Wafayāt al-aʿyān*, 6:181. Nāqiṭ designates an assistant adding the vowel marks in a copied Qurʾān.

89. Al-Khaṭīb al-Baghdādī, *Taʾrīkh Baghdād*, 16:225; Ibn Khallikān, *Wafayāt al-aʿyān*, 6:177–178.

90. Al-Farrāʾ, *Maʿānī al-Qurʾān*, ed. Aḥmad Yūsuf al-Najātī and Muḥammad ʿAlī al-Najjār, 3 vols. (Cairo: Maṭbaʿat Dār al-Kutub al-Miṣriyya, 1955–1972). The chapter headings of *The Definitions* are preserved in Ibn al-Nadīm, *Fihrist*, 74 / pt. 1, 200, and Ibn al-Qifṭī, *Inbāh al-ruwāt*, 3:4, and 16–17, no. 814.

91. For a brief overview of the Baghdad book culture, see Kennedy, "Baghdad as a Center of Learning."

92. Ibn al-Nadīm, *Fihrist*, 23 / pt. 1, 48; Karabacek, *Arab Paper*, 24.

93. Adrian Johns, *The Nature of the Book: Print and Knowledge in the Making* (Chicago: University of Chicago Press, 1998). Shawkat Toorawa coined the term *bookmen;* see Toorawa, *Ibn Abī Ṭāhir Ṭayfūr*, 14–15, 55–57.

94. Dana Sajdi, "Print and Its Discontents: A Case for Pre-print Journalism and Other Sundry Print Matters," in "Nation and Translation in the Middle East," ed. Samah Selim, special issue, *The Translator: Studies in Intercultural Communication* 15, no. 1 (2009): 105–138. See also Bloom, *Paper before Print.*

95. For a nuanced gradation of these functions, see Sebastian Günther, "Assessing the Sources." On the concept of authorship, see also Lale Behzadi and Jaakko Hämeen-Anttila, eds., *Concepts of Authorship in Pre-modern Arabic Texts* (Bamberg, Germany: Bamberg University Press, 2015).

96. On the currency correspondence, see Lutz Ilisch, "Reichswährung und Regionalwährung nach der Münzreform ʿAbd al-Maliks im islamischen Osten," in *Die Grenzen der Welt: Arabica et Iranica ad honorem Heinz Gaube*, ed. Lorenz Korn, Eva Ortmann, and Florian Schwartz (Wiesbaden, Germany: Reichert, 2008), 167–179; A. S. Ehrenkreutz, "Money," in *Wirtschaftsgeschichte des Vorderen Orients*

in islamischer Zeit, ed. Berthold Spuler, HdO, pt. 1, vol. 6, sect. 6 (Leiden, Netherlands: Brill, 1977), 84–97; Eliyahu Ashtor, "Essai sur les prix et les salaires dans l'empire califien," *RSO* 36 (1961): 16–69, esp. 25, 48–49. The indicated rates are approximations, as local currencies could differ. In the anecdote with al-Rashīd and al-Aṣmaʿī, one *dīnar* equals twenty-four *dirhams* (Marzubānī, *Muqtabas,* 134–136), and for taxation purposes, Abū ʿUbayd equates one *dīnar* with ten *dirhams* in his *Types of Dues,* written 215 / 830. The rounded figures in both currencies also carried symbolic value.

97. Al-Āmidī, *al-Muwāzana bayna shiʿr Abī Tammām wa-l-Buḥturī,* ed. al-Sayyid Aḥmad Ṣaqr (Cairo: Dār al-Maʿārif, 1379 / 1960), 1:20–21.

98. On Diʿbil, see Iṣbahānī, *Aghānī,* 20:75–76; *GAS,* 2:529–532. On Abū Tammām, see al-Ṣūlī, *Life and Times of Abū Tammām,* xxiii, with further examples and references cited there. For the presystematic phase of practical criticism, see Beatrice Gruendler, "Abstract Aesthetics and Practical Criticism in Ninth-Century Baghdad," in *Takhyīl: The Imaginary in Classical Arabic Poetics,* ed. Marlé Hammond and Geert Jan van Gelder (Oxford: Gibb Memorial Trust, 2008), 196–220.

99. Sīrāfī, *Akhbār al-naḥwiyyīn,* 50.

100. For a general survey of scholars' circumstances, see Rudolf Sellheim, "Gelehrte und Gelehrsamkeit im Reiche der Chalifen," in *Festgabe für Paul Kirn zum 70. Geburtstag dargebracht von Freunden und Schülern,* ed. Ekkehard Kaufmann (Berlin: Erich Schmidt, 1961), 54–79.

101. Iṣbahānī, *Aghānī,* 23:440–441.

102. The *Catalogue* (*Fihrist,* 363–367 / pt. 2, 321–332, i.e., *maqāla* 8.1) lists among those engaged in the translation (*taʿrīb*) of popular fiction: Jabala b. Sālim, for Persian tales (364 / pt. 2, 325), ʿAlī b. Dāwūd, the secretary of caliph Hārūn's wife Zubayda, for Indian tales and as author of fables (364 / pt. 2, 324, 326); and al-Aṣbagh b. ʿAbd al-ʿAzīz b. Sālim al-Sijistānī (364 / pt. 2, 326).

103. Ibn al-Nadīm, *Fihrist,* 363 / pt. 2, 322. For a detailed study of the fragment, see Nabia Abbott, "A Ninth-Century Fragment of the 'Thousand Nights': New Light on the Early History of the Arabian Nights," *Journal of Near Eastern Studies* 8 (1949): 129–164.

104. For a study of the fragment, see D. S. Rice, "The Oldest Illustrated Arabic Manuscript," *Bulletin of the School of Oriental and African Studies* 22 (1959): 207–220. On the motif of posthumous reunion and translated examples of stories, see Beatrice Gruendler, "'That You Be Brought Near': Union beyond the Grave in the Arabic Literary Tradition," in *Love after Death,* ed. Bernhard Jussen and Ramie Targoff (Berlin: De Gruyter, 2014), 71–95.

105. Ibn al-Nadīm, *Fihrist,* 367 / pt. 2, 331.

106. Ḥabīb Zayyāt, *al-Wirāqa wa-ṣināʿat al-kitāba* (Beirut: Dār al-Ḥamrāʾ, 1992), 31.

107. Al-Khaṭīb al-Baghdādī, *Taʾrīkh Baghdād,* 16:225; Ibn Khallikān, *Wafayāt al-aʿyān,* 6:177–178.

108. Zubaydī, *Ṭabaqāt al-naḥwiyyīn,* 199; al-Khaṭīb al-Baghdādī, *Ta'rīkh Baghdād,* 14:393; Ibn al-Qifṭī, *Inbāh al-ruwāt,* 2:13; Schoeler, *The Oral and the Written,* 54–58, English trans. of Schoeler, "Weiteres zur Frage der mündlichen oder schriftlichen Überlieferung der Wissenschaften im frühen Islam," *Der Islam* 66 (1989): 38–67, esp. 57–62.

109. Al-Khaṭīb al-Baghdādī, *Ta'rīkh Baghdād,* 14:400.

110. Ibid., 14:405.

111. Ibid.

112. Zubaydī, *Ṭabaqāt al-naḥwiyyīn,* 199; al-Khaṭīb al-Baghdādī, *Ta'rīkh Baghdād,* 14:401; Ibn al-Qifṭī, *Inbāh al-ruwāt,* 2:19.

113. Al-Khaṭīb al-Baghdādī, *Ta'rīkh Baghdād,* 14:401.

114. Marzubānī, *Muqtabas,* 315; al-Khaṭīb al-Baghdādī, *Ta'rīkh Baghdād,* 14:393.

115. Al-Khaṭīb al-Baghdādī, *Ta'rīkh Baghdād,* 14:400. See also the variant in Ibn al-Qifṭī, *Inbāh al-ruwāt,* 2:18, which replaces Yaḥyā with Ibn Rāhawayhi.

116. For another page, see the illustration in Ibn al-Nadīm, *Fihrist,* ed. Sayyid, pt. 1, 179–180.

117. Zubaydī, *Ṭabaqāt al-naḥwiyyīn,* 201; al-Khaṭīb al-Baghdādī, *Ta'rīkh Baghdād,* 14:401–402.

118. Lughawī, *Marātib al-naḥwiyyīn,* 93.

119. Abū ʿUbayd, *al-Amthāl al-sā'ira,* published in alphabetical order as first part of *al-Tuḥfa al-bahiyya wa-l-ṭurfa al-shāhiyya* (Istanbul: Maṭbaʿat al-Jawā'ib, 1302/1885) / ed. Abd al-Majīd Qaṭāmish (Damascus: Dār al-Ma'mūn li-l-Turāth, 1400/1980) / ed. Iḥsān ʿAbbās and ʿAbdalmajīd ʿAbdīn, as *Faṣl al-maqāl fī sharḥ Kitāb al-Amthāl,* with commentary of Abū ʿUbayd al-Bakrī (Beirut: Dār al-Amāna, 1971).

120. Lughawī, *Marātib al-naḥwiyyīn,* 93

121. Ibid.; al-Khaṭīb al-Baghdādī, *Ta'rīkh Baghdād,* 14:394; Ibn al-Qifṭī, *Inbāh al-ruwāt,* 2:14. For the printed version, see Abū ʿUbayd, *al-Gharīb al-muṣannaf,* ed. Ramaḍān ʿAbdattawwāb (Cairo: Maktabat al-Thaqāfa al-Dīniyya, 1989), and the manuscripts MS Yale L-116, Nemoy no. 145 (beginning at fol. 216), dated A.H. 490 and MS Milano Ambrosiana, H 139, dated A.H. 384, complete.

122. ʿAbdattawwāb, *Kitāb al-Gharīb al-muṣannaf,* 28, 135–137. On the synonymic-semantic thesaurus, see also Baalbaki, *Arabic Lexicographical Tradition,* 46–48, 268–272, 274–277.

123. For Abū ʿUbayd's model, see Ibn al-Nadīm, *Fihrist,* 57 / pt. 1, 145.

124. ʿAbdattawwāb, *Kitāb al-Gharīb al-muṣannaf,* 83–137.

125. The subheadings of chapter 7, "Horses," are similar but not identical to those of Abū ʿUbayda's *Kitāb al-Khayl.* Likewise, the subheadings of chapter 24 resemble this earlier work in including motion and social behavior. From chapter 19 onward, the order varies in the manuscripts, and the Tunis manuscript, deemed closest to the original by ʿAbdattawwāb, *Kitāb al-Gharīb al-muṣannaf,* is followed here.

126. Various editions exist: Abū ʿUbayd, *al-Amwāl,* ed. M. Ḥāmid al-Fiqī (Cairo: Maṭbaʿat ʿAbd al-Laṭīf al-Ḥijāzī, 1353 / [1934–1935]) / ed. Muḥammad Khalīl Harrās (Cairo: Maktabat al-Kulliyyāt al-Azhariyya, 1388 / 1968; rpt., Beirut: Dār al-Kutub al-ʿIlmiyya, 1406 / 1986) / ed. Dār al-Ḥadātha (Beirut: Dār al-Ḥadātha, 1408 / 1988). In English, see Abū ʿUbayd, *The Book of Revenue,* trans. Imran Ahsan Khan Nyazee (Reading, UK: Garnet, 2002), and *The Book of Finance,* trans. Noor Mohammad Ghiffari (New Delhi: Adam Publishers, 2007). See also the studies of Andreas Görke, *Das Kitāb al-Amwāl des Abū ʿUbaid al-Qāsim b. Sallām: Entstehung und Überlieferung eines frühislamischen Rechtswerkes* (Princeton, NJ: Darwin Press, 2003); and Jens Scheiner, "Steuern und Gelehrsamkeit in der frühen ʿAbbāsidenzeit: Das *Kitāb al-amwāl* des Abū ʿUbaid al-Qāsim b. Sallām. Teil 1: Abū ʿUbaids Steuersystematik und die Rolle des Herrschers. Teil 2: Abū ʿUbaids juristische Argumentation," *ZDMG* 162 (2012): 317–352, 653–693.

127. *Amwāl,* n. 115, *ḥadīth* no. 393.

128. Ibid., n. 212.

129. Ibid., n. 234, *ḥadīth* no. 1753.

130. See Scheiner, "Steuern und Gelehrsamkeit."

131. The masculine pronoun is deliberate and reflects the fact that no female book author is recorded from the third / ninth century.

132. Ibn al-Anbārī, *Nuzha,* 110–111 / 159–160; Yāqūt, *Muʿjam al-udabāʾ,* 15:77–78. For a discussion of this event, see Chapter 3, section "The Stationer-Disciple."

133. Al-Khaṭīb al-Baghdādī, *Taʾrīkh Baghdād,* 14:395–396; Zubaydī, *Ṭabaqāt al-naḥwiyyīn,* 110.

134. Muḥammad b. Aḥmad al-Dhahabī, *Siyar aʿlām al-nubalāʾ,* ed. Shuʿayb al-Arnāʾūṭ and Ḥusayn al-Asad (Beirut: Muʾassasat al-Risāla, 1402–1405 / 1982–1985), 10:507.

135. Lughawī, *Marātib al-naḥwiyyīn,* 94.

136. Ibn al-Nadīm, *Fihrist,* 78 / pt. 1, 215; al-Khaṭīb al-Baghdādī, *Taʾrīkh Baghdād,* 14:393; Ibn al-Qifṭī, *Inbāh al-ruwāt,* 2:13.

137. Al-Khaṭīb al-Baghdādī, *Taʾrīkh Baghdād,* 14:393; Ibn al-Qifṭī, *Inbāh al-ruwāt,* 2:13.

138. Al-Khaṭīb al-Baghdādī, *Taʾrīkh Baghdād,* 14:393, and a variant in Zubaydī, *Ṭabaqāt al-naḥwiyyīn,* 199. Al-Khaṭīb al-Baghdādī attributes the quote to Ibn Durustawayh, and al-Zubaydī to al-Jāḥiẓ.

139. Al-Khaṭīb al-Baghdādī, *Taʾrīkh Baghdād,* 14:394; Ibn al-Qifṭī, *Inbāh al-ruwāt,* 2:14.

140. Al-Khaṭīb al-Baghdādī, *Taʾrīkh Baghdād,* 14:403–404; Ibn al-Qifṭī, *Inbāh al-ruwāt,* 2:19.

141. Lughawī, *Marātib al-naḥwiyyīn,* 93.

142. See Görke, *Kitāb al-Amwāl,* 37.

143. Al-Khaṭīb al-Baghdādī, *Ta'rīkh Baghdād,* 14:406.

144. Ibid., 14:397; Ibn al-Qifṭī, *Inbāh al-ruwāt,* v2:17–18. Another formula for the "license to transmit," *ḥaqq al-riwāya,* survives in the word *baccalaureate.* See R. Y. Ebied and M. J. L. Young, "New Light on the Origin of the Term 'Baccalaureate,'" *Islamic Quarterly* 18 (1974): 3–7.

145. Al-Khaṭīb al-Baghdādī, *Ta'rīkh Baghdād,* 14:397. See also the variant with Yaḥyā b. Maʿīn as the book's first hearer, al-Khaṭīb al-Baghdādī, *Ta'rīkh Baghdād,* 14:396, identical with Ibn al-Qifṭī, *Inbāh al-ruwāt,* 2:16.

146. On social mobility through book authorship, see also Kennedy, "Baghdad as a Center of Learning," 103.

147. Al-Khaṭīb al-Baghdādī, *Ta'rīkh Baghdād,* 14:397, identical with Ibn al-Qifṭī, *Inbāh al-ruwāt,* 2:17.

148. Marzubānī, *Muqtabas,* 315; al-Khaṭīb al-Baghdādī, *Ta'rīkh Baghdād,* 14:393.

149. On the *Types of Dues,* see Görke, *Kitāb al-Amwāl;* on the *Famous Proverbs,* see Sellheim, "Gelehrte und Gelehrsamkeit," 56–58, 63, 81; and on *Classified Rare Words,* see ʿAbdattawwāb, *Kitāb al-Gharīb al-muṣannaf.*

150. Schoeler, *The Oral and the Written,* 57, English trans. of Schoeler, "Weiteres zur Frage."

151. Al-Khaṭīb al-Baghdādī, *Ta'rīkh Baghdād,* 14:393.

152. On Abū ʿUbayd's orally made mistakes, see Lughawī, *Marātib al-naḥwiyyīn,* 93; on his accuracy in writing, see Zubaydī, *Ṭabaqāt al-naḥwiyyīn,* 199–200.

153. Zubaydī, *Ṭabaqāt al-naḥwiyyīn,* 201–202; Ibn al-Nadīm, *Fihrist,* 78 / pt. 1, 215–216. For a shorter version, see al-Khaṭīb al-Baghdādī, *Ta'rīkh Baghdād,* 14:403.

154. Ibn al-Nadīm, *Fihrist,* 78 / pt. 1, 215–216.

155. Jāḥiẓ, *Ḥayawān,* 1:79–82.

156. Al-Khaṭīb al-Baghdādī, *Ta'rīkh Baghdād,* 14:404–405.

157. See Scheiner, "Steuern und Gelehrsamkeit."

158. See Görke, *Kitāb al-Amwāl,* 33, 60.

159. See al-Khaṭīb al-Baghdādī, *Ta'rīkh Baghdād,* 14:394, for the positive appraisal, and for the negative, 14:403, identical with Ibn al-Qifṭī, *Inbāh al-ruwāt,* 2:19–20. Görke, *Kitāb al-Amwāl,* sees the point of criticism instead in Abū ʿUbayd's clustering of *ḥadīth.*

160. Pseudo-Jāḥiẓ, *al-Maḥāsin wa-l-aḍdād,* ed. Gerlof van Vloten (Amsterdam: Oriental Press, [1974]) / ed. Muḥammad A. Khānjī (Cairo: Maṭbaʿat al-Saʿāda, 1906), 7; al-Jāḥiẓ, *al-Risāla fī l-jidd wa-l-hazl,* in *Rasā'il al-Jāḥiẓ,* ed. ʿAbdassalām M. Hārūn, vol. 1 (Beirut: Dār al-Jīl, 1411 / 1991), 225–278.

161. For three book addicts, al-Jāḥiẓ, the vizier al-Fatḥ b. Khāqān, and the judge Ismāʿīl b. Isḥāq, see Ibn al-Nadīm, *Fihrist,* 108 / pt. 1, 578.

162. See Zayyāt, *Wirāqa;* Maya Shatzmiller, *Labour in the Medieval Islamic World* (Leiden, Netherlands: Brill, 1994); Chapter 3.

2. POETS

1. Iṣbahānī, *Aghānī,* 20:73, 82–83. The same source cites his uncle's intervention to negotiate his release from prison (20:86).

2. Ibid., 20:141.

3. Ibid., 20:82, 96–97.

4. Ibid., 20:74.

5. Ibid., 20:79.

6. Ibid., 20:91–92.

7. Ibid., 20:96–97. This did not hinder him from later denying authorship of the satire to avoid the repercussions (20:98, 110). Ibrāhīm b. al-Mahdī once admitted that he was the author in order to save the poet and later disclaimed this as a white lie.

8. Ibid., 20:81.

9. Ibid., 20:98–99.

10. Ibid., 20:143–145.

11. As related by himself; see ibid., 20:102–103.

12. Ibid., 20:87.

13. Ibid., 20:84.

14. ʿAbdallāh Ibn al-Muʿtazz, *Ṭabaqāt al-shuʿarāʾ*, ed. ʿAbdassaṭṭār A. Farrāj (Cairo: Dār al-Maʿārif, 1375 / 1956; rpt., 1981), 265–66; Iṣbahānī, *Aghānī,* 20:88–89.

15. Iṣbahānī, *Aghānī,* 20:77–78.

16. Ibid., 20:122, 131, 133–135.

17. Even though its most current meaning is "book," the word *kitāb* can stand for a piece of writing of any length, ranging from a one-page letter to a multivolume work. On the rise of letter writing as concomitant with book writing, see Cook, "Opponents of Writing," 480–481.

18. Iṣbahānī, *Aghānī,* 20:101–102, 141–142.

19. Ibid., 20:88–87, 142.

20. Ibid., 20:115–116.

21. Ibid., 20:143–144.

22. On Ṭāhirid literary patronage in general, see Clifford Edmund Bosworth, "The Tahirids and Arabic Culture," *Journal of Semitic Studies* 14 (1969): 45–79; on their patronage of Ibn al-Rūmī, see Beatrice Gruendler, *Medieval Arabic Praise Poetry: Ibn al-Rūmī and the Patron's Redemption* (London: RoutledgeCurzon 2003).

23. Iṣbahānī, *Aghānī,* 20:118–120. In a variant, the satire was prompted by Diʿbil's being denied entry by the door keeper, and he reacted with violence (20:120).

24. Ibid., 20:117–118.

25. Ibid., 20:141.

26. Ibid., 20:127–128 with a variant, 20:129–130.

27. Ibid., 20:125–127.

28. Ibid., 20:100.

29. For Marwān's recitation, see ibid., 10:85–87; for Di'bil's draft poem, 20:100.

30. Ibid., 20:124–127.

31. Ibid., 20:90.

32. Ibid., 20:69–70, 93. Al-Ma'mūn knew how to take satire, and rather than going overboard with punishing the poet, he had it dealt with in kind (20:130–132). He also enjoyed Di'bil's other poetry and recited his homecoming poem whenever he returned from a journey (20:106–108, 135–139).

33. Ibid., 20:110.

34. Ibid., 20:76–77.

35. Ṣūlī, *Life and Times of Abū Tammām,* §33 / *Akhbār Abī Tammām,* 63.

36. See Schoeler, *The Oral and the Written,* 28–44, English trans. of Schoeler, "Die Frage der mündlichen oder schriftlichen Überlieferung der Wissenschaften im frühen Islam," *Der Islam* 62 (1985): 201–230; and Cook, "Opponents of Writing," 476–479.

37. Iṣbahānī, *Aghānī,* 20:128–129.

38. Ibn Sharaf al-Qayrawānī, *Masā'il al-intiqād* [as *Questions de critique littéraire*], ed. and trans. Charles Pellat (Algiers: Carbonel, 1953), 30–31.

39. Leon Zolondek, ed., *Di'bil b. 'Alī: The Life and Writings of an Early 'Abbāsid Poet* (Lexington: University Press of Kentucky, 1961).

40. For the first description, see Ibn al-Mu'tazz, *Ṭabaqāt al-shu'arā',* 147, and Zolondek, *Di'bil b. 'Alī,* 143, no. 31 (the numbers refer to the passages Zolondek assembled from literary sources). For the second description, see Ṣūlī, *Life and Times of Abū Tammām,* §34.1 / *Akhbār Abī Tammām,* 63; and Abū 'Ubaydallāh Muḥammad b. 'Imrān al-Marzubānī, *al-Muwashshaḥ fī ma'ākhidh al-'ulamā' 'alā al-shu'arā',* ed. Muḥammad 'Alī al-Bijāwī (Cairo: Dār Nahḍat Miṣr li-l-Ṭibā'a wa-l-Nashr wa-l-Tawzī', n.d.), 372 / ed. Muḥammad Ḥ. Shamsaddīn (Beirut: Dār al-Kutub al-'Ilmiyya, [1415] / 1995), 339 (both editions are cited hereafter, in this order, separated by a slash).

41. Ibn al-Mu'tazz, *Ṭabaqāt al-shu'arā',* 147; Zolondek, *Di'bil b. 'Alī,* 143, no. 31.

42. Incipit "Unter dem Felsen am Wege / Erschlagen liegt er, / In dessen Blut / Kein Tau herabträuft." For a study on Goethe's version, see Wolfhart Heinrichs, "Ta'abbaṭa Sharran, Goethe, Shākir," in *Reflections on Reflections: Near Eastern Writers Reading Literature,* ed. Angelika Neuwirth and Andreas Islebe (Wiesbaden, Germany: Reichert, 2006), 191–252, esp. 197.

43. Zolondek, *Di'bil b. 'Alī,* 150–151, no. 52.

44. On the poet, see Beatrice Gruendler, "Abū Tammām," in *EI3,* first published online and in print 2007, accessed December 21, 2019, http://dx.doi.org/10.1163/1573-3912_ei3_SIM_0035. For the ode, see Abū Tammām, *Dīwān bi-sharḥ al-Khaṭīb al-Tibrīzī,* ed. Muḥammad 'Abduh 'Azzām (Cairo: Dār al-Ma'ārif, 1407 / 1987), vol. 1, no. 3.

45. On Abu Tammām, see Gruendler, "Abū Tammām," and further references cited there; on the controversy about his modern style, Gruendler, "Modernity in the Ninth Century: The Controversy around Abū Tammām," *Studia Islamica* 112 (2017): 131–148.

46. Ṣūlī, *Life and Times of Abū Tammām,* §122.1 / *Akhbār Abī Tammām,* 244; Āmidī, *Muwāzana,* 1:19.

47. On Abū Sulmā (Salama) Muknif al-Madanī (alive late second / eighth or early third / ninth century), see *GAS,* 2:601.

48. On Muḥammad b. Mūsā al-Barbarī, see Fleischhammer, *Quellen des Kitāb al-Aghānī,* 95–96. On the event, see Ṣūlī, *Life and Times of Abū Tammām,* §94.1 / *Akhbār Abī Tammām,* 199–201. The two variants of the account contain small additions. The first, in Iṣbahānī, *Aghānī,* 16:315–316, adds explanatory detail and emphasizes Diʿbil's accusation by turning it into more vivid direct speech and using the intensive adjectival form *sarūq,* "arch-thief." The chain of transmission is independent from the other sources; it cites Abū l-ʿAbbās Aḥmad b. Waṣīf and the author's paternal cousin Abū ʿAbdallāh Aḥmad b. al-Ḥasan b. Muḥammad al-Iṣbahānī, both of whom cite the narrator Muḥammad b. Mūsā al-Barbarī. The second variant, in Marzubānī, *Muwashshaḥ,* 407–409 / 367–368, adds three further verses, two of which also appear in Abū Tammām's ode. The verses' later addition supports al-Ḥasan b. Wahb's argument that they were planted in the account to discredit Abū Tammām. The *isnād* depends on al-Ṣūlī, who cites Muḥammad b. Mūsā al-Barbarī. In the account's translation, variant formulations and additions are given in brackets.

49. This verse is echoed in the wording and rhyme of hemistich no. 192:21b and the meaning of hemistich 22a in Abū Tammām's ode, see n. 52.

50. *Kaʾanna Banī l-Qaʿqāʿi yawma wafātihī / nujūmu samāʾin kharra min baynihā l-badru.*

51. Āmidī, *Muwāzana,* 1:72–73. In this variant, Diʿbil recites Muknif's ode without narrative frame and then describes the reaction of the narrator al-Yazīdī. The *isnād* cites Ibn al-Jarrāḥ, who cites al-Yazīdī, although it does not appear in the printed edition of Ibn al-Jarrāḥ's *Waraqa.* The narrator must be a later member of Yazīdī family, since the more famous Abū Muḥammad, a poet, died 202 / 817. See *GAS,* 2:610.

52. The poem is a lament of general Muḥammad b. Ḥumayd al-Ṭūsī; see Abū Tammām, *Dīwān,* vol. 4, no. 192. The accusation concerns verses 2–3 and 14–15.

53. This verse is also identified as a borrowing of Muslim's motif of a patron's death, making people averse to travel and causing travelers to return home, which is based in turn on al-Nābigha's motif of the patron's death making the riding beasts go astray in the night; see Āmidī, *Muwāzana,* 1:79–80. Both this and the verbatim theft appear in al-Āmidī's list of Abū Tammām's thefts as "what I come across in people's books about his thefts and what I deduced and extracted myself" (*Muwāzana,* 1:59).

54. Ṣūlī, *Life and Times of Abū Tammām,* §94.2 / *Akhbār Abī Tammām,* 201.

55. See the example recounted, ibid., §61.1–61.4 / 108–114; and the digests mentioned, ibid. §61.4 / 114. This practice is discussed by Gruendler, "Abstract Aesthetics," 213–220, which includes a translation of the account, whose events are datable to the lifetime of Ibrāhīm b. al-ʿAbbās al-Ṣūlī (d. 243 / 857), one of the participants.

56. Between Muslim b. al-Walīd and his opponent Ibn Qanbar there was a long-lasting exchange of poetic flytings with tribal undertones, which had been started by al-Ṭirimmāḥ (d. c. 105–112 / 724–730) of the western tribe of Ṭayyiʾ, to whom al-Farazdaq (d. c. 114 / 732) of the eastern tribe of Tamīm had responded. After the death of al-Ṭirimmāh, Ibn Qanbar of the Tamīm continued to satirize him, which Muslim b. al-Walīd found objectionable and retorted. The exchange eventually widened to include the whole of the Quraysh, on the side of the Tamīm, and the Helpers (Anṣār), on the side of the Ṭayyiʾ, and shifted focus from purely tribal banter to the two groups' status in Islam. Ibn Qanbar, taking the side of the Quraysh, produced vicious attacks on the Anṣār, to which Muslim eventually stopped responding. The complete *akhbār* on this are found in Iṣbahānī, *Aghānī,* 18:342–354. For a discussion and translation of select *akhbār,* see Gruendler, "Abbasid Poets and the Qur'ān."

57. Ṣūlī, *Life and Times of Abū Tammām,* §94.1 / *Akhbār Abī Tammām,* 244; Marzubānī, *Muwashshaḥ,* 377 / 344; Āmidī, *Muwāzana,* 1:19.

58. See Felix Klein-Franke, "The *Ḥamāsa* of Abū Tammām, Part 1," *JAL* 2 (1971): 13–36; and Klein-Franke, "The *Ḥamāsa* of Abū Tammām, Part 2," *JAL* 3 (1972): 141–178. On this book, see section below, "Abū Tammām and His Books."

59. Āmidī, *Muwāzana,* 1:112 and 123.

60. See Iṣbahānī, *Aghānī,* 20:74–75.

61. For al-Aṣmaʿī crediting al-Ḥasan b. Muṭayr al-Asadī with the verse, see Iṣbahānī, *Aghānī,* 20:77. For Abū Hiffān conceding it to Diʿbil, see 20:75–76.

62. Iṣbahānī, *Aghānī,* 20:135–39.

63. Ṣūlī, *Life and Times of Abū Tammām,* §34.1 / *Akhbār Abī Tammām,* 63; Marzubānī, *Muwashshaḥ,* 372 / 339.

64. Al-Ṣūlī identifies and refutes these critics in his introductory epistle. See Ṣūlī, *Life and Times of Abū Tammām,* §§2.1–24.14 / *Akhbār Abī Tammām,* 3–46.

65. See Gruendler, "Meeting the Patron," 62–64, 80–85.

66. Ṣūlī, *Life and Times of Abū Tammām,* §69.1–4 / *Akhbār Abī Tammām,* 121–125; Abū Tammām, *Dīwān,* vol. 1, no. 15.

67. Marzubānī, *Muwashshaḥ,* 381 / 346.

68. Ṣūlī, *Life and Times of Abū Tammām,* §69.6–28 / *Akhbār Abī Tammām,* 125–138.

69. For the caliphal session, see Iṣbahānī, *Aghānī,* 20:106–108; for the gubernatorial one, 20:135–136.

70. Ibid., 13:108–109.

71. See Chapter 1, section "Inescapable, Imperfect Books."

72. On the dog bite, see Abū ʿUbaydallāh Muḥammad b. ʿImrān al-Marzubānī, *Muʿjam al-shuʿarāʾ*, ed. ʿAbdassaṭṭār A. Farrāj (Baghdad: Dār Iḥyāʾ al-Kutub al-ʿArabiyya, [1379] / 1960), 109; and Zolondek, *Diʿbil b. ʿAlī*, 164, no. 85. On the banquet brawl, see Ibn al-Jarrāḥ, *Waraqa*, 13–14; and Zolondek, *Diʿbil b. ʿAlī*, 153–154, no. 58. On the bridge brawl, see Ibn al-Jarrāḥ, *Man ismuhū ʿAmr min al-shuʿarāʾ*, ed. ʿAbd al-ʿAzīz b. Nāṣir al- Māniʿ (Riaḍ: Jāmiʿat al-Malik Saʿūd, 1431 / 2011), 200–201; Marzubānī, *Muʿjam*, 28; and Zolondek, *Diʿbil b. ʿAlī*, 161, no. 76. For the verse on the rich miser by the poet al-Mustahill b. al-Kumayt, see Ibn al-Jarrāḥ, *Waraqa*, 83; Marzubānī, *Muʿjam*, 453; and Zolondek, *Diʿbil b. ʿAlī*, 171–172, no. 109. For the couplet by the poet Ibn Kunāsa comparing matrimony with a cross, see Ibn al-Jarrāḥ, *Waraqa*, 87; Zolondek, *Diʿbil b. ʿAlī*, 170, no. 102.

73. Abū Tammām, *Sharḥ Dīwān al-Ḥamāsa li-Abī-ʿAlī Aḥmad b. M. b. al-Ḥasan al-Marzūqī*, ed. Aḥmad Amīn and ʿAbdassalām Hārūn (Cairo: Maṭbaʿat Lajnat at-Taʾlīf wa-l-Tarjama wa-l-Nashr, 1371–1372 / 1951–1953; rpt., Beirut: Dār al-Jīl, 1411 / 1991), 2:1513, no. 642; Zolondek, *Diʿbil b. ʿAlī*, 177, no. 124.

74. Ibn al-Jarrāḥ, *Waraqa*, 89–90; and Zolondek, *Diʿbil b. ʿAlī*, 151, no. 54.

75. Ibn al-Jarrāḥ, *Waraqa*, 91; and Zolondek, *Diʿbil b. ʿAlī*, 154, no. 59.

76. Zolondek, *Diʿbil b. ʿAlī*, 160–161, no. 74. ʿAmr b. al-ʿĀṣ was a contemporary of Muḥammad and an astute politician. He led the conquest of Egypt, which he governed until his death; see A. J. Wensinck, "ʿAmr b. al-ʿĀṣ," in *EI2*, 1:541.

77. On Diʿbil's statement, see Ibn al-Muʿtazz, *Ṭabaqāt al-shuʿarāʾ*, 322; and Zolondek, *Diʿbil b. ʿAlī*, 151, no. 53. On Ibn Abī Umayya, see al-Khaṭīb al-Baghdādī, *Taʾrīkh Baghdād*, 2:433–434, no. 419; Zolondek, *Diʿbil b. ʿAlī*, 169, no. 99; and *GAS*, 2:607–608. A client *(mawlā)* was a convert to Islam, which entailed a relationship to the Muslim at whose hands he had converted.

78. Zolondek, *Diʿbil b. ʿAlī*, 167, no. 93.

79. Ibn Qutayba was one of the great Sunnī polygraphs of the third / ninth century, being both a theologian and a writer of *adab;* see Gérard Lecomte, "Ibn Ḳutayba," in *EI2*, 3:844–847.

80. Zolondek, *Diʿbil b. ʿAlī*, 125–132.

81. For the best boast, namely, about the victory of the early Muslims at the battle of Badr, see Zolondek, *Diʿbil b. ʿAlī*, 167, no. 92; for the best satirical verse, see 148, no. 45. For the truest verse, praising the Prophet by the Companion Anas [b. Abī Anas] b. Zunaym al-Kinānī, see Zolondek, *Diʿbil b. ʿAlī*, 138, no. 18 has the verse only. For the worst poetic lie, namely, al-Muhalhil's hyperbole about battle noise heard across the whole of the Arabian Peninsula, see Zolondek, *Diʿbil b. ʿAlī*, 175, no. 118.

82. Zolondek, *Diʿbil b. ʿAlī*, 129.

83. ʿAmr b. Naṣr al-Qiṣāfī was a Basran poet and convert to Islam who composed praise poems for Caliph Hārūn al-Rashīd and his successors. See *GAS*, 2:526;

Ibn al-Muʿtazz, *Ṭabaqāt al-shuʿarāʾ*, 305 (here the comment is transmitted by Diʿbil's son Ḥusayn); Ibn al-Jarrāḥ, *Waraqa*, 7–8; and Zolondek, *Diʿbil b. ʿAlī*, 162, no. 79. On the *mukhaḍram* poet, see 162, no. 90. On Abū l-ʿUdhāfir, see Ibn al-Jarrāḥ, *Waraqa*, 4; and Zolondek, *Diʿbil b. ʿAlī*, 177, no. 123.

84. For a story *(qiṣṣa)* of a poet returning from the front to save a woman of his neighborhood from an unwelcome suitor, see Zolondek, *Diʿbil b. ʿAlī*, 153, no. 57; for the lovers' death, see 180, no. A III.

85. Ṣūlī, *Life and Times of Abū Tammām*, §122.2 / *Akhbār Abī Tammām*, 244; Marzubānī, *Muwashshaḥ*, 377 / 344.

86. See Ṣūlī, *Life and Times of Abū Tammām*, §§90, 95.1 / *Akhbār Abī Tammām*, 183, 202.

87. See Ṣūlī, *Life and Times of Abū Tammām*, §64.1 / *Akhbār Abī Tammām*, 115–116.

88. Iṣbahānī, *Aghānī*, 18:328. Muslim b. al-Walīd, also called Ṣarīʿ al-Ghawānī (Slain by the Beauties), was a pioneer of the modern style of poetry in Abbasid times; see *GAS*, 2:528–529.

89. Ibn Thawāba was an assistant to the viziers of the caliphs al-Muhtadī (r. 255–256 / 869–870) and al-Muʿtamid (r. 356–379 / 870–892) and a talented stylist and poet. Being of Christian background, he tried to gain social acceptance by hosting an illustrious circle of poets and literati. For his request to the Banū Nawbakht, see Ṣūlī, *Life and Times of Abū Tammām*, §10.1–2 / *Akhbār Abī Tammām*, 15–16.

90. On Abū Tammām, see Ibn al-Muʿtazz, *Ṭabaqāt al-shuʿarāʾ*, 285, and on famous poets, 47.

91. On Abū Nuwās, one of the most famous poets of the early ʿAbbāsid period, who made the wine song (*khamriyya*) a genre of its own, see Ewald Wagner, "Abū Nuwās," in *EI2*, 1:143–144; and *GAS*, 2:543–550.

92. Ṣūlī, *Life and Times of Abū Tammām*, §86.3 / *Akhbār Abī Tammām*, 173; and Iṣbahānī, *Aghānī*, 18:335. In the variant in *Aghānī*, the poet swears not to pray before having memorized the *dīwān*s, which takes him two months, and he is found at home sitting before them, but not in the act of composing.

93. He did so by intermediary of a reciter, due to his own rough voice. See Iṣbahānī, *Aghānī*, 20:113.

94. The account appears only in the commentary by al-Tibrizī (died 502 / 1109), and it is improbable that the entire work was completed in that short time span. On the account, see Suzanne P. Stetkevych, *Abū Tammām and the Poetics of the ʿAbbāsid Age* (Brill: Leiden, Netherlands, 1991), 282–283; for a literary analysis of selected chapters of the *Ḥamāsa*, 287–356.

95. Four further anthologies by AbuTammām have not survived. See *GAS*, 2:558.

96. Āmidī, *Muwāzana*, 1:59.

97. Ibid., 1:38.

98. See Ṣūlī, *Life and Times of Abū Tammām*, §110.1 / *Akhbār Abī Tammām*, 230–232.

99. See beginning of previous section, p. 96.

100. Iṣbahānī, *Aghānī,* 13:119–121.

101. Ibid., 13:107–108, 110–111. See also the variant, Ibn Abī Ṭāhir, *Kitāb Baghdād,* ed. ʿIzzat al-ʿAṭṭār al-Ḥusaynī (Cairo: Maktabat al-Khānjī, 1368 / 1949), 89–90.

102. Iṣbahānī, *Aghānī,* 13:109–110.

103. For the letter sent during sickness, ibid., 13:118; for the letter during disgrace, 13:119.

104. Ibid., 13:109.

105. Ibid., 13:113–114. In a variant, the caliph invites him by letter (13:109).

106. Ibid., 13:109–10, with a variant, 13:109.

107. Ibid., 13:112.

108. Ibid., 13:111.

109. Ibid., 13:116.

110. Ibn Abī Ṭāhir, *Kitāb Baghdād,* 87–88. On Arab readers of Persian books, see also Gutas, *Greek Thought, Arabic Culture,* 50. The account describes the language of the consulted books as Persian, without specifying whether this meant Middle Persian (Pahlavi) or New Persian (Fārsī). The latter language hardly appears in written sources before the fourth-tenth century, whereas translations from Pahlavi into Arabic are well documented since the second / eighth century. The Pahlavi originals of these translations are mostly lost; one exception is a Pahlavi preface of the fable collection *Kalīla wa-Dimna,* which was recently discovered by Daniel Sheffield. For a recent study of a lost Pahlavi royal chronicle mentioned in the Arabic sources, see Jaakko Hämeen-Anttila, *Khwadāynāmag: The Middle Persian Book of Kings* (Leiden, Netherlands: Brill, 2018).

111. On the late antique cosmopolis, see Garth Fowden, *Before and After Muḥammad: The First Millennium Refocused* (Princeton, NJ: Princeton University Press, 2014); and Isabel Toral, *Al-Ḥīra: Eine arabische Kulturmetropole im spätantiken Kontext* (Leiden, Netherlands: Brill, 2014).

112. Iṣbahānī, *Aghānī,* 13:117.

113. On al-ʿAttābī's concision, see ibid., 13:112; and on recording his statements, 13:113.

114. Ibid., 13:116.

3. STATIONERS

1. On the adoption and production of paper in the Arab world, see Bloom, "Papermaking,"; Bloom, *Paper before Print,* 47–89; Gacek, *Arabic Manuscripts,* 186–193; Déroche et al., *Islamic Codicology,* 49–52; Pedersen, *Arabic Book,* 60–62; Grohmann, *Arabische Paläographie,* 1:98–105; and Huart and Grohmann, "Kāghad." See also the older studies by Loveday, *Islamic Paper,* and Karabacek, *Arab Paper.*

2. See Bloom, *Paper before Print,* 47; Hugh Kennedy, *The Great Arab Conquests: How the Spread of Islam Changed the World We Live In* (Philadelphia: Da Capo Press, 2007), 295; and Valerie Hansen, *The Silk Road: A New History* (Oxford: Oxford University Press, 2012), 16, 118, 138.

3. See Valerie Hansen, *Silk Road,* 5, 116–120, 129–138. In Turkestan, paper is attested since the second century C.E.; see Pedersen, *Arabic Book,* 60n14.

4. For the paper types, see Gacek, *Arabic Manuscripts,* 191–192, based on Ibn al-Nadīm's *Catalogue,* for the officials supplying their labels, see Karabacek, *Arab Paper,* 24, and for the introduction of paper in Baghdad, see Grohmann, *Arabische Paläographie,* 1:100 and Huart and Grohmann, "Kāghad."

5. See al-Yaʿqūbī, Ibn Wāḍiḥ, *Kitāb al-Buldān,* ed. M. J. de Goeje (Leiden, Netherlands: Brill 1892), 245, translated in al-Yaʿqūbi, *The Works of Ibn Wāḍiḥ al-Yaʿqūbī: An English Translation,* ed. Matthew S. Gordon et al. (Leiden, Netherlands: Brill, 2018), 1:78; and Kennedy, "Baghdad as a Center of Learning," 93. The booksellers were relocated outside Baghdad on the section of the road leading from the southeastern Basra Gate to its crossing of the Sarat Canal shortly before the Ḥarrānī Archway. See the map by Guy Le Strange, reproduced in Jacob Lassner, *The Topography of Baghdad in the Early Middle Ages: Texts and Studies* (Detroit, MI: Wayne State University Press, 1970), 202, nos. 47, 50.

6. Houari Touati, *L'armoire à sagesse: Bibliothèques et collections en Islam* (Paris: Aubier, 2003), 207–209.

7. For a list of Christian codices from the third / ninth century, see the Introduction, based on Déroche, "Manuscrits arabes datés." On Syriac books, see Chrysi Kotsifou, "Books and Book Production in the Monastic Communities of Byzantine Egypt," in *The Early Christian Book,* ed. William E. Klingshirn and Linda Safran (Washington, DC: Catholic University of America Press, 2007), 48–66; and Joel T. Walker, "Books and Readers in East-Syrian Monastic Tradition," in *Commutatio et Contentio: Studies in the Late Roman, Sasanian, and Early Near East in Memory of Zeev Rubin,* ed. Henning Börm and Josef Wiesehöfer (Düsseldorf, Germany: Wellem, 2012), 305–345.

8. See Arbache, *Évangile arabe selon Saint Luc* on Mt. Sinai, Codex Sinaiticus Ar. 72, and an Arabic version of the Acts of the Apostles also from St. Catherine Cloister, Mt. Sinai, Codex Sinaiticus Ar. 154, at Déroche, "Manuscrits arabes datés," 354–355 and fig. 22. Codex Vaticanus Arabicus 13, a collection of Gospel portions and Pauline letters, contains Greek indications of the liturgical calendar and reading notes showing its use by Greek-speaking clerics. See Schulthess, *Manuscrits arabes des lettres de Paul,* 129–144 and figs. 2a and b.

9. Shābushtī, *Kitāb al-Diyārat.* One example is Dayr Zurāra near Kūfa, where some poets interrupted their pilgrimage (159–161).

10. Shatzmiller, *Labour in the Medieval Islamic World,* 236–238, 279–281; Pedersen, *Arabic Book,* 47.

11. On the genre of the biographical dictionary, see Cooperson, *Classical Arabic Biography;* M. J. L. Young, "Arabic Biographical Writing," in *Religion, Learning and Science in the Abbasid Period,* ed. M. J. L. Young, J. D. Lathan, and R. B. Serjeant (Cambridge: Cambridge University Press, 1990), 168–187; and Wadad al-Qadi, "Biographical Dictionaries: Inner Structure and Cultural Significance," in *The Book in the Islamic World,* ed. George N. Atiyeh (Albany: State University of New York Press, 1995), 93–122. On Mamluk biographical dictionaries specifically, see Thomas Bauer, "Literarische Anthologien der Mamlukenzeit," in *Die Mamluken: Studien zu ihrer Geschichte und Kultur: Zum Gedenken an Ulrich Haarmann (1942–1999),* ed. Stephan Conermann and Anja Pistor-Hatam (Schenefeld, Germany: EB-Verlag, 2003), 71–122.

12. Muḥammad b. Aḥmad al-Dhahabī, *Taʾrīkh al-islām wa-ṭabaqāt al-mashāhīr wa-l-aʿlām,* ed. ʿUmar ʿA. al-Tadmurī, 52 vols. (Beirut: Dār al-Kitāb al-ʿArabī, 1407–1416 / 1987–1995).

13. The numbers of listed stationers—many of whom were *also* scholars, as that trade alone did not warrant their inclusion—grouped in half-century increments (to even out generational gaps) are respectively two (150–200 H), thirteen (200–250 H), twenty-six (250–300 H), twenty-eight (300–350 H), and thirty-eight (350–400 H). In percentages this means a rise from 0.2 percent to nearly 2 percent of the total number of biographies per twenty-year period. Those average at 953 individuals, with 667 as the lowest and 1,232 as the highest number. The biographies have been digitally extracted by Maxim Romanov. For his quantitative analysis and approach to this work, see Maxim Romanov, "Toward the Digital History of the pre-Modern Muslim World: Developing Text-mining Techniques for the Study of Arabic Biographical Collections," in *Analysis of Ancient and Medieval Texts and Manuscripts: Digital Approaches,* ed. Tara L Andrews and Caroline Macé (Turnhout: Brepols Publishers, 2014), 229–244 and "Algorithmic Analysis of Medieval Arabic Biographical Collections," *Speculum* 92 (2017): 226–246.

14. On women scholars, see Mohammad Akram Nadwi, *al-Muḥaddithāt: The Woman Scholars in Islam* (Oxford: Interface Publications, 2007).

15. An independent thinker and initially a Muʿtazilate, he was later accused of heresy, like his friend and student Ibn al-Rāwandī (d. end of third / ninth century). His books treat the Shīʿa, the branches of Christianity, and further religions and sects; see Ibn al-Nadīm, *Fihrist,* 216 / pt. 1, 600, *GAS,* 1:620, and Samuel M. Stern, "Abū ʿĪsā Muḥammad b. Hārūn al-Warrāq," in *EI2,* 1:130.

16. The death date, partial in al-Dhahabī, is complete in al-Khaṭīb al-Baghdādī, *Taʾrīkh Baghdād,* 12:396–497.

17. See also al-Khaṭīb al-Baghdādī, *Taʾrīkh Baghdād,* 3:102–103.

18. The long genealogy is owed to his famous ancestor ʿAmr b. Dīnār, a leading theologian, traditionist, and Muftī of Mecca. See Ṣafadī, *al-Wāfī bi-l-wafayāt,* 23:217–219.

19. On him, see also al-Khaṭīb al-Baghdādī, *Ta'rīkh Baghdād,* 7:419–420, no. 3377. He is not to be confused with the reputed Qur'ān reciter of the same name, Abū Ya'qūb Isḥāq b. Ibrāhīm al-Muqri' (d. 286/899-900) on whom, see 7: 417, no. 3374, and Christopher Melchert and Asma Afsaruddin. "Reciters of the Qur'an," in *EQ,* 4: 386–393, esp. 390. The reciter's brother mentioned there but lacking an entry of his own is Aḥmad b. Ibrāhīm al-Warrāq (27/1).

20. On him, see al-Khaṭīb al-Baghdādī, *Ta'rīkh Baghdād,* 7:430, no. 3390.

21. On him, see *GAS,* 1:186. He was the only one to transmit al-Shāfi'ī's *al-Mabsūṭ.*

22. See Introduction, section "Dearth of Artifacts."

23. For a recent study of transmission documents (*ijāza*), see Andreas Görke and Konrad Hirschler, eds., *Manuscript Notes as Documentary Sources* (Würzburg, Germany: Ergon, 2011). On personal registers, see Garret Davidson, "Carrying on the Tradition: An Intellectual and Social History of Post-canonical Hadith Transmission" (PhD diss., University of Chicago, 2014), 209–231.

24. On the gradual acceptance of recording Ḥadīth in writing at the beginning of the third/ninth century, see Schoeler, "Mündliche Thora und Ḥadīṯ"; Cook, "Opponents of Writing."

25. See Ṣafadī, *al-Wāfī bi-l-wafayāt,* 19:416.

26. On him, see *GAS,* 1:95. The Prophet's biography had been compiled by Ibn Isḥāq and redacted by Ibn Hishām.

27. On al-Athram, see *GAL,* 1:107, where he is described characteristically as al-Aṣma'ī's student, without any surviving works of his own. On the event, see al-Khaṭīb al-Baghdādī, *Ta'rīkh Baghdād,* 15:341; Ibn al-Anbārī, *Nuzha,* 86/107; and Pedersen, *Arabic Book,* 44, based on a later source.

28. Yāqūt, *Mu'jam al-udabā',* 15:77; Ṣafadī, *al-Wāfī bi-l-wafayāt,* 22:214–215.

29. Ismā'īl headed the bureaus of chancellery, secret correspondence (*sirr*), and estates under Caliph al-Rashīd's vizier al-Faḍl b. al-Rabī' (187–193/803–809) and the bureau of *sirr* under the same vizier under Caliph al-Amīn (193–198/809–814). See Dominique Sourdel, *Le vizirat 'abbāside de 749 à 936 (132 à 324 de l'Hégire)* (Damascus: Institut Français de Damas, 1959–1960), 1:185–186, 190–191. The works of Abū 'Ubayda included linguistic issues in Scripture and the Prophetic tradition, pre-Islamic and Islamic history, poetry, proverbs, grammar and linguistic solecisms, and lexicographical monographs. See the survey in chapter 1, section "Dramatis Personae."

30. Khaṭīb al-Baghdādī, *Ta'rīkh Baghdād,* 13:594–595; Ibn al-Qifṭī, *Inbāh al-ruwāt,* 2:319–320. A slightly shorter version appears in Ibn al-Anbārī, *Nuzha,* 126–127/159–160; Yāqūt, *Mu'jam al-udabā',* 15:77–78; Ṣafadī, *al-Wāfī bi-l-wafayāt,* 22:214.

31. This is the only case encountered so far of distributed copying of single books, though in large and rapid copying commissions several scribes are often mentioned as being engaged together.

32. See Max Weisweiler, "Das Amt des Mumstamlī in der arabischen Wissenschaft," *Oriens* 4 (1951), 27–57.

33. Ibn al-Qifṭī, *Inbāh al-ruwāt,* 2:319–320.

34. See Yāqūt, *Muʿjam al-udabāʾ*, 18:40–94, esp. 42; Pederson, *Arabic Book*, 50.

35. On ʿUbaydallāh b. Mūsā, see note 25 and see previous section "The Stationer-Disciple." On Khalaf b. Hishām al-Bazzāz, see *GAS*, 1:12, where his *nisba* is given as al-Bazzār (not to be confused with the famous traditionist Muḥammad b. al-Muẓaffar al-Bazzāz, d. 286 / 899; *GAS*, 1:204–205) and Melchert and Afsaruddin, "Reciters," 4:389. On Abū Bakr al-Ḥumaydī, see *GAS*, 1:101–102. On Abū Nuʿaym al-Faḍl Ibn Dhakwān, see *GAS*, 1:101 (where his patronym is given as Ibn Dukayn). On Isḥāq Ibn Rāhawayh, see *GAS*, 1:109–110 (he collected an enormous amount of Ḥadīth, both in writing and by memorization, claiming to know all his books by heart, and it was he who suggested to al-Bukhārī to summarize all extant Ḥadīth collections). On Dāwūd b. Rāshid [al-Khwārazmī], see Ṣafadī, *al-Wāfī bi-l-wafayāt*, 13:470 (where his patronym is given as Rashīd). On the litterateur and essayist al-Jāḥiẓ, see Charles Pellat, al-Djāḥiẓ," in *EI2*, 3:385–387. On Abū Dāwūd al-Sijistānī (not to be confused with the grammarian with the same *nisba*), see *GAS*, 1:149–152. On Abū Yaḥyā ʿAbd al-Karīm b. al-Haytham al-Dayrʿaqūlī, see Ṣafadī, *al-Wāfī bi-l-wafayāt*, 19:96; and al-Khaṭīb al-Baghdādī, *Taʾrīkh Baghdād*, 11:78 (the short entry mentions nonetheless that "he wrote a lot"). On Muḥammad b. Jarīr al-Ṭabarī, see *GAS*, 1:323–328.

36. The cases in which a stationer's *samāʿ* from the author of the book(s) he reproduces is mentioned are 26 / 7, 27 / 1, 29 / 4, 31 / 5, and 35 / 1. In the other cases (28 / 7, 28 / 9, 32 / 3, and 33 / 11), no such audition is mentioned.

37. Yaḥyā b. Yaḥyā b. Kathīr al-Maṣmūdī, an Andalusian jurisconsult of Berber descent, produced one the most widespread and commented recensions of the Ḥadīth collection *al-Muwaṭṭaʾ* by Mālik b. Anas (d. 179 / 796). See *GAS*, 1:459.

38. On him and his brother, a reputed Qurʾān reciter, see note 19.

39. Mālik b. Sulaymān al-Harawī is not found in the major biographical dictionaries. Saʿīd b. Manṣūr is the author of a less well-known but very early Ḥadīth collection. See *GAS*, 2:104; and Muḥammad Z. Siddiqi, *Ḥadīth Literature: Its Origin, Development, and Special Features* (Cambridge: Islamic Texts Society, 1993), 71.

40. See Nefeli Papoutsakis, *Desert Travel as a Form of Boasting: A Study of Dū r-Rumma's Poetry* (Wiesbaden, Germany: Harrassowitz, 2009), 6.

41. For the *rāwī* of Muslim b. al-Walīd, see Iṣbahānī, *Aghānī*, 18:328; on the *rāwī* of ʿUmāra b. Aqīl, see 23:440–441 and chapter 1, section "Intellectual Property versus Entrepreneurship."

42. He is not found in the major biographical dictionaries and not to be confused with Muḥammad b. Habīb, the Baghdadian philologist and historian of pre-Islamic and early Islamic lore and genealogy, author of *al-Muḥabbar*, and source of the *Naqāʾiḍ Jarīr wa-l-Farazdaq*. See Ilse Lichtenstaedter, "Muḥammad b. Ḥabīb," in *EI2*, 7:401–402.

43. See Gruendler, "Stability and Change," 111–112.

44. See Beatrice Gruendler, "al-ʿAskarī, Abū Ahmad," in *EI3*, first published online and in print 2009, consulted accessed December 31, 2019, http://dx.doi.org /10.1163/1573-3912_ei3_COM_22689.

45. Ibn al-Nadīm, *Fihrist,* 62 / pt. 1, 159.

46. Ibid., 62 / pt. 1, 159–160; al-Sīrāfī, *Akhbār al-naḥwiyyīn,* 68; Ibn al-Anbārī, *Nuzha,* 127 / 160; slightly shortened, Ibn al-Qifṭī, *Inbāh al-ruwāt,* 4:320. Ibn al-Nadīm appends Ibn al-Sikkīt's explanation of the proverb.

47. "He had in his possession corrected books . . . and vocalized [the texts] he recorded in them" *(kāna ṣāḥiba kutubin muṣaḥḥahatin . . . wa-ḍabaṭa mā ḍammanahā);* Yāqūt, *Muʿjam al-udabāʾ,* 15:77; Ṣafadī, *al-Wāfī bi-l-wafayāt,* 22:214–215. On the reductive writing system and the consequences associated with its usage, see Gruendler, "Stability and Change."

48. Yāqūt, *Muʿjam al-udabāʾ,* 15:77; Ṣafadī, *al-Wāfī bi-l-wafayāt,* 22:214–215.

49. Yāqūt, *Muʿjam al-udabāʾ,* 15:77.

50. Jāḥiẓ, *Ḥayawān,* 1:41.

51. On al-Rabīʿ, see *GAS,* 1:487–488. On the colophon, see the editor's introduction in Muḥammad b. Idrīs al-Shāfiʿī, *al-Risāla,* ed. Aḥmad Muḥammad Shākir (Cairo: Maṭbaʿat Muṣṭafā al-Bābī al-Ḥalabī, 1940), 17. See also the bilingual edition, al-Shāfiʿī, *The Epistle on Legal Theory,* ed. and trans. Joseph E. Lowry (New York: New York University Press, 2013), esp. xxx–xxxi.

52. The *mustamlī* was a scholar's assistant, and the designation derives from the verb *istamlā,* "to ask for, take, or receive dictation." Such an assistant would take a scholar's work down in writing and therefore needed to have a degree of knowledge of the subject. At times he also fulfilled other services, such as passing on the lecture of the scholar to a large crowd (*muballigh, mulqī*) or dictating his work to students in a separate class (*muktib, muʿīd*), so the activities were broader than the profession's literal designation. *Mustamlī*s might specialize in Prophetic tradition, *adab,* or linguistic disciplines. In these aspects and their bridging of scholarship and craft, they resembled the *warrāqūn,* and some also served simultaneously as *warrāq* to their employer. The difference between *mustamlī* and *warrāq* was that the dissemination of the former was from oral to written text, and of the latter from written to written text. See Weisweiler, "Amt des Mumstamlī."

53. Ḥabīb Zayyāt instead sees a sequence in *wirāqa* from copying the Qurʾān, then Ḥadith, and then other topics. See Zayyāt, *Wirāqa,* 10.

54. Cf. also Maḥmūd al-Warrāq, *Dīwān,* ed. Walīd Qaṣṣāb (Beirut: Dār Ṣādir, 1422 / 2001), 131, where the poem appears in six verses with slight variations and is included among those attributed to the poet in literary sources.

55. For his writings, see note 15.

56. See Ibn al-Nadīm, *Fihrist,* 209 / pt. 1, 582 for a stationer of al-Jāḥiẓ, Abū Yaḥyā Zakariyyāʾ b. Yaḥyā b. Sulaymān, besides stationer no. 32 / 3. Two servants of the historian al-Wāqidī (d. 207 / 823) copied day and night, lowering the prices of his books, which had sold before for as much as 2,000 *dīnār*s each; see 111 / pt. 1, 308. Al-Wāqidī also had a secretary, Muḥammad b. Saʿd (d. 230 / 845), who transmitted his works and turned his master's compilations *(taṣnīfāt)* into redacted

books *(ta'līfāt).* He is best known for his biographical dictionary of Ḥadīth transmitters; see 111–112 / pt. 1, 310; and J. W. Fück, "Ibn Sa'd," in *EI2,* 3:922–924.

57. See Charles Pellat, "Mathālib," in *EI2,* 6:828–829.

58. The trend to assert the cultural superiority of Iranians over non-Arabs (referred to as *shu'ūbiyya*), nonetheless found expression in the Arabic language. Susanne Enderwitz, "Shu'ūbiyya," in *EI2,* 9:513–516.

59. The early Abbasids had essentially adopted the Sasanian administrative and bureaucratic state apparatus, including the function of the secretary. Gutas, *Greek Thought, Arabic Culture,* 56.

60. Ibn al-Nadīm, *Fihrist,* 183 / pt. 1, 325–327; Yāqūt, *Mu'jam al-udabā',* 12:192–196; Ṣafadī, *al-Wāfī bi-l-wafayāt,* 19:558–559.

61. The *bayt al-ḥikma* was not, as has often been claimed, an academy or a center for translation activities. Dimitri Gutas and Kevin van Bladel, "Bayt al-Ḥikma," in *EI3,* first published online and in print 2009, accessed February 22, 2013, http://referenceworks.brillonline.com/entries/encyclopaedia-of-islam-3/bayt-al-hikma-COM_22882.

62. Aḥmad b. Abī Khālid acted as al-Ma'mūn's vizier without carrying the title, from 202 / 818 until his death. A onetime Barmakid protégé, he gained the good graces of the subsequent vizier al-Faḍl b. Sahl (d. 202 / 818), whom he succeeded. Sourdel, *Vizirat 'abbāside,* 1:219–225, 732; and Dominique Sourdel, "Aḥmad ibn Abī Khālid al-Aḥwal," in *EI2,* 1:271–272.

63. Jahshiyārī, *Wuzarā',* ed. Ibrāhīm Ṣāliḥ, 479; the emphasis is the author's. The event does not appear in the preserved portion of this work, but in the appendix of Ṣāliḥ's edition, based on Yāqūt, *Mu'jam al-udabā',* 12:192–193. See also Zayyāt, *Wirāqa,* 33–34; and Pedersen, *Arabic Book,* 49.

64. Often, a request for dictation was made openly. See, e.g., Iṣbahānī, *Aghānī,* 3:184–185 (the transmitters Khalaf b. Abī 'Amr b. al-'Alā' and Khalaf al-Aḥmar requested diction from the poet Bashshār); 4:16–17 (in the circle of the philologist Ibn al-A'rābī, an unidentified man received recitation of *madīḥ* by the poet Abū l-'Amaythal and wrote it down); 4:43–44, 46–47 (Ja'far al-Muhallabī asks Abū l-'Amaythal to recite a *zuhd* poem and takes it down); 4:48–49 (a passing old man, overhearing Abū l-'Amaythal's recitation of a *zuhd* poem in a mosque, writes it down); 10:67 (in his gathering, 'Ubaydallāh b. Sulaymān b. Wahb has verses of two secretaries from his family recited by another member of the circle and recorded in writing); and 10:94–95 (in an audience with caliph al-Amīn, the aging poet Marwān b. Abī Ḥafṣa (d. after 240 / 854 or 247 / 861) is consulted about poetic criticism and answers in verse, and the narrator, an *adīb,* writes this down). Occasionally such a request was made in private, e.g., the philologist al-Mubarrad, having heard an excellent wine poem by Abū Tammām, visits the poet-prince Ibn al Mu'tazz, who dictates it to him from memory on request; see al-Ṣūlī, *Life and Times of Abū Tammām* § 91.1–2 / *Akhbār Abī Tammām,* 184.

65. See Iṣbahānī, *Aghānī,* 23:433–434.

66. See al-Ṣūlī, *Life and Times of Abū Tammām,* §61.4 / *Akhbār Abī Tammām,* 114 and chapter 2, section "The Accusation, Version Two."

67. See al-Ṣūlī, *Life and Times of Abū Tammām,* §10.1–2 / *Akhbār Abī Tammām,* 15–16 and chapter 2, section "Diʿbil on Abū Tammām."

68. For the first definition of the Arabic notebook, see Schoeler, *Genesis of Literature in Islam,* 21–24, and in further detail, Schoeler, *The Oral and the Written,* 28–44.

69. For poets' collected works, see Ibn al-Muʿtazz, *Ṭabaqāt al-shuʿarāʾ,* 47, and on Abū Tammān, see 285. As for ancient poetry, Ibn al-Muʿtazz states that it circulated widely and people were bored with it (86). See also chapter 2, section "Diʿbil on Abū Tammām."

70. The change from gold to silver currency implies a twenty- to twenty-five–fold drop in price. See al-Ṣūlī, *Life and Times of Abū Tammām,* §27 / *Akhbār Abī Tammām,* 55–56.

71. Bloom, *Paper before Print,* 57, 79.

72. The event must have occurred prior to the death of al-Riyāshī (d. c. 257 / 871), who appears in the account.

73. However, as Leder, "Grenzen der Rekonstruktion" has shown, it cannot be assumed that every title cited stands for an actual book.

74. On the definition of *abjad,* see Peter T. Daniels, "Fundamentals of Grammatology," *JAOS* 110 (1990): 727–730.

75. On this genre, see ʿAbdattawwāb, *Laḥn al-ʿāmma;* and Georgine Ayoub, "Laḥn," in *Encyclopedia of Arabic Language and Linguistics,* ed. Kees Versteegh (Leiden, Netherlands: Brill, 2007), 2:628–634.

76. On him, see *GAS,* 8:129–136, 9:137–138.

77. Grammarians' prestige was reflected in their employment as tutors by the elite. After al-Kisāʾī (d. 189 / 805) and al-Farrāʾ, the Kufan Ibn al-Sikkīt still served as tutor for a caliph's sons; among the Basrans, Quṭrub, Ibn al-Aʿrābī, al-Riyāshī, and Abū ʿUbayda tutored sons of high dignitaries. See Gérard Troupeau, "La grammaire à Bagdād du IX au XIIIe siècle," *Arabica* 9 (1962): 397–405; and Sellheim, "Gelehrte und Gelehrsamkeit," 59–61, 63–64.

78. Ibn al-Sikkīt, *Iṣlāḥ al-mantiq,* ed. A. M. Shākir and ʿAbdassalām M. Hārūn (Cairo: Dār al-Maʿārif, 1368 / 1949).

79. "He was the better of the two men in [book] writing" *(kāna aḥsana l-rajulayni taʾlīfan);* Lughawī, *Marātib al-naḥwiyyīn,* 95. See also al-Marzubānī, *Muqtabas,* 319–320; Ibn Khallikān, *Wafayāt al-aʿyān,* 6:395.

80. The manuscript, Library of al-Manṣūra no. 4580, bearing a reading statement of the grammarian Ibn Fāris (d. 395 / 1004) dated 372 / 982 and which was used for the printed edition, seems to have been lost, however.

81. Although the work exists only in a later versification and countless commentaries, the sources unanimously credit Quṭrub with its invention. See Gruendler, "Stability and Change," 113–116.

82. Yāqūt, *Mu'jam al-udabā'*, 19:52–54. On *qimaṭr,* see Gacek, *Arabic Manuscript Tradition,* 119.

83. He was 'Abdallāh b. Muḥammad b. Rustam al-Lughawī. See Zubaydī, *Ṭabaqāt al-naḥwiyyīn,* 208; al-Khaṭīb al-Baghdādī, *Ta'rīkh Baghdād,* 16:398; Ibn al-Qifṭī, *Inbāh al-ruwāt,* 4:394. He also appears in the chain of transmission in al-Tibrīzī's revision. See Ibn al-Sikkīt, *Iṣlāḥ al-mantiq,* 3. On the profession of *mustamlī,* see note 52.

84. Sīrāfī, *Akhbār al-naḥwiyyīn,* 68; Ibn al-Nadīm, *Fihrist,* 64 / pt. 1, 166–167; Ibn al-Anbārī, *Nuzha,* 153 / 199–200. Note the following variants: "read [*yaqra'u*] the book," and "I [i.e., Ibn Durayd] told [al-Riyāshī] what he had said" (Ibn al-Nadīm, *Fihrist,* 64 / pt. 1, 166–167); "He was told about what that man had said" (Ibn al-Anbārī, *Nuzha,* 153 / 199–200). A *jerboa* is desert rodent that appears on the typical menu of the Bedouin. For a humorous account of a Bedouin inviting a field-working grammarian to a meal of *jerboa,* see Beatrice Gruendler, "*Al-ḥanīn ilā l-awṭān* and Its Alternatives in Classical Arabic Literature," in *Representations and Visions of Homeland in Modern Arabic Literature,* ed. Sebastian Günther and Stephan Milich (Hildesheim, Germany: Georg Olms, 2016), 1–41.

85. On him, see *GAS,* 8:96–97.

86. Ibn al-Anbārī, *Nuzha,* 153 / 199.

87. Zubaydī, *Ṭabaqāt al-naḥwiyyīn,* 97.

88. Thus, al-Shaybānī (d. c. 205 / 820) allegedly did not share his dictionary: "His *Kitāb al-Jīm* has no transmission, because Abū 'Amr [al-Shaybānī] withheld it from people, and no one read it before him" (Lughawī, *Marātib al-naḥwiyyīn,* 91–92). Werner Diem, "Das Kitāb al-Ǧīm des Abū 'Amr aš-Šaibānī: Ein Beitrag zur arabischen Lexikographie" (PhD diss., Universität München, 1968), 33–34, 92, confirms the book's lack of a reception. Likewise, Abū 'Amr al-Harawī (d. 255 / 869) kept his similarly titled work to himself until it was destroyed in the flooding of an army camp; see Ibn al-Anbārī, *Nuzha,* 151–152 / 196–197. The abovementioned *Kitāb Sībawayhi* was transmitted only after the death of its author; see Monique Bernards, *Changing Traditions: Al-Mubarrad's Refutation of Sībawayh and the Subsequent Reception of the* Kitāb (Leiden, Netherlands: Brill, 1977), 5.

89. See Ibn al-Nadīm, *Fihrist,* 58 / pt. 1, 166–167 for the former amount, and al-Khaṭīb al-Baghdādī, *Ta'rīkh Baghdād,* 14:22–23 for the latter. See, further, Zubaydī, *Ṭabaqāt al-naḥwiyyīn,* 99; Ibn al-Anbārī, *Nuzha,* 153 / 199.

90. Lughawī, *Marātib al-naḥwiyyīn,* 67.

91. Zubaydī, *Ṭabaqāt al-naḥwiyyīn,* 97; al-Khaṭīb al-Baghdādī, *Ta'rīkh Baghdād,* 14:22–23.

92. Zubaydī, *Ṭabaqāt al-naḥwiyyīn,* 97.

93. Ibn al-Anbārī, *Nuzha,* 154 / 201.

94. Lughawī, *Marātib al-naḥwiyyīn,* 76. The epithet "Khūzistānī," given to the Persian-born Sībawayhi, is meant to be derogatory. Ibn al-Sikkīt (hailing from a

village in Khuzistan, a region in southwestern Iran) once identified himself in a class with the same unflattering non-Arab *nisba,* and the inquiring teacher, al-Farrā', felt ashamed to have exposed an honest student. Ibn al-Nadīm, *Fihrist,* 79 (here misread as *khūdhī*) / pt. 1, 219; Ibn Khallikān, *Wafayāt al-aʿyān,* 6:396.

95. Ibn Khallikān, *Wafayāt al-aʿyān,* 6:396, 400; al-Khaṭīb al-Baghdādī, *Ta'rīkh Baghdād,* 16:400; Ibn al-Qifṭī, *Inbāh al-ruwāt,* 4:53; Ibn al-Anbārī, *Nuzha,* 139–140 / 179; Ibn al-Sikkīt, *Iṣlāḥ al-mantiq,* 9.

96. Bernards, *Changing Traditions,* 54, 87–93. All subsequent studies in the field would refer to it.

97. Al-Sīrāfī, who also recorded the above dispute in the book market, noted carefully who read Sībawayhi's *Kitāb,* which portion of it, how many times, and under whose direction.

98. Mathematically, twelve readings are possible, but certain vowel combinations (*fiʿil, fiʿul, fuʿil*) rarely occur in the Arabic language. Wolfdietrich Fischer, *Grammatik des klassischen Arabisch* (Wiesbaden, Germany: Harrassowitz, 1987), 35, §62.

99. Ibn Khalllikān, *Wafayāt al-aʿyān,* 6:400.

100. Al-Tibrīzī remarks in the preface of his revision, "Most of what it contains is the language in use, which one must know and take care to memorize." Ibn al-Sikkīt, *Iṣlāḥ al-mantiq,* 13.

101. James E. Montgomery, "Of Models and Amanuenses: The Remarks on the *Qaṣīda* in Ibn Qutayba's *Kitāb al-Shiʿr wa-l-shuʿarā',*" in *Islamic Reflections and Arabic Musings: Studies in Honour of Professor Alan Jones,* ed. Robert Hoyland and Philip F. Kennedy (Oxford: Gibb Memorial Trust, 2004), 1–47, esp. 40.

102. Such a procedure is suggested by Tharwat ʿUkāsha for two of Ibn Qutayba's other books and deserves further investigation. Where Ibn Qutayba criticizes a predecessor, such as Abū ʿUbayd's *Gharīb al-ḥadīth,* in his own work on the subject, he does so openly. See Gérard Lecomte, *Ibn Qutayba (mort en 276/889): L'homme, son oeuvre, ses idées* (Damascus: Institut Français de Damas, 1965), 203. This should not, however, be regarded as plagiarism, as the rearranging of transmitted material was a standard practice of scholarship as well as *adab,* and the failure to mention his sources (as was usual in scholarship) may have been the practical choice of an author writing for a broader public that was not interested in this.

103. Ibn al-Sikkīt, *Iṣlāḥ al-mantiq,* 12.

104. Al-Tibrīzī, *Kitāb Tahdhīb Iṣlāḥ al-manṭiq,* ed. Muḥammad Badr al-Dīn al-Naʿsānī (Cairo: Maṭbaʿat al-Saʿāda, 1325 / 1907). See Ibn al-Sikkīt, *Iṣlāḥ al-mantiq,* 13–14.

105. Thus Lecomte describes Ibn Qutayba (*Ibn Qutayba,* 64).

106. See Elias Muhanna, *The World in a Book: Al-Nuwayrī and the Islamic Encyclopedic Tradition* (Princeton, NJ: Princeton University Press, 2018), 108–112. For an English excerpt, see Shihab al-Dīn al-Nuwayrī, *The Ultimate Ambition in the Arts of Erudition: A Compendium of Knowledge from the Classical Islamic World,* trans. Elias Muhanna (New York: Penguin Books, 2016), 103–115, 289.

4. BOOK OWNERS AND READERS

1. He produced well-corrected books and contacted scholars with them (*ṣāḥibu kutubin muṣaḥḥaḥatin laqiya bihā l-ʿulamāʾ*). As author, he composed *Mathālib al-ʾArab, al-Nawādir,* and *Gharīb al-ḥadīth. GAS,* 1:271; al-Khaṭīb al-Baghdādī, *Taʾrīkh Baghdād,* 14:269, no. 671.

2. See Ibn al-Nadīm, *Fihrist,* 125 / pt. 1, 344–346, and 130 / pt. 1, 361–362.

3. Ibid., 123 / pt. 1, 339, and 130 / pt. 1, 361–361.

4. On early Arabic libraries, see Bloom, "Literary and Oral Cultures," 668–681, esp. 678; Youssef Eche, *Les bibliothèques arabes publiques et semi-publiques en Mésopotamie, en Syrie, et en Égypte au moyen age* (Damascus: Institut Français de Damas, 1967); and Olga Pinto, "The Libraries of the Arabs during the Time of the Abbasids," *Islamic Culture* 3 (1929): 210–248. On the role of libraries in intellectual life, see Toorawa, *Ibn Abī Ṭāhir Ṭayfūr,* 13–14. For recent monographs on later libraries, see Konrad Hirschler, *Medieval Damascus: Plurality and Diversity in an Arabic Library: The Ashrafīya Library Catalogue* (Edinburgh: Edinburgh University Press, 2017); and Boris Liebrenz, *Die Rifāʿīya aus Damaskus: Eine Privatbibliothek im osmanischen Syrien und ihr kulturelles Umfeld* (Leiden, Netherlands: Brill, 2016).

5. Touati, *L'armoire à sagesse,* 47–48. For values and conversion rates between *dirhams* and *dīnārs*, see Chapter 1, section "Intellectual Property versus Entrepreneurship."

6. For an in-depth study of the composition and agenda of this magnum opus by al-Jāḥiẓ, including a detailed table of contents and a partial translation of the introduction, see James Montgomery, *Al-Jāḥiẓ: In Praise of Books* (Edinburgh: Edinburgh University Press, 2016).

7. For the information on mulberry bast paper as more resistant to bookworms, I am indebted to Adam Gacek (personal communication).

8. Jāḥiẓ, *Ḥayawān,* 1:55–56. On this section, see also Montgomery, *Al-Jāḥiẓ,* 164 and 447.

9. Jāḥiẓ, *Ḥayawān,* 1:52–54. See also Montgomery, *Al-Jāḥiẓ,* 447.

10. One of al-Maʾmūn's leading generals and governor of Jibāl, Ādharbāyjān, and Armenia, he helped put down the revolt of Bābak al-Khurramī before he was himself executed for sedition.

11. Iṣbahānī, *Aghānī,* 23:427–429, citing the poet himself via Muḥammad b. ʿAbdallāh b. Ādam al-ʿAbdī via al-ʿAnazī (d. 290 / 902), via al-Ṣūlī (d. 335 / 946 or 947). On Farwa b. Ḥumayḍa al-Asadī, see *GAS,* 2:526.

12. See Gutas, *Greek Thought, Arab Culture.*

13. Miskawayh, *al-Ḥikma al-khālida: Jāvīdān khirad,* ed. ʿAbdarraḥmān Badawī (Tehran: Intishārāt Dānishgāh Tehran, 1377 / 1999; rpt. of Cairo, 1952), 5–6. On this work, see Charles Pellat, "D̲j̲āwīd̲h̲ān K̲h̲irad," in *EI2* supp., 263–264.

14. Of Zoroastrian background and having grown up in a village near Kūfa, al-Ḥasan b. Sahl became secretary of taxes under his brother al-Faḍl's vizierate (196–202 / 812–817), then his successor as vizier (202–211 / 817–826) and governor for al-Ma'mūn (r. 197–218 / 813–833). See Dominique Sourdel, "Al-Ḥasan b. Sahl," in *EI2,* 3:243–244; Sourdel, *Vizirat ʿabbāside,* 1:214–218.

15. Miskawayh, *Jāvīdān khirad,* 21.

16. For a published library catalogue from the eighth / fourteenth century, see Hirschler, *Medieval Damascus.*

17. Namely, the one by ʿAlī b. Muḥammad al-Kūfī, to whom he also devotes an entry describing him as avid transmitter and book collector (*rāwiya wa-jammāʿatu kutubin*). Ibn al-Nadīm, *Fihrist,* 101 / pt. 1, 277, and 87 / pt. 1, 241. Another written source is Ibn Muqla's lists of eloquent men (*Fihrist,* 138 / pt. 1, 389).

18. Miskawayh, *Jāvīdān khirad,* 21–22.

19. The son of a Zoroastrian father who converted to Islam, al-Faḍl himself converted in 190 / 806 (six years before taking the vizierate). He is the most Iranian and pro-*mawālī* of the Abbasid viziers and was therefore stopped by the Arab and ʿIrāqī aristocracy. See Dominique Sourdel, "Al-Faḍl b. Sahl b. Zadhānfarūkh," in *EI2,* 2:731–732.

20. Kābulistān is equated with Kābul by the geographer and historian Yāqūt; see his *Muʿjam al-buldān,* ed. Muhammad ʿAbdarraḥmān al-Marʿashlī (Beirut: Dār Iḥyā' al-Turāth alʿArabī, n.d.), 4:111.

21. Miskawayh, *Jāvīdān khirad,* 19–20. The Arch is the last standing remnant of the Sasanian palace in this former capital of their empire. It is also the subject of a famous ode of the poet al-Buḥturī, who interpreted it as a warning of the ephemerality of earthly rule. The "Great Persian" refers to the mythical Iranian king Hushang (Ūshahanj) as whose testament (*waṣiyya,* 21) Ibn Miskawayh identifies the original *Jāvīdān khirad* and quotes it in his preface (6–18).

22. Ibid., 20–21.

23. See note 13.

24. Ibid., 6–7.

25. See, for example, al-Aṣmaʿī asking students for the poetry of al-Sayyid al-Ḥimyarī. Iṣbahānī, *Aghānī,* 7:227, 230. For his borrowing of Abū ʿUbayda's *Explanatory Re-writing,* see Chapter 1, section "A Book Author."

26. See Gruendler, "Abbasid Poets and the Qur'ān," 137–169, esp. 139, 159.

27. The term *zandaqa* means more precisely dualism, but it was used in Abbasid times as a catchall for heretical beliefs.

28. Ibn al-Muʿtazz, *Ṭabaqāt al-shuʿarā',* 22.

29. See Gruendler, "Farewell to Ghazal," 137–172, esp. 145–146.

30. Ṣūlī, *Life and Times of Abū Tammām,* xiv. The poet would compose another ode on the public burning of Bābak's corpse and those of two other rebels suspended on crosses (xiv).

31. Ṭabarī, *Ta'rīkh al-rusul wa-l-mulūk,* 9:104–110, esp. 107–108. As for the other cited book, *Kitāb Marwak,* the printed edition spells it as *Kitāb Mazdak,* but the former spelling has been established by Jaakko Hämeen-Anttila, who identified it as another Sasanian book of wisdom. Hämeen-Anttila, *Khwadāynāmag,* 35–36, 36n.

32. See Ibn Qutayba, *Adab al-kātib* (Cairo: Maktabat al-Saʿāda, 1382 / 1963), 2–5; and Gérard Lecomte, "L'introduction du Kitāb *Adab al-kātib* d'Ibn Qutayba," in *Mélanges Louis Massignon,* ed. Institut Français de Damas (Damascus: Institut Français de Damas, 1957), 3:47–65.

33. On the illustrations of *Kalila wa-Dimna,* see Anna Contadini, *A World of Beasts: A Thirteenth-Century Illustrated Arabic Book on Animals (the Kitāb Naʿt al-Ḥayawān) in the Ibn Bakhtīshūʿ Tradition* (Leiden, Netherlands: Brill, 2012); Bernard O'Kane, *Early Persian Painting: Kalīla and Dimna Manuscripts of the Late Fourteenth Century* (London: Tauris, 2003); Julian Raby, "Between Sogdia and the Mamluks: A Note on the Earliest Illustrations to *Kalīla wa Dimna,*" *Oriental Art* 33 (1987): 381–398; and the Islamic Painted Page, a database of Islamic Arts of the Book, Universität Hamburg, accessed March 9, 2020, http://www.islamicpaintedpage.com. The dating of the Geniza fragment is supplied by Dr. Ben Outhwaite, Head of Genizah Research Unit, Cambridge University Library. For a comparative chart of scripts of dated third / ninth century codices, see Déroche, "Manuscrits arabes datés," reproduced as fig. 1a and b.

34. See Hämeen-Anttila, *Khwadāynāmag,* 36.

35. For three book addicts—al-Jāḥiẓ, the vizier al-Fatḥ b. Khāqān, and the judge Ismāʿīl b. Isḥāq—see Ibn al-Nadīm, *Fihrist,* 130 / pt. 1, 361 and 208 / pt. 1, 578 (the account recurs with different *isnād*), and a further—the judge and theologian al-Ḥasan b. Ziyād al-Lu'lu'ī (d. 204 / 819)—Jāḥiẓ, *Ḥayawān,* 1:52–53 and Montgomery, *Al-Jāḥiẓ,* 446.

36. For more detail, see Introduction, section "Book Formats, Literary Sources, and Method."

37. See Francesco Gabrieli, "Ibn al-Muqaffaʿ, in *EI2,* 3:883–885; Michael Cooperson, "Ibn al-Muqaffaʿ," in *The Biographical Encyclopedia of Islamic Philosophy,* ed. Oliver Leaman (London: Thoemmes, 2006), 1:280–286; and István T. Kristó-Nagy, *La pensée d'Ibn al-Muqaffaʿ: Un "agent double" dans le monde persan et arabe* (Paris: Éditions de Paris, 2013). On the ascription of the translation of the *Logic (al-Manṭiq)* to him, see Kristó-Nagy, *La pensée,* 175–179.

38. Added chapters mentioned by al-Yaʿqūbī are "The Trial of Dimna" and "The Traveller and the Goldsmith," here called "The Turtle, the Tiger, the Monkey, and the Carpenter," elsewhere also referred to as "The Snake, the Monkey, and the Tiger." The chapter sequence is close to type D after the classification of François de Blois, attested for instance in the MS Paris, Bibliothèque nationale de France arabe 3466, dated 845 / 1450.

39. For the quote, see al-Yaʿqūbī, *Works of Ibn Wāḍiḥ al-Yaʿqūbī,* 2:351. See also 1:45, 3:1101–1102.

40. Ibn al-Nadīm, *Fihrist,* 364 / pt. 2, 325–326.

41. Al-Jāḥiẓ, *Dhamm akhlāq al-kuttāb,* in *Rasāʾil al-Jāḥiẓ,* ed. ʿAbdassalām M. Hārūn (Beirut: Dār al-Jīl, 1411 / 1991) 2:183–209. The *Book of Mazdak* was also translated by Ibn al-Muqaffaʿ. For the correction of the title to *Kitāb Marwak,* see note 31.

42. Ibn al-Nadīm, *Fihrist,* 140 / pt. 1, 391.

43. Ibid., 364 / pt. 2, 326.

44. On the recording of the textual material of the Qurʾān, see Burton, "Collection of the Qurʾān." On the Qurʾān's oral transmission, see Gade, "Recitation of the Qurʾan," Melchert and Afsaruddin. "Reciters of the Qurʾan," and the recent study by Nasser, *The Transmission of the Variant Readings of the Qurʾān.*

45. For an example, see Introduction, note 36.

46. See Dan Sheffield, "New Evidence for the Middle Persian Prototype of *Kalīla wa-Dimna*" (paper presented at the 227th meeting of the American Oriental Society, Los Angeles, March 17–20, 2017).

47. Ibn al-Nadīm, *Fihrist,* 364 / pt. 2, 324.

48. Furthermore, Ibn Miskawayh (*Jāwīdān khirad,* 89–100) culled all the wisdom sayings from that same chapter and retitled them as "*ḥikam al-Hind.*" See Beatrice Gruendler, "Les versions de *Kalīla wa-Dimna:* Une transmission et une circulation mouvantes," in *Énoncés sapientiels et littérature exemplaire: Une intertextualité complexe,* ed. Marie-Sol Ortola (Nancy, France: Éditions Universitaires de Lorraine, 2013), 385–416.

49. On these and related questions regarding *Kalīla wa-Dīmna,* see Beatrice Gruendler et al., "An Interim Report on the Editorial and Analytical Work of the AnonymClassic Project," *Medieval Worlds,* forthcoming.

50. Abū ʿAbdallāh M. b. al-Ḥusayn b. ʿUmar al-Yamanī, *Muḍāhāt Kitāb Kalīla wa-Dimna bi-mā ashbahahā min ashʿār al-ʿarab,* ed. M. Yūsuf Najm (Beirut: Dār al-Thaqāfa, [1961]). The word *zabad* also occurs in the Qurʾān, Sūrat al-Raʿd / 17:13.

51. See Leder, *Story-Telling* and Toral, "Erzählen im arabischen *adab.*"

52. Jāḥiẓ, *Ḥayawān,* 1:57.

53. See also a further anonymous quote about the benefits of books preserving knowledge over time. Ibid., 1:72–73.

54. Ibid., 1:79–82.

55. See Montgomery, *Jāḥiẓ,* 161–171 and 444–451 for the argument and a paraphrase of Jāḥiẓ, *Ḥayawān,* 1:50–62, respectively.

56. This is the book's older Arabic title, based on Persian *Hazār afsāne,* before it became *Alf layla wa-layla.* See Abbott, "A Ninth-Century Fragment" and Aboubakr Chraïbi, *Les Mille et une nuits: Histoire du texte et classification des contes* (Paris: L'Harmattan, 2008), 23–45.

CONCLUSION

1. The waning resistance has been assumed to have been geographically broadly by Gregor Schoeler, whereas Michael Cook finds an even earlier acceptance in most regions, but lingering resistance in the city of Basra. See Schoeler, *The Oral and the Written,* 28–44, translated from "Mündliche Thora und Ḥadīṯ"; Cook, "Opponents of Writing," 447–450, 489–491.

2. Kashouh, *Arabic Versions of the Gospels,* 291–292 (family Q), 462–464 (family T).

3. Notably the MSS Oxford, Bodleian Pococke 400, Paris, Bibliothèque nationale de France, arabe 5881 and arabe 3471. The practice appears in manuscripts since the fourteenth century.

4. See, for instance, the intertwining of written and oral practices shown by Michael T. Clanchy, *From Memory to Written Record: England 1066–1307* (Oxford: Blackwell, 1979); and Joyce Coleman, *Public Reading and Reading Public in Late Medieval England and France* (Cambridge: Cambridge University Press, 1996).

5. See John Guillory, "Genesis of the Media Concept," *Critical Inquiry* 36 (2010): 321–362, esp. 326, 337.

6. On al-Jāḥiẓ, see Montgomery, "Al-Jāḥiẓ's Kitāb al-Bayān wa-l-tabyīn," 128. On Isḥāq b. Ibrāhīm Ibn Wahb al-Kātib, see Paul L. Heck, *The Construction of Knowledge in Islamic Civilization: Qudāma b. Jaʿfar and His Kitāb al-Kharāj wa-ṣināʿat al-kitāba* (Leiden, Netherlands: Brill, 2002), 79–85.

7. For the standard theory, see Bauer, "Arabische Kultur"; and for knowledge classification, Wolfhart Heinrichs, "The Classification of the Sciences and the Consolidation of Philology in Classical Islam," in *Centres of Learning: Learning and Location in Pre-modern Europe and the Near East,* ed. Jan W. Drijvers and Alasdair A. Macdonald (Leiden, Netherlands: Brill, 1995), 119–139.

BIBLIOGRAPHY

PRIMARY SOURCES

al-ʿAbbās b. al-Aḥnaf. *Dīwān*. Edited by M. Ṭarrād. Beirut: Dār al-Kitāb al-ʿArabī, 1997.

Abū Tammām. *Sharḥ Dīwān al-Ḥamāsa li-Abī ʿAlī Aḥmad b. M. b. al-Ḥasan al-Marzūqī*. Edited by Aḥmad Amīn and ʿAbdassalām Hārūn. 4 pts. in 2 vols. Cairo: Maṭbaʿat Lajnat at-Taʾlīf wa-l-Tarjama wa-l-Nashr, 1951–1953. Reprint, Beirut: Dār al-Jīl, 1991.

———. *Dīwān bi-Sharḥ al-Khaṭīb al-Tibrīzī*. Edited by Muḥammad ʿAbduh ʿAzzām. 4 vols. Cairo: Dār al-Maʿārif, 1987.

Abū l-Ṭayyib al-Lughawī. *See* al-Lughawī.

Abū l-ʿAmaythal ʿAbdallāh b. Khulayd. *Kitāb al-Maʾthūr fīmā ttafaqa lafẓuhū wa-khtalafa maʿnāhu*, published as *Kitāb al-Maʾthūr: Das Buch der Wörter mit gleichem Laut und verschiedener Bedeutung*. Edited by Fritz Krenkow. London: Probsthain, 1925.

Abū ʿUbayd. *The Book of Finance*. Translated by Noor Mohammad Ghiffari. New Delhi: Adam Publishers, 2007.

———. *The Book of Revenue*. Translated by Imran Ahsan Khan Nyazee. Reading, UK: Garnet, 2002.

———. *Gharīb al-ḥadīth.* Edited by Ḥusayn Muḥammad M. Sharaf. 6 pts. Cairo: Majmaʿ al-Lugha al-ʿArabiyya, 1999.

———. *Al-Gharīb al-muṣannaf.* Edited by Ramaḍān ʿAbdattawwāb. Cairo: Maktabat al-Thaqāfa al-Dīniyya, 1989.

———. *Al-Amwāl.* Edited by M. Ḥāmid al-Fiqī. Cairo: Maṭbaʿat ʿAbd al-Laṭīf al-Ḥijāzī, [1934–1935]. / Edited by Muḥammad Khalīl Harrās. Cairo: Maktabat al-Kulliyyāt al-Azhariyya, 1388 / 1968. Reprint, Beirut: Dār al-Kutub al-ʿIlmiyya, 1986. / Edited by Dār al-Ḥadātha. Beirut: Dār al-Ḥadātha, 1408 / 1988.

———. *Al-Amthāl al-sāʾira.* Published in alphabetical order as first part of *al-Tuḥfa al-bahiyya wa-l-ṭurfa al-shāhiyya.* Istanbul: Maṭbaʿat al-Jawāʾib, 1885. / Edited by Abd al-Majīd Qaṭāmish. Damascus: Dār al-Maʾmūn li-l-Turāth, 1980. / As *Faṣl al-maqāl fī sharḥ Kitāb al-Amthāl.* Edited by Iḥsān ʿAbbās and ʿAbdalmajīd ʿAbdīn, with commentary by Abū ʿUbayd al-Bakrī. Beirut: Dār al-Amāna, 1971.

Abū ʿUbayda. *Majāz al-Qurʾān.* Edited by Fuat Sezgin., 2 vols. Cairo: al-Khānjī, 1954–1962. / Edited by Fuat Sezgin. Facsimile ed. Frankfurt: Institute for the History of Arabic-Islamic Science at the Johann Wolfgang Goethe University, 2010.

———. *Al-Khayl.* Edited by Fritz Krenkow. Hyderabad, India, 1939–1940. Reprint, 1981.

———. *Ayyām al-ʿarab qabla l-Islām li-Abī ʿUbayda: Multaqaṭāt min al-kutub wa-l-makhṭūṭāt.* Edited by ʿĀdil Jāsim al-Bayātī. Baghdad: Dār al-Jaḥiẓ li-l-Ṭibāʿa wa-l-Nashr, 1976.

———. *Naqāʾiḍ Jarīr wa-l-Farazdaq.* Edited by A. A. Bevan. Leiden, Netherlands: 1905–1912. Reprint, Baghdad, n.d. / Edited by M. I. ʿA. al-Ṣāwī. 2 vols. Cairo, 1935.

al-Āmidī. *Al-Muwāzana bayna shiʿr Abī Tammām wa-l-Buḥturī.* Edited by al-Sayyid Aḥmad Ṣaqr. 2 vols. Cairo: Dār al-Maʿārif, 1960.

al-Aṣmaʿī, ʿAbdalmalik b. Qurayb. *Fuḥūlat al-shuʿarāʾ.* Edited and translated by Charles Torrey. *ZDMG* 65 (1911): 487–516. Reprint, Beirut: Dār al-Kitāb al-Jadīd, 1971. / As *Suʾālāt Abī Ḥātim al-Sijistānī li-l-Aṣmaʿī wa-radduhū ʿalayhi Fuḥūlat al-shuʿarāʾ.* Edited by Muḥammad ʿA. Salāma. Cairo: Maktabat al-Thaqāfa al-Dīniyya, 1994.

———. *Al-Khayl.* Edited by August Haffner. *Sitzungsberichte der Kaiserlichen Akademie der Wissenschaften in Wien, Philosophisch-Historische Classe,* 132, 10, Vienna: Tempsky, 1895. / Edited by Nūrī Ḥammūdī al-Qaysī. Baghdad: Maṭbaʿat al-Ḥukūma, 1970.

al-Bandanījī, Abū Bishr al-Yamān b. Abī l-Yamān. *Al-Taqfiya fī l-lugha.* Edited by Khalīl Ibrāhīm al-ʿAṭiyya. Baghdad: al-Jumhūriyya al-ʿIrāqiyya, Wizārat al-Awqāf, 1976.

al-Dhahabī, Muḥammad b. Aḥmad. *Taʾrīkh al-Islām wa-ṭabaqāt al-mashāhīr wa-l-aʿlām.* Edited by ʿUmar ʿA. al-Tadmurī. 52 vols. Beirut: Dār al-Kitāb al-ʿArabī, 1987–1995.

———. *Siyar aʿlām al-nubalāʾ.* Edited by Shuʿayb al-Arnāʾūṭ and Ḥusayn al-Asad. 23 vols. Beirut: Muʾassasat al-Risāla, 1982–1985.

al-Farrāʾ. *Maʿānī al-Qurʾān.* Edited by Aḥmad Yūsuf al-Najātī and Muḥammad ʿAlī al-Najjār. 3 vols. Cairo: Maṭbaʿat Dār al-Kutub al-Miṣriyya, 1955–1972.

Ibn ʿAbdrabbih. *Al-ʿIqd al-farīd.* Edited by M. Saʿīd al-ʿAryān. 8 vols. Cairo: Dār al-Fikr, 1940.

Ibn Abī Ṭāhir. *Kitāb Baghdād.* Edited by ʿIzzat al-ʿAṭṭār al-Ḥusaynī. Cairo: Maktabat al-Khānjī, 1949.

Ibn al-Anbārī, Abū l-Barakāt. *Nuzhat al-alibbāʾ.* Edited by Ibrāhīm al-Sāmarrāʾī. Baghdad: Maṭbaʿat al-Maʿārif, 1959. / Edited by Muḥammad Abū l-Faḍl Ibrāhīm. Cairo: Dār Nahḍat Miṣr li-l-Ṭabʿ wa-l-Nashr, 1967.

Ibn al-Athīr. *Al-Kāmil fī l-taʾrīkh.* Edited by C. J. Tornberg. 12 vols. Leiden, Netherlands: Brill, 1851–1876. Reprint, Beirut: Dār Ṣādir, 1965–1967.

Ibn Ḥajar al-ʿAskalānī. *Al-Iṣāba fū tamyīz al-ṣaḥāba.* Edited by ʿAlī Muḥammad al-Bijāwī. 8 vols. Cairo: Dār Nahḍa Miṣr li-t-Ṭabʿ wa-l-Nashr, 1970–1972.

Ibn al-Jarrāḥ, Abū ʿAbdallāh M. b. Dāwūd. *Man ismuhū ʿAmr min al-shuʿarāʾ.* Edited by ʿAbd al-ʿAzīz b. Nāṣir al-Māniʿ. Riyadh: Jāmiʿat al-Malik Saʿūd, 2011.

———. *Al-Waraqa.* Edited by ʿAbdalwahhāb ʿAzzām and ʿAbdassattār A. Farrāj. Cairo: Dār al-Maʿārif, 1953.

Ibn Khallikān. *Wafayāt al-aʿyān.* Edited by Iḥsān ʿAbbās. 8 vols. Beirut: Dār Ṣādir, 1977. Reprint, Beirut: Dār al-Thaqāfa, n.d.

Ibn al-Muʿtazz, ʿAbdallāh. *Ṭabaqāt al-shuʿarāʾ.* Edited by ʿAbdassattār A. Farrāj. Cairo: Dār al-Maʿārif, 1956. Reprint, 1981.

Ibn al-Nadīm. *Fihrist.* Edited by Riḍā Tajaddud. Amman: Dār al-Masīra, 1988. Reprint of Tehran, 1971. / Edited by Ayman Fuʾād Sayyid. 2 pts. in 4 vols. London: al-Furqan Islamic Heritage Foundation, 2009.

Ibn al-Qifṭī. *Inbāh al-ruwāt ʿalā anbāh al-nuḥāt.* Edited by Muḥammad Abū l-Faḍl Ibrāhīm. 4 vols. Cairo: Maṭbaʿat Dār al-Kutub, 1950–1974. Reprint, Cairo: Dār al-Fikr al-ʿArabī, 1986.

Ibn Qutayba. *Adab al-kātib.* Cairo: Maktabat al-Saʿāda, 1963.

Ibn Sharaf al-Qayrawānī. *Masāʾil al-intiqād.* As *Questions de critique littéraire.* Edited and translated by Charles Pellat. Algiers: Carbonel, 1953.

Ibn al-Sikkīt, *Iṣlāḥ al-manṭiq.* Edited by A. M. Shākir and ʿAbdassalām M. Hārūn. Cairo: Dār al-Maʿārif, 1949.

al-Iṣbahānī, Abū l-Faraj. *Al-Aghānī.* Edited by Muḥammad Qumayḥa. 25 vols. Beirut: Dār al-Thaqāfa, 1955. Reprint, 1981.

al-Jāḥiẓ, ʿAmr b. Baḥr. *Al-Risāla fī l-jidd wa-l-hazl.* In *Rasāʾil al-Jāḥiẓ,* edited by ʿAbdassalām M. Hārūn, vol. 1, 225–278. Beirut: Dār al-Jīl, 1991.

———. *Dhamm akhlāq al-kuttāb*. In *Rasāʾil al-Jāḥiẓ*, edited by ʿAbdassalām M. Hārūn, vol. 2, 183–209. Beirut: Dār al-Jīl, 1991.

———. *Al-Ḥayawān*. Edited by ʿAbdassalām M. Hārūn. 7 vols. Beirut: Dār Iḥyāʾ al-Turāth al-ʿArabī, 1938. Reprint, 1969.

al-Jahshiyārī, Abū ʿAbdallāh M. b. ʿAbdūs. *Al-Wuzarāʾ*. Edited by Hans von Mžik, based on unicate MS Vienna Cod. mixt. 916, dated 1151. Leipzig: Harrassowitz, 1926–1928. / Edited by Ibrāhīm Ṣāliḥ. Abu Dhabi: National Library Cultural Foundation, 2009.

al-Jumaḥī, Muḥammad b. Sallām. *Ṭabaqāt fuḥūl al-shuʿarāʾ*. Edited by Maḥmūd M. Shākir. 2 vols. Cairo: Maṭbaʿat al-Madanī, n.d.

al-Khaṭīb al-Baghdādī, Aḥmad b. ʿAlī. *Taʾrīkh Baghdād*. Edited by Bashshār ʿAwwār Maʿrūf. 17 vols. Beirut: Dār al-Gharb al-Islāmī, 2001.

———. *Taqyīd al-ʿilm*. Edited by Youssef Eche. Damascus, 1949.

al-Lughawī, Abū l-Ṭayyib ʿAbd al-Wāḥid b. ʿAlī. *Marātib al-naḥwiyyīn*. Edited by Muḥammad Abū l-Faḍl Ibrāhīm. Cairo: Maṭbaʿat Nahḍat Miṣr, 1954.

Maḥmūd al-Warrāq. *Dīwān*. Edited by Walīd Qaṣṣāb. Beirut: Dār Ṣādir, 2001.

al-Marzubānī, Abū ʿUbaydallāh Muḥammad b. ʿImrān. *Al-Muwashshaḥ fī maʾākhidh al-ʿulamāʾ ʿalā l-shuʿarāʾ*. Edited by Muḥammad ʿAlī al-Bijāwī (Cairo: Dār Nahḍat Miṣr li-l-Ṭibāʿa wa-l-Nashr wa-l-Tawzīʿ, n.d.) / Edited by Muḥammad Ḥ. Shamsaddīn. Beirut: Dār al-Kutub al-ʿIlmiyya, 1995.

———. *Nūr al-qabas al-mukhtaṣar min al-Muqtabas fī akhbār al-nuḥāt wa-l-udabāʾ wa-l-shuʿarāʾ wa-l-ʿulamāʾ*. Recension of Yūsuf b. Aḥmad al-Yaghmurī (d. 726/1326). Edited by Rudolf Sellheim. Wiesbaden, Germany: Steiner, 1964.

———. *Muʿjam al-shuʿarāʾ*. Edited by ʿAbdassaṭṭār A. Farrāj. Baghdad: Dār Iḥyāʾ al-Kutub al-ʿArabiyya, 1960.

Miskawayh. *Al-Ḥikma al-khālida: Jāvīdān khirad*. Edited by ʿAbdarraḥmān Badawī. Tehran: Intishārāt Dānishgāh Tehran, 1999. Reprint of Cairo, 1952.

al-Nuwayrī, Shihab al-Dīn. *The Ultimate Ambition in the Arts of Erudition: A Compendium of Knowledge from the Classical Islamic World*. Translated by Elias Muhanna. New York: Penguin Books, 2016.

Pseudo-Jāḥiẓ. *Al-Maḥāsin wa-l-aḍdād*. Edited by Gerlof van Vloten. Amsterdam: Oriental Press, [1974]. / Edited by Muḥammad A. al-Khānjī. Cairo: Maṭbaʿat al-Saʿāda, 1906.

al-Ṣafadī. *Al-Wāfī bi-l-wafayāt* [*Das biographische Lexikon des Ṣalāḥaddīn Ḫalīl ibn Aibak aṣ-Ṣafadī*]. Edited by Helmut Ritter et al. Istanbul: Deutsche Morgenländische Gesellschaft and Franz Steiner, 1931–2013.

al-Shābushtī. *Al-Diyārat*. Edited by Kūrkīs ʿAwwād. Baghdad: Maṭbaʿat al-Maʿārif, 1951.

al-Shāfiʿī, Muḥammad b. Idrīs. *The Epistle on Legal Theory*. Edited and translated by Joseph E. Lowry. New York: New York University Press, 2013.

———. *Al-Risāla*. Edited by Aḥmad Muḥammad Shākir. Cairo: Maṭbaʿat Muṣṭafā al-Bābī al-Ḥalabī, 1940.

al-Sīrāfī. *Akhbār al-naḥwiyyīn al-baṣriyyīn*. Edited by Ṭāhā Muḥammad al-Zaynī and Muḥammad ʿAbdalmunʿim al-Khafājī. Cairo: Muṣṭafā al-Bābī al-Ḥalabī, 1955.

al-Ṣūlī, Abū Bakr. *The Life and Times of Abū Tammām by Abū Bakr Muḥammad ibn Yaḥyā al-Ṣūlī, Preceded by al-Ṣūlī's Epistle to Abū l-Layth Muzāḥim ibn Fātik*. Edited and translated by Beatrice Gruendler. Library of Arabic Literature. New York: New York University Press, 2015. / *Akhbār Abī Tammām*. Edited by Khalīl Muḥammad ʿAsākir, Muḥammad ʿAbduh ʿAzzām, and Naẓīr al-Islām al-Hindī. Cairo: Lajnat al-Taʾlīf wa-l-Tarjama wa-l-Nashr, 1937. Reprint, Beirut: Dār al-Āfāq al-Jadīda, [1980].

———. *Adab al-kuttāb*. Edited by M. Bahjat al-Atharī, Cairo: al-Maṭbaʿa al-Salafiyya, 1922–1923. / Edited by Aḥmad Ḥ. Basaj. Beirut: Dār al-Kutub al-ʿIlmiyya, 1994.

al-Ṭabarī. *Taʾrīkh al-rusul wa-l-mulūk*. Edited by Muḥammad Abū l-Faḍl Ibrāhīm. 10 vols. Cairo: Dār al-Maʿārif, 1960–1968.

al-Tibrīzī. *Kitāb Tahdhīb Iṣlāḥ al-manṭiq*. Edited by Muḥammad Badr al-Dīn al-Naʿsānī. Cairo: Maṭbaʿat al-Saʿāda, 1907.

al-Yamanī, Abū ʿAbdallāh M. b. al-Ḥusayn b. ʿUmar. *Muḍāhāt Kitāb Kalīla wa-Dimna bi-mā ashbahahā min ashʿār al-ʿarab*. Edited by M. Yūsuf Najm. Beirut: Dār al-Thaqāfa, [1961].

al-Yaʿqūbī, Ibn Wāḍiḥ. *The Works of Ibn Wāḍiḥ al-Yaʿqūbī: An English Translation*. Edited by Matthew S. Gordon, Chase F. Robinson, Everett K. Rowson, and Michael Fishbein. 3 vols. Leiden, Netherlands: Brill, 2018.

———. *Kitāb al-Buldān*. Edited by M. J. de Goeje. Leiden, Netherlands: Brill 1892.

Yāqūt. *Muʿjam al-udabāʾ*. Edited by D. S. Margoliouth. 20 vols. London: Luzac, 1923–1931. Reprint, Baghdad, 1964; Beirut: Dār Iḥyāʾ al-Turāth al-ʿArabī, n.d.

———. *Muʿjam al-buldān*. Edited by Muhammad ʿAbdarraḥmān al-Marʿashlī. 4 vols. Beirut: Dār Iḥyāʾ al-Turāth alʿArabī, n.d.

al-Zubaydī. *Ṭabaqāt al-naḥwiyyīn wa-l-lughawiyyīn*. Edited by M. Abū l-Faḍl Ibrāhīm. Cairo: Dār al-Maʿārif, 1973. Reprint, 1984.

CRITICAL LITERATURE

Abbott, Nabia. "A Ninth-Century Fragment of the 'Thousand Nights': New Light on the Early History of the *Arabian Nights*." *Journal of Near Eastern Studies* 8 (1949): 129–164.

ʿAbdattawwāb, Ramaḍān. *Laḥn al-ʿāmma wa-l-taṭawwur al-lughawī*. Cairo: Dār al-Maʿārif, 1967.

———. *Das Kitāb al-Gharīb al-muṣannaf von Abū ʿUbaid und seine Bedeutung für die nationalarabische Lexikographie.* Heppenheim, Germany: Wolf, 1962.

Ali, Samer. *Arabic Literary Salons in the Islamic Middle Ages: Poetry, Public Performance, and the Presentation of the Past.* Notre Dame, IN: University of Notre Dame Press, 2010.

Almagor, Ella. "The Early Meaning of *Majāz* and the Nature of Abū ʿUbayda's Exegesis." In *Studia Orientalia Memoriae D. H. Baneth Dedicata,* edited by Joshua Blau, Shlomo Pines, Meir Jacob Kister, and Shaul Shaked, 307–326. Jerusalem: Magnes Press, 1979.

Arbache Samir. *L'Évangile arabe selon Saint Luc: Texte du VIII siècle, copié en 897. Édition et traduction.* Paris: Éditions Safran, 2012.

Ashtor, Eliyahu. "Essai sur les prix et les salaires dans l'empire califien." *RSO* 36 (1961): 16–69.

Auchterlonie, Paul. *Arabic Biographical Dictionaries: A Summary Guide and Bibliography.* Durham, UK: Middle East Libraries Committee, 1987.

Ayoub, Georgine. "Laḥn." In *Encyclopedia of Arabic Language and Linguistics,* edited by Kees Versteegh, Mushira Eid, Alaa Elgibali, Manfred Woidich, and Andrzej Zaborski, vol. 2, 628–634. Leiden, Netherlands: Brill, 2007.

Baalbaki, Ramzi. *The Arabic Lexicographical Tradition: From the 2nd/8th to the 12th/18th Century.* Leiden, Netherlands: Brill, 2014.

———. *The Legacy of the Kitāb: Sībawayhi's Analytical Methods within the Context of the Arabic Grammatical Theory.* Leiden, Netherlands: Brill, 2008.

Bagnall, Roger S. *Early Christian Books in Egypt.* Princeton, NJ: Princeton University Press, 2009.

Bauer, Thomas. "Arabische Kultur." In *Rhetorik: Begriff–Geschichte–Internationalität,* edited by Gert Ueding, 283–300. Tübingen, Germany: Max Niemeyer, 2005.

———. "Literarische Anthologien der Mamlukenzeit." In *Die Mamluken: Studien zu ihrer Geschichte und Kultur: Zum Gedenken an Ulrich Haarmann (1942–1999),* edited by Stephan Conermann and Anja Pistor-Hatam, 71–122. Schenefeld, Germany: EB-Verlag, 2003.

———. *Das Pflanzenbuch des Ḥanīfa ad-Dīnawarī: Inhalt, Aufbau, Quellen.* Wiesbaden, Germany: Harrassowitz, 1988.

Bearman, Peri J., Thierry Bianquis, C. E. Bosworth, Emeri van Donzel, and Wolfhart P. Heinrichs, eds. *Encyclopaedia of Islam.* 2nd ed. 12 vols. with indices. Leiden, Netherlands: Brill, 1960–2005.

Beeston, A. F. L., T. M. Johnston, R. B. Serjeant, and G. R. Smith, eds. *Arabic Literature to the End of the Umayyad Period.* The Cambridge History of Arabic Literature. Cambridge: Cambridge University Press, 1983.

Behrens-Abouseif, Doris. *The Book in Mamluk Egypt and Syria (1250–1517): Scribes, Libraries, and Markets.* Leiden, Netherlands: Brill, 2018.

Behzadi, Lale, and Jaakko Hämeen-Anttila, eds. *Concepts of Authorship in Pre-modern Arabic Texts.* Bamberg, Germany: Bamberg University Press, 2015.
Bernards, Monique. *Changing Traditions: Al-Mubarrad's Refutation of Sībawayh and the Subsequent Reception of the* Kitāb. Leiden, Netherlands: Brill, 1977.
Blair, Sheila. *Islamic Calligraphy.* Edinburgh: Edinburgh University Press, 2006.
Blair, Sheila, and Jonathan Bloom, eds. *By the Pen and What They Write: Writing in Islamic Art and Culture.* New Haven, CT: Yale University Press, 2017.
Blois, François de. *Burzoy's Voyage to India and the Origin of the Book of* Kalilah wa Dimnah. London: Royal Asiatic Society, 1990.
Bloom, Jonathan. "How Paper Changed the Literary and Visual Culture of the Islamic Lands." In Blair and Bloom, *By the Pen and What They Write,* 107–127.
———. "Papermaking: The Historical Diffusion of an Ancient Technique" In *Mobilities of Knowledge,* edited by Heike Jöns, Peter Mensburger, and Michael Hefferman, 51–66. Cham, Switzerland: Springer, 2017.
———. "Literary and Oral Cultures." In *The New Cambridge History of Islam.* Vol. 4, *Islamic Cultures and Societies to the End of the Eighteenth Century,* edited by Robert Irwin, 668–681. Cambridge: Cambridge University Press, 2011.
———. *Paper before Print: The History and Impact of Paper in the Islamic World.* New Haven, CT: Yale University Press, 2001.
Bosworth, Clifford Edmund. "The Tahirids and Arabic Culture." *Journal of Semitic Studies* 14 (1969): 45–79.
Brockelmann, Carl, *Geschichte der arabischen Litteratur.* 2 vols. and 3 suppl. vols. Leiden, Netherlands: Brill, 1996.
Burton, John. "Collection of the Qurʾān," In McAuliffe, *EQ,* vol. 1, 351–361.
Carter, Michael G. *Sībawayhi.* Oxford: Tauris, 2004.
Chraïbi, Aboubakr. *Les Mille et une nuits: Histoire du texte et classification des contes.* Paris: L'Harmattan, 2008.
Clanchy, Michael T. *From Memory to Written Record: England 1066–1307.* Oxford: Blackwell, 1979.
Coleman, Joyce. *Public Reading and Reading Public in Late Medieval England and France.* Cambridge: Cambridge University Press, 1996.
Cook, Michael. "The Opponents of the Writing of Tradition in Early Islam." *Arabica* 44 (1997): 437–530.
Cooperson, Michael. "Ibn al-Muqaffaʿ." In *The Biographical Encyclopedia of Islamic Philosophy,* edited by Oliver Leaman, vol. 1, 280–286. London: Thoemmes, 2006.
———. *Classical Arabic Biography.* Cambridge: Cambridge University Press, 2000.
Contadini, Anna. *A World of Beasts: A Thirteenth-Century Illustrated Arabic Book on Animals (the Kitāb Naʿt al-Ḥayawān) in the Ibn Bakhtīshūʿ Tradition.* Leiden, Netherlands: Brill, 2012.
Daniels, Peter T. "Fundamentals of Grammatology." *JAOS* 110 (1990): 727–730.

Davidson, Garret. "Carrying on the Tradition: An Intellectual and Social History of Post-canonical Hadith Transmission." PhD diss., University of Chicago, 2014.

David-Weill, Jean. *Le Djâmi' d'Ibn Wahb.* 2 vols. Cairo: Institut Français d'Archéologie Orientale, 1939–1941.

De Goeje, M. J. "Beschreibung einer alten Handschrift von Abû 'Obaid's Ġarîb-al-ḥadîṯ." *ZDMG* 18 (1864): 781–807.

Dehaene, Stanislas. *Reading in the Brain: The New Science of How We Read.* New York: Penguin Books, 2009.

Déroche, François. *Qur'āns of the Umayyads: A First Overview.* Leiden, Netherlands: Brill, 2014.

———. *Le livre manuscrit arabe: Préludes à une histoire.* Paris: Bibliothèque nationale de France, 2004.

———. *The Abbasid Tradition: Qur'ans of the 8th to the 10th Centuries AD.* London: Nour Foundation, 1992.

———. "Les manuscrits arabes datés du IIIe / IXe siècle." *REI* 55–57 (1987–1989): 343–379.

Déroche, François et al. *Islamic Codicology: An Introduction to the Study of Manscripts in Arabic Script.* Translated by Deke Dusinberre, and David Razinowicz. London: al-Furqan Islamic Heritage Foundation, 2015.

Déroche, François et al. *Manuel de codicologie des manuscrits en écriture arabe.* Paris: Bibliothèque nationale de France, 2000.

Diem, Werner. "Das Kitāb al-Ǧīm des Abū 'Amr aš-Šaibānī: Ein Beitrag zur arabischen Lexikographie." PhD diss., Universität München, 1968.

Donner, Fred. *Narratives of Islamic Origins: The Beginnings of Islamic Historical Writing.* Princeton, NJ: Darwin Press, 1998.

Drory, Rina. "The Abbasid Construction of the *Jāhiliyya:* Cultural Authority in the Making." *Studia Islamica* 83 (1996): 33–49.

Duri [al-Dūrī], Abdal'aziz. "*Dīwān* 1. The Caliphate." In Bearman et al., *EI2,* vol. 2, 323–237.

Ebied, R. Y., and M. J. L. Young. "New Light on the Origin of the Term 'Baccalaureate.'" *Islamic Quarterly* 18 (1974): 3–7.

Eche, Youssef. *Les bibliothèques arabes publiques et semi-publiques en Mésopotamie, en Syrie, et en Égypte au moyen age.* Damascus: Institut Français de Damas, 1967.

Egan, Ronald. "To Count Grains of Sand on the Ocean Floor: Changing Perceptions of Books and Learning in the Song Dynasty." In *Knowledge and Text Production in An Age of Print: China, 900–1400,* edited by Lucille Chia and Hilde De Weerdt, 33–62. Leiden, Netherlands: Brill, 2011.

Ehrenkreutz, A. S. "Money." In *Wirtschaftsgeschichte des Vorderen Orients in islamischer Zeit,* edited by Berthold Spuler, HdO, pt. 1, vol. 6., sect. 6, 84–97. Leiden, Netherlands: Brill, 1977.

El-Hibri, Tayeb. *Reinterpreting Islamic Historiography: Hārūn al-Rashīd and the Narrative of the ʿAbbāsid Caliphate.* New York: Cambridge University Press, 1999.

Enderwitz, Susanne. "Shuʿūbiyya." In Bearman et al., *EI2,* vol. 9, 513–516.

Faulstich, Werner. *Das Medium als Kult: Von den Anfängen bis zur Spätantike (8. Jahrhundert).* Göttingen, Germany: Vandenhoeck and Ruprecht, 1997.

Fischer, Wolfdietrich. *Grammatik des klassischen Arabisch.* Wiesbaden, Germany: Harrassowitz, 1987.

Fishman, Talya. "Guarding Oral Transmission: Within and between Cultures." In "Oral Tradition in Judaism, Christianity and Islam," edited by Werner H. Kelber and Paula Sanders. Special issue, *Oral Tradition* 25, no. 1 (2010): 41–56.

Fleet, Kate, Gudrun Krämer, Denis Matringe, John Nawas, and Everett Rowson, eds. *Encyclopaedia of Islam.* 3rd ed. 57 vols. to date. Leiden, Netherlands: Brill, 2007–.

Fleischhammer, Manfred. *Die Quellen des Kitāb al-Aghānī.* Wiesbaden, Germany: Harrassowitz, 2004.

Fowden, Garth. *Before and after Muhammad: The First Millennium Refocused.* Princeton, NJ: Princeton University Press, 2014.

Fück, J. W. "Ibn Saʿd." In Bearman et al., *EI2,* vol. 3, 922–923.

Gabrieli, Francesco. "Ibn al-Muqaffaʿ." In Bearman et al., *EI2,* vol. 3, 883–885.

Gacek, Adam. *Arabic Manuscripts: A Vademecum for Readers.* Leiden, Netherlands: Brill, 2012.

———. *The Arabic Manuscript Tradition: A Glossary of Technical Terms.* Leiden, Netherlands: Brill, 2001, supp. 2008.

———. "Technical Practices and Recommendations Recorded by Classical and Post-Classical Arabic Scholars concerning the Copying and Correction of Manuscripts." In *Les manuscrits du Moyen-Orient: Essais de codicologie et de paléographie, Actes du Colloque d'Istanbul, Istanbul, 26–29 mai 1986,* edited by François Déroche, 51–60 and plates xx b–xxxii b. Paris: Institut Français d'Études Anatoliennes d'Istanbul, 1989.

Gade, Anna M. "Recitation of the Qurʾān," In McAuliffe, *EQ,* vol. 4, 367–385.

Gibb., H. A. R. "Abū ʿUbayda." In Bearman et al., *EI2,* vol. 1, 158.

Görke, Andreas. *Das Kitāb al-Amwāl des Abū ʿUbaid al-Qāsim b. Sallām: Entstehung und Überlieferung eines frühislamischen Rechtswerkes.* Princeton, NJ: Darwin Press, 2003.

Görke, Andreas, and Konrad Hirschler, eds. *Manuscript Notes as Documentary Sources.* Würzburg, Germany: Ergon, 2011.

Griffith, Sidney H. *The Bible in Arabic: The Scriptures of the "People of the Book" in the Language of Islam.* Princeton, NJ: Princeton University Press, 2013.

———. "The Gospel in Arabic: An Inquiry into Its Appearance in the First Abbasid Century." *Oriens Christianus* 67 (1983): 126–167.

Grohmann, Adolf. *Arabische Paläographie.* 2 vols. Vienna: Hermann Böhlau, 1967–1971.

Gruendler, Beatrice. "Abbasid Poets and the Qur'ān." In *The Qur'an and Adab: The Shaping of Literary Traditions in Classical Islam,* edited by Nuha Alsha'ar, 137–169. Oxford: Oxford University Press, 2017.

———. "Modernity in the Ninth Century: The Controversy around Abū Tammām." *Studia Islamica* 112 (2017): 131–148.

———. "*Al-ḥanīn ilā l-awṭān* and Its Alternatives in Classical Arabic Literature." In *Representations and Visions of Homeland in Modern Arabic Literature,* edited by Sebastian Günther and Stephan Milich, 1–41. Hildesheim, Germany: Georg Olms, 2016.

———. "Aspects of Craft in the Arabic Book Revolution." In *Globalization of Knowledge in the Post-antique Mediterranean, 700–1500,* edited by Jürgen Renn and Sonja Brentjes, 31–66. London: Routledge, 2016.

———. "'That You Be Brought Near': Union beyond the Grave in the Arabic Literary Tradition." In *Love after Death,* edited by Bernhard Jussen and Ramie Targoff, 71–95. Berlin: De Gruyter, 2014.

———. "Les versions de *Kalīla wa-Dimna:* Une transmission et une circulation mouvantes." In *Énoncés sapientiels et littérature exemplaire: Une intertextualité complexe,* edited by Marie-Sol Ortola, 385–416. Nancy, France: Éditions Universitaires de Lorraine, 2013.

———. *Book Culture before Print: The Early History of Arabic Media.* Occasional Papers of the Margaret Weyerhaeuser Jewett Chair of Arabic. Beirut: American University of Beirut, 2012.

———. "Stability and Change in Arabic Script." In *The Shape of Script: How and Why Writing Systems Change,* edited by Stephen D. Houston, 93–111. Santa Fe, NM: School of Advanced Research, 2012.

———. "Farewell to Ghazal: Convention and Danger of the Arabic Love Lyric." In *Poetry and History: The Value of Poetry in Reconstructing Arab History,* edited by Ramzi Baalbaki, Saleh Said Agha, and Tarif Khalidi, 137–172. Beirut: American University of Beirut, 2011.

———. "Pre-modern Arabic Philologists: Poets' Friends or Foes?" *Geschichte der Germanistik* 39 / 40 (2011): 7–21.

———. "Abū Tammām." In Fleet et al., *EI3,* first published online and in print 2009. Accessed December 21, 2019. http://dx.doi.org/10.1163/1573-3912_ei3_SIM_0035.

———. "Al-ʿAskarī, Abū Aḥmad." In Fleet et al., *EI3,* first published online and in print 2009. Accessed December 31, 2019. http://dx.doi.org/10.1163/1573-3912_ei3_COM_22689.

———. "*Tawqīʿ* (Apostille): Verbal Economy in Verdicts of Tort Redress." In *The Weaving of Words: Approaches to Classical Arabic Literature,* edited by Lale Behzadi and Vahid Behmardi, 101–129. Beirut: Ergon, 2009.

———. "Abstract Aesthetics and Practical Criticism in Ninth-Century Baghdad." In *Takhyīl: The Imaginary in Classical Arabic Poetics,* edited by Marlé Hammond and Geert J. van Gelder, 196–220. Oxford: Gibb Memorial Trust, 2008.

———. "Meeting the Patron: An *Akhbār* Type and Its Implications for *Muḥdath* Poetry." In *Ideas, Images, Methods of Portrayal: Insights into Arabic Literature and Islam,* edited by Sebastian Günther, 59–88. Wiesbaden, Germany: Harrassowitz, 2005.

———. "Verse and Taxes: The Function of Poetry in Selected Literary *Akhbār* of the Third / Ninth Century." In *On Fiction and Adab in Medieval Arabic Literature,* edited by Philip F. Kennedy, 85–124. Wiesbaden, Germany: Harrassowitz, 2005.

———. *Medieval Arabic Praise Poetry: Ibn al-Rūmī and the Patron's Redemption.* London: RoutledgeCurzon, 2003.

———. "Sheets." In McAuliffe, *EQ,* vol. 4, 587–589.

Gruendler, Beatrice et al. "An Interim Report on the Editorial and Analytical Work of the AnonymClassic Project." *Medieval Worlds,* forthcoming.

Guillory, John. "Genesis of the Media Concept" *Critical Inquiry* 36 (2010): 321–362.

Günther, Sebastian. "Assessing the Sources of Classical Arabic Compilations: The Issue of Categories and Methodologies." *BJMES* 32 (2005): 75–98.

———. *Quellenuntersuchungen zu den „Maqātil al-Ṭālibiyyīn" des Abū l-Faraj al-Isfahānī (gest. 356/967).* Hildesheim, Germany: Georg Olms, 1991.

Gutas, Dimitri. "On Graeco-Arabic Epistolary 'Novels.'" Review of *The Correspondence between Aristotle and Alexander the Great,* by Miklós Maróth. *MEL* 12 (2009): 59–70.

———. *Greek Thought, Arabic Culture: The Graeco-Arabic Translation Movement in Baghdad and Early ʿAbbāsid Society (2nd–4th / 8th–10th centuries).* London: Routledge, 1989.

Gutas, Dimitri, and Kevin van Bladel. "Bayt al-Ḥikma." In Fleet et al., *EI3,* first published online and in print 2009. Accessed February 22, 2013. http://referenceworks.brillonline.com/entries/encyclopaedia-of-islam-3/bayt-al-hikma-COM_22882.

Hämeen-Anttila, Jaakko. *Khwadāynāmag: The Middle Persian Book of Kings.* Leiden, Netherlands: Brill, 2018.

Hansen, Valerie. *The Silk Road: A New History.* Oxford: Oxford University Press, 2012.

Heck, Paul L. *The Construction of Knowledge in Islamic Civilization: Qudāma b. Jaʿfar and His* Kitāb al-Kharāj wa-ṣināʿat al-kitāba. Leiden, Netherlands: Brill, 2002.

Heinrichs, Wolfhart. "Ta'abbaṭa Sharran, Goethe, Shākir." In *Reflections on Reflections: Near Eastern Writers Reading Literature,* edited by Angelika Neuwirth and Andreas Islebe, 191–252. Wiesbaden, Germany: Reichert, 2006.

———. "The Classification of the Sciences and the Consolidation of Philology in Classical Islam." In *Centres of Learning: Learning and Location in Pre-modern Europe and the Near East,* edited by Jan W. Drijvers and Alasdair A. Macdonald, 119–139. Leiden, Netherlands: Brill, 1995.

———. "Contacts between Scriptural Hermeneutics and Literary Theory in Islam: The Case of Majāz." *Zeitschrift für Geschichte der Arabisch-Islamischen Wissenschaften* 7 (1991): 253–284.

———. "On the Genesis of the *Ḥaqīqa-Majāz* Dichotomy." *Studia Islamica* 59 (1984): 111–140.

———. "Prosimetrical Genres in Classical Arabic Literature." In *Prosimetrum: Crosscultural Perspectives on Narrative in Prose and Verse,* edited by Joseph Harris and Karl Reichl, 249–275. Cambridge: D. S. Brewer, 1997.

Hirschler, Konrad. *Medieval Damascus: Plurality and Diversity in an Arabic Library: The Ashrafiya Library Catalogue.* Edinburgh: Edinburgh University Press, 2017.

Huart, Clément, and Adolf Grohmann. "Kāhgad." In Bearman et al., *EI2,* vol. 4, 419–420.

Hunger, Herbert. *Schreiben und Lesen in Byzanz: Die byzantinische Buchkultur.* Munich: Beck, 1989.

Ilisch, Lutz. "Reichswährung und Regionalwährung nach der Münzreform ʿAbd al-Maliks im islamischen Osten." In *Die Grenzen der Welt: Arabica et Iranica ad honorem Heinz Gaube,* edited by Lorenz Korn, Eva Ortmann, and Florian Schwartz, 167–179. Wiesbaden, Germany: Reichert, 2008.

Jaeger, Ludwig, and Georg Stanitzek, eds. *Transkribieren: Medien, Lektüre.* Munich: Fink, 2002.

Johns, Adrian. *The Nature of the Book: Print and Knowledge in the Making.* Chicago: University of Chicago Press, 1998.

Juynboll, Gautier H. A. *Encyclopedia of Canonical Hadīth.* Leiden, Netherlands: Brill, 2007.

Karabacek, Joseph von. *Arab Paper.* Translated by Don Baker and Suzy Dittmar. London: Islington Books, 2001. Originally published as "Das arabische Papier," in *Mitteilungen aus der Sammlung Papyrus Erzherzog Rainer,* 87–91. Vienna, 1897.

Kashouh, Hikmat. *The Arabic Versions of the Gospels: The Manuscripts and Their Families.* Arbeiten zur Neutestamentlichen Textforschung 42. Berlin: De Gruyter, 2012.

Kennedy, Hugh. "Baghdad as a Center of Learning and Book Production." In Blair and Bloom, *By the Pen and What They Write,* 89–103.

———. *The Great Arab Conquests: How the Spread of Islam Changed the World We Live In.* Philadelphia: Da Capo Press, 2007.

———. *When Baghdad Ruled the Muslim World: The Rise and Fall of Islam's Greatest Dynasty.* Philadelphia: Da Capo Press, 2004.

Khoury, Raif G. *Wahb b. Munabbih, Der Heidelberger Papyrus PSR Heid Arab 23, pt. 1: Leben und Werk des Dichters, pt. 2: Faksimiletafeln.* Wiesbaden, Germany: Harrassowitz, 1972.

Klein-Franke, Felix. "The *Ḥamāsa* of Abū Tammām, Part 2." *JAL* 3 (1972): 141–178.

———. "The *Ḥamāsa* of Abū Tammām, Part 1." *JAL* 2 (1971): 13–36.

Kotsifou, Chrysi. "Books and Book Production in the Monastic Communities of Byzantine Egypt." In *The Early Christian Book,* edited by William E. Klingshirn and Linda Safran, 48–66. Washington DC: Catholic University of America Press, 2007.

Kristó-Nagy, István T. *La pensée d'Ibn al-Muqaffaʿ: Un "agent double" dans le monde persan et arabe.* Paris: Éditions de Paris, 2013.

Lane, E. W. *Arabic-English Lexicon.* London: Williams and Norgate, 1877. Reprint, Cambridge: Islamic Texts Society, 1984.

Lassner, Jacob. *The Topography of Baghdad in the Early Middle Ages: Texts and Studies.* Detroit, MI: Wayne State University Press, 1970.

Lecomte, Gérard. *Ibn Qutayba (mort en 276/889): L'homme, son oeuvre, ses idées.* Damascus: Institut Français de Damas, 1965.

———. "Ibn Ḳutayba." In Bearman et al., *EI2,* vol. 3, 844–847.

———. "L'introduction du Kitāb *Adab al-kātib* d'Ibn Qutayba." In *Mélanges Louis Massignon,* edited by Institut Français de Damas, vol. 3, 47–65. Damascus: Institut Français de Damas, 1957.

Leder, Stefan, ed. *Story-Telling in the Framework of Non-fictional Arabic Literature.* Wiesbaden, Germany: Harrassowitz, 1998.

———. "Conventions of Fictional Narration in Learned Literature." In Leder, *Story-Telling,* 34–60.

———. "Grenzen der Rekonstruktion alten Schrifttums nach den Angaben im Fihrist." In *Ibn an-Nadîm und die mittelalterliche arabische Literatur: Beiträge zum 1. Johann Wilhelm Fück–Kolloquium Halle 1987,* 21–31. Wiesbaden, Germany: Harrassowitz, 1996.

———. "The Literary Use of Khabar: A Basic Form of Historical Writing." In *The Byzantine and Early Islamic Near East.* Vol. 1, *Problems in Literary Source Material,* edited by Averil Cameron and Lawrence I. Conrad, 277–315. Princeton, NJ: Darwin Press, 1992.

Leemhuis, Frederik. "Codices of the Qur'ān." In McAuliffe, *EQ,* vol. 1, 347–351.

Lewis, Bernard. "Al-Aṣmaʿī." In Bearman et al., *EI2,* vol. 1, 717–719.

Lichtenstaedter, Ilse. "Muḥammad b. Ḥabīb." In Bearman et al., *EI2,* vol. 7, 401–402.

Liebrenz, Boris. *Die Rifāʿīya aus Damaskus: Eine Privatbibliothek im osmanischen Syrien und ihr kulturelles Umfeld.* Leiden, Netherlands: Brill, 2016.

Loveday, Helen. *Islamic Paper: A Study of an Ancient Craft.* London: Don Baker Memorial Fund, 2001.

Maqdisi, George. *The Rise of Colleges: Institutions of Learning in Islam and the West.* Edinburgh: Edinburgh University Press, 1981.

Marogy, Amal E. *Kitāb Sībawayhi: Syntax and Pragmatics.* Leiden, Netherlands: Brill, 2010.

Maróth, Miklós. *The Correspondence between Aristotle and Alexander the Great: An Anonymous Greek Novel in Letters in Arabic Translation.* Piliscaba, Hungary: Avicenna Institute of Middle East Studies, 2006.

McAuliffe, Jane D., ed. *Encyclopaedia of the Qur'ān,* 5 vols. with index. Leiden, Netherlands: Brill, 2001 / 2006

Melchert, Christopher and Asma Afsaruddin. "Reciters of the Qur'an," In McAuliffe, *EQ,* vol. 4, 386–393.

Montgomery, James E. *Al-Jāḥiẓ: In Praise of Books.* Edinburgh: Edinburgh University Press, 2016.

———. "Al-Jāḥiẓ's Kitāb al-Bayān wa-l-tabyīn." In *Writing and Representation in Medieval Islam,* edited by Julia Bray, 91–152. London: Routledge, 2006.

———. "Of Models and Amanuenses: The Remarks on the *Qaṣīda* in Ibn Qutayba's *Kitāb al-Shiʿr wa-l-shuʿarā'.*" In *Islamic Reflections and Arabic Musings: Studies in Honour of Professor Alan Jones,* edited by Robert Hoyland and Philip F. Kennedy, 1–47. Oxford: Gibb Memorial Trust, 2004.

Muhanna, Elias. *The World in a Book: Al-Nuwayrī and the Islamic Encyclopedic Tradition.* Princeton, NJ: Princeton University Press, 2018.

al-Musawi, Muhsin J. *The Medieval Islamic Republic of Letters: Arabic Knowledge Construction.* Notre Dame, IN: University of Notre Dame Press, 2015.

Nadwi, Mohammad Akram. *Al-Muḥaddithāt: The Woman Scholars in Islam.* Oxford: Interface Publications, 2007.

Nasser, Shady Hekmat. *The Transmission of the Variant Readings of the Qur'ān: The Problem of Tawātur and the Emergence of Shawādhdh.* Leiden, Netherlands: Brill, 2013.

Nielsen, Henrik Skov, James Phelan, and Richard Walsh. "Ten Theses about Fictionality." *Narrative* 23, no. 1 (January 2015): 61–73.

O'Kane, Bernard. *Early Persian Painting: Kalila and Dimna Manuscripts of the Late Fourteenth Century.* London: Tauris, 2003.

Papoutsakis, Nefeli. *Desert Travel as a Form of Boasting: A Study of D̲ū r-Rumma's Poetry.* Wiesbaden, Germany: Harrassowitz, 2009.

Pedersen, Johannes. *The Arabic Book.* Translated by Geoffrey French. Princeton, NJ: Princeton University Press, 1984.

Pellat, Charles. "al-Djāḥiẓ." In Bearman et al., *EI2,* vol. 3, 385–387.

———. "D̲jāwīd̲h̲ān K̲h̲irad." In Bearman et al., *EI2* supp., 263–264.

———. "Mathālib." In Bearman et al., *EI2,* vol. 6, 828–829.

Pinto, Olga. "The Libraries of the Arabs during the Time of the Abbasids." *Islamic Culture* 3 (1929): 210–248.

al-Qadi, Wadad. "Biographical Dictionaries: Inner Structure and Cultural Significance." In *The Book in the Islamic World,* edited by George N. Atiyeh, 93–122. Albany: State University of New York Press, 1995.

———. "Early Islamic State Letters: The Question of Authenticity." In *The Byzantine and Early Islamic Near East.* Vol. 1, *Problems in Literary Source Material,* edited by Averil Cameron and Lawrence I. Conrad, 215–275. Princeton: Darwin Press, 1992.

Rabbat, Nasser. "Ribāṭ." In Bearman et al., *EI2,* vol. 8, 493–506.

Raby, Julian. "Between Sogdia and the Mamluks: A Note on the Earliest Illustrations to *Kalīla wa Dimna.*" *Oriental Art* 33, no. 4 (1987): 381–398.

Rice, D. S. "The Oldest Illustrated Arabic Manuscript." *Bulletin of the School of Oriental and African Studies* 22 (1959): 207–220.

Robinson, Chase F. *Islamic Historiography.* Cambridge: Cambridge University Press, 2003.

Romanov, Maxim. "Algorithmic Analysis of Medieval Arabic Biographical Collections." *Speculum* 92 (2017): 226–246.

———. "Toward the Digital History of the pre-Modern Muslim World: Developing Text-mining Techniques for the Study of Arabic Biographical Collections." In *Analysis of Ancient and Medieval Texts and Manuscripts: Digital Approaches,* edited by Tara L Andrews and Caroline Macé, 229–44. Turnhout: Brepols Publishers, 2014.

Roper, Geoffrey. "The History of the Book in the Muslim World." In *The Oxford Companion to the Book,* edited by Michael F. Suarez, S. J. Woudhuysen, and H. R. Woudhuysen, 524–552. Oxford: Oxford University Press, 2010.

Rosenthal, Franz. *Man versus Society in Medieval Islam.* Edited by Dimitri Gutas. Leiden, Netherlands: Brill, 2015.

———. "Muslim Social Values and Literary Criticism: Reflections on the Ḥadīth of Umm Zarʿ." *Oriens* 34 (1994): 31–56. Reprinted in Rosenthal, *Man versus Society in Medieval Islam,* 909–940.

———. "The Technique and Approach of Muslim Scholarship." *Analecta Orientalia* 24 (1947): 1–74.

Sajdi, Dana. "Print and Its Discontents: A Case for Pre-print Journalism and Other Sundry Print Matters." In "Nation and Translation in the Middle East," edited by Samah Selim. Special issue, *The Translator: Studies in Intercultural Communication* 15, no. 1 (2009): 105–138.

Saliba, George [Jūrj Ṣalībā]. *Al-Fikr al-ʿilmī al-ʿarabī: Nashʾatuhū wa-taṭawwuruhū.* Tripoli: Markaz al-Dirāsāt al-Masīḥiyya al-Islāmiyya, Jāmiʿat al-Balimand, 1998.

Scheiner, Jens. "Steuern und Gelehrsamkeit in der frühen ʿAbbāsidenzeit: Das *Kitāb al-amwāl* des Abū ʿUbaid al-Qāsim b. Sallām. Teil 1: Abū ʿUbaids Steuersystematik und die Rolle des Herrschers. Teil 2: Abū ʿUbaids juristische Argumentation." *ZDMG* 162 (2012): 317–352, 653–693.

Schmidt, Nora. *Philologische Kommentarkulturen: Abū ʿUbaidas Maǧāz al-Qurʾān im Licht spätantiken Exegesewissens.* Wiesbaden, Germany: Harrassowitz, 2016.

Schoeler, Gregor. *The Genesis of Literature in Islam: From the Aural to the Read.* Revised and enlarged ed. of *Écrire et transmettre dans les débuts de l'Islam,* in collaboration with and translated by Shawkat M. Toorawa. Edinburgh: Edinburgh University Press, 2009.

———. *The Oral and the Written in Early Islam.* Translated by Uwe Vagelpohl, with a preface by James E. Montgomery. New York: Routledge, 2006.

———. *Écrire et transmettre dans les débuts de l'Islam.* Paris: Presses Universitaires de France, 2002.

———. *Charakter und Authentie der muslimischen Überlieferung über das Leben Mohammeds.* Berlin: Walter de Gruyter, 1996.

———. "Mündliche Thora und Ḥadīṯ: Überlieferung, Schreibverbot, Redaktion." *Der Islam* 66 (1989): 213–241.

———. "Weiteres zur Frage der mündlichen oder schriftlichen Überlieferung der Wissenschaften im frühen Islam." *Der Islam* 66 (1989): 38–67.

———. "Die Frage der mündlichen oder schriftlichen Überlieferung der Wissenschaften im frühen Islam," *Der Islam* 62 (1985): 201–230.

Schulthess, Sara. "Les manuscrits arabes des lettres de Paul: La reprise d'un champ de recherche négligé" PhD diss., l'Université de Lausanne / Radboud Universiteit Nijmegen, 2016. Online component: https://digi.vatlib.it/view/MSS_Vat.ar.13.

Sellheim, Rudolf. "Gelehrte und Gelehrsamkeit im Reiche der Chalifen." In *Festgabe für Paul Kirn zum 70. Geburtstag dargebracht von Freunden und Schülern,* edited by Ekkehard Kaufmann, 54–79. Berlin: Erich Schmidt, 1961.

Sezgin, Fuat. *Geschichte des arabischen Schrifttums* (*GAS*). 17 vols. to date. Leiden, Netherlands: Brill, 1967–).

Shatzmiller, Maya. *Labour in the Medieval Islamic World.* Leiden, Netherlands: Brill, 1994.

Sheffield, Dan. "New Evidence for the Middle Persian Prototype of *Kalīla wa-Dimna.*" Paper presented at the 227th meeting of the American Oriental Society, Los Angeles, March 17–20, 2017.

Shoshan, Boaz. "On Popular Literature in Medieval Cairo." *Poetics Today* 14, no. 1 (Summer 1993): 349–365.

Siddiqi, Muhammad Z. *Ḥadīth Literature: Its Origin, Development, and Special Features.* Cambridge: Islamic Texts Society, 1993.

Smith, John Maynard, and Eörs Szathmáry. *The Origins of Life: From the Birth of Life to the Origins of Language.* Oxford: Oxford University Press, 1999.

Sourdel, Dominique. "Aḥmad b. Abī Khālid al-Aḥwal." In Bearman et al., *EI2,* vol. 1, 271–272.

———. "Al-Faḍl b. Sahl b. Zadhānfarūkh." In Bearman et al., *EI2,* vol. 2, 731–732.

———. "Al-Ḥasan b. Sahl." In Bearman et al., *EI2,* vol. 3, 243–244.

———. *Le vizirat ʿabbāside de 749 à 936 (132 à 324 de l'Hégire).* Damascus: Institut Français de Damas, 1959–1960.

Stetkevych, Suzanne P. *Abū Tammām and the Poetics of the ʿAbbāsid Age.* Brill: Leiden, Netherlands, 1991.

Stern, Samuel M. "Abū ʿĪsā Muḥammad b. Hārūn al-Warrāq." In Bearman et al., *EI2,* vol. 1, 130.

Stewart, Devin. "Abū l-Faraj Muḥammmad ibn Isḥāq Ibn al-Nadīm." In *Essays in Arabic Literary Biography 925–1350,* edited by Terri DeYoung and Mary St. Germain, 129–142. Wiesbaden, Germany: Harrassowitz, 2011.

Toorawa, Shawkat. *Ibn Abī Ṭāhir Ṭayfūr and Arabic Writerly Culture: A Ninth-Century Bookman in Baghdad.* London: RoutledgeCurzon, 2005.

Toral, Isabel. "Erzählen im arabischen *adab:* Zwischen Fiktionalität und Faktualität." In *Faktuales und Fiktionales Erzählen: Interdisziplinäre Perspektiven,* edited by Monika Fludernik, Nicole Falkenhayer, and Julia Steiner, 59–76. Würzburg, Germany: Ergon Verlag, 2018.

———. *Al-Ḥīra: Eine arabische Kulturmetropole im spätantiken Kontext.* Leiden, Netherlands: Brill, 2014.

Touati, Houari. *L'armoire à sagesse: Bibliothèques et collections en Islam.* Paris: Aubier, 2003.

Troupeau, Gérard. "La grammaire à Bagdād du IX au XIIIe siècle." *Arabica* 9 (1962): 397–405.

Ullmann, Manfred. *Aufs Wasser schreiben.* Munich: Verlag der Bayerischen Akademie der Wissenschaften and Beck, 1989.

Vernay-Nouri, Annie and Eloïse Brac de la Perrière, eds. *The Journeys of Kalila and Dimna: Itineraries of Fables in the Arts and Literature of the Islamic World.* Leiden, Netherlands: Brill, forthcoming.

Versteegh, Kees. *The Arabic Language.* Edinburgh: Edinburgh University Press, 1997.

Wagner, Ewald. "Abū Nuwās." In Bearman et al., *EI2,* vol. 1, 143–144.

Walker, Joel T. "Books and Readers in East-Syrian Monastic Tradition." In *Commutatio et Contentio, Studies in the Late Roman Sasanian, and Early Near East: In memory of Zeev Rubin*, edited by Henning, Börm, and Josef Wiesehöfer, 305–345. Düsseldorf: Wellem 2012.

Wansbrough, John. "*Majāz al-Qurʾān:* Periphrastic Exegesis." *Bulletin of the School of Oriental and African Studies* 33 (1970): 247–266.

Webb, Peter. *Al-Maqrīzī's al-Khabar ʿan al-bashar.* Vol. 5, sections 1–2, *The Arab Thieves: Critical Edition, Annotated Translation and Study.* Leiden, Netherlands: Brill, 2019.

Weisweiler, Max. "Das Amt des Mustamlī in der arabischen Wissenschaft." *Oriens* 4 (1951): 27–57.

Wensinck, A. J. "ʿAmr b. al-ʿĀṣ." In Bearman et al., *EI2,* vol. 1, 541.

Werkmeister, Walter. *Quellenuntersuchungen zum Kitāb al-ʿIqd al-farīd des Andalusiers Ibn ʿAbdrabbih (246/860–328/940).* Berlin: Schwarz, 1983.

Wild, Stefan. *Self-Referentiality in the Qurʾān.* Wiesbaden, Germany: Harrassowitz, 2006.

Young, M. J. L. "Arabic Biographical Writing In *Religion, Learning and Science in the Abbasid Period,* edited by M. J. L. Young, J. D. Latham, and R. B. Serjeant, 168–187. The Cambridge History of Arabic Literature. Cambridge: Cambridge University Press, 1990.

Zayyāt, Ḥabīb. *Al-Wirāqa wa-ṣināʿat al-kitāba.* Beirut: Dār al-Ḥamrāʾ, 1992. Reprint of articles first published in *al-Mashriq,* 1947 and 1954.

Zolondek, Leon, ed. *Diʿbil b. ʿAlī: The Life and Writings of an Early ʿAbbāsid Poet.* Lexington: University Press of Kentucky, 1961.

Zwettler, Michael. *The Oral Tradition of Classical Arabic Poetry: Its Character and Implications.* Columbus: Ohio State University Press, 1978.

ONLINE RESOURCES

Arabic Papyrology Database
https://www.apd.gwi.uni-muenchen.de/apd/project.jsp

Bibliothèque Nationale de France Gallica
https://gallica.bnf.fr/accueil/en/content/accueil-en

Codex Vatican Ar. 13 (see also Schulthess)
https://digi.vatlib.it/view/MSS_Vat.ar.13

Corpus Coranicum
https://corpuscoranicum.de/

Hill Museum and Manuscript Library
http://hmml.org/script_collection/islamic-collection-manuscript-page/

Islamic Manuscripts Reference Library
http://www.islamicmanuscripts.info/reference/index.html

Islamic Painted Page: A Database of Islamic Arts of the Book, Universität Hamburg
http://www.islamicpaintedpage.com/

Orient Digital, Staatsbibliothek zu Berlin
http://orient-digital.staatsbibliothek-berlin.de/content/index.xml

VHMML School Arabic Paleography
https://www.vhmmlschool.org/arabic

ACKNOWLEDGMENTS

It has taken a long time to write this short book. My move between continents and academic systems, from Yale University to Freie Universität Berlin in 2014, was only part of the reason. Going through the large amount of Arabic sources started earlier than that and has taken longer, and it was necessary to understand the kinds of reactions and controversies surrounding the use of the earliest Arabic books. After those years of work, I have selected from my readings only a small fraction, which to my mind best exemplify this transformative period of the Arabic-Islamic civilization—whose impulses have been received in Europe since the Middle Ages.

My interest has always been the way Arabic literature, particularly poetry, "worked" within a society, what exactly made it the effective mode of action as described by countless sources. The relevance of the various types of media involved became clear to me only gradually in the course of my investigations and then formed part of the undergraduate course "From Pictograph to Pixel: Changing Ways of Human Communication," which I created and taught at Yale University from 2005 to 2012, together with an Egyptologist and a computer scientist. This made me realize even more the enormous impact the emergence of Arabic book culture had for the next millennium—and not only for the sphere of Arabic language culture but also for adjacent civilizations to the east and west.

And—although colleagues in the field of Arabic studies were aware of this phenomenon—it had not been communicated to a public beyond the field. This is what I wanted to do, and to do in a way that would make the book accessible not only to scholars of Near Eastern studies but to any interested reader. My inspiration and encouragement for writing this type of book were Hermione Lee's incomparable biographies of well-known and lesser-known female British authors, although her elegant style remains unmatched.

In the process, I have had many conversations with colleagues from Yale, Berlin, and many other places who have inspired me and helped me develop my ideas, and it is a pleasure to express my gratitude to them: Thomas Bauer, Lale Behzadi, Ann Blair, Aboubakr Chraïbi, Anne Eusterschulte, Michael Fischer, Regula Forster, Mark Geller, Jan van Ginkel, Dimitri Gutas, Jaakko Hämeen-Anttila, Valerie Hansen, Konrad Hirschler, John Huehnergard, Andrew Johnston, Alicia Kennedy, Verena Klemm, István Kristó-Nagy, Ulrich Marzolph, James Montgomery, Glenn W. Most, Bilal Orfali, Beate Pongratz-Leisten, Tahera Qutbuddin, Dana Sajdi, Devin Stewart, Shawkat Toorawa, Isabel Toral, Anita Traninger, Anders Winroth, and Christopher Wood. My work with all the team members of the Anonym-Classic Project at Freie Universität Berlin has been a constant source of joy and a true factory of ideas.

I thank Maxim Romanov for sharing with me his digitized version of al-Dhahabī's *Taʾrīkh al-islām* and extracting all entries on stationers, and Yousry El-Seadawy, doctoral candidate at the Berlin Graduate School Muslim Cultures and Societies of Freie Universität Berlin, for sharing with me his doctoral research on early Arabic codices, especially the manuscript of Shafiʿī's *Risāla* (Cairo, Dār al-Kutub uṣūl al-fiqh 41). To Ben Outhwaite, Head of Genizah Research Unit, Cambridge University Library, I owe the dating of T-S Ar. 40.9.

Research on this book was supported by the Institute of Advanced Studies (Wissenschaftskolleg) in Berlin, which gave me the time and support to fully devote myself to reading sources during my fellowship in 2010 to 2011 and permitted me to host James Montgomery for a working session. Part of the research was done with the support of an Advanced Grant by the European Research Council under grant agreement no. 742635. I further thank my anonymous readers for their thorough comments on all levels of the first draft, Sharmila Sen for accepting the book for Harvard University Press, Heather Hughes for all her support with logistical matters, Graciela Galup for the elegant cover and interior book design, Cheryl Hirsch for her great care in the production phase, Anne Davidson for her thorough copy editing, and Ruslan Pavlyshyn for his accuracy in compiling the index.

I am grateful to the following libraries for giving permission to use images of codices from their collections: Heidelberger Papyrussammlung, Österreichische Nationalbibliothek, Cambridge University Library, the Bodleian Library of the University of Oxford, the Vatican Apostolic Library, Beyazit State Library, and the Egyptian National Library (Dār al-Kutub al-Miṣriyya). I also owe thanks to Éditions Geuthner for permission to reproduce the chart of early scripts from the article by François Déroche, "Les manuscrits arabes datés du IIIe / IXe siècle," *REI* 55–57 (1987–1989): 343–379; and to the Austrian Academy of Sciences (Österreichische Akademie der Wissenschaften) for permission to reproduce Adolf Grohmann's photograph of the papyrus notebook. To Ramzi Baalbaki I am indebted for allowing republication of much of the text of my published lecture *Book Culture before Print: The Early History of Arabic Media* (The American University of Beirut, The Margaret Weyerhaeuser Jewett Chair of Arabic, Occasional Papers, 2012) in Chapter 1.

It is my regret that some people did not see the completion of this book: David Brennan, with whom I much discussed it; Wolfhart Heinrichs, from whom I learned more than I can say; and my father, who bought me my first book and accompanied with interest, advice, and support each and every step in my life. I thank my mother for her unfailing love, my brother Matthias, who is my best critic, and my sister Nausikaa, whose creativity is a constant inspiration. And I could never have completed this book without the love, encouragement, and gracious patience of Normand.

CONTENTS IN DETAIL, FIGURES, AND LISTS

INDEX OF NAMES AND WORKS

INDEX OF SUBJECTS AND TERMS

141; of a vizier, 107, 116. *See also* Arabic stationer; Qur'ān
cosmopolitanism, Abbasid, 5, 8, 145
cosmopolitan knowledge, 145
court, caliphal, 39, 156; literary gatherings at, 82, 93; literati at, 90–91, 145; poetic recitation at, 101
craft (*ṣināʿa*, pl. *ṣināʿāt*), 113–114, 129, 143, 161–163, 165
craftspeople, 60, 103–106, 113, 120–121, 132, 136, 138–141. *See also* Arabic stationer
critical reflection, 159
criticism, practical, 61, 93
culture, breeding, also adages, edifying, educational, and entertaining literature, literary arts, lore (*adab*, pl. *ādāb*), 72, 80, 102, 128, 130–131, 143–144, 149, 152, 157–158, 161–162; circulation of, 131; fictionality in, 162; as polite letters, 56; quotations of, 157; *adab* tradition, 139
currencies, conversion of, 30, 60–61, 188n96
currency, monetary, 30, 60–61

ḍabṭ. *See* vocalization by paraphrase
database: thematic, 97; use of book as, 34, 88, 99, 102; use of library as, 145
debate, oral, 89, 135
destruction: of texts, 82; of written materials, 23
dictation (*imlā'*, pl. *amālī*), 23, 51; assistant *(mustamlī)*, 125, 134, 204n52; as book format, 26, 155; in book production, 58–59; book promotion through, 134; part of title, 155; request for, 131, 205n64; sessions, 11, 26, 134; teaching by, 50–51, 58–59. *See also* Arabic book
dictionary: biographical, 12, 27, 42, 96, 118, 136; lexicographical, 71; of modern poets, 132; part of title, 48; of prophetic tradition (Ḥadīth), 73; thematic (thesaurus), 67
ḍidd (pl. *aḍdād*). *See* words signifying a term and its opposite
digest. *See* Arabic book: abridgment
dīnār, conversion, 30, 60–61. *See also* prices
dirham, conversion, 30, 60–61. *See also* prices
discourse, elegant *(ḥadīth mūniq)*, 162
dissemination, of writings, 119–120; of knowledge, 139; non-dissemination by books, 150, 155; oral and written, 122; through teaching, 138. *See also* bimodality; control
dīwān (pl. *dawāwīn*). *See* collected works
dīwān of the Arabs, 41. *See also* register
documents, legal, 81
draft version. *See* Arabic poetry

encyclopedia, 132, 166
epistle (*risāla*, pl. *rasā'il*), 27, 102, 155–156, 158; part of title, 8, 13–15, 22, 124, 126–127, 161
epithet of provenance, profession *(nisba)*, 112
errors: books about, 56, 122, 133–134, 136–138; in copying *(taṣḥīf)*, 24, 55; frequent *(laḥn al-ʿāmma)*, 24, 133; linguistic *(laḥn)*, 37, 41
ethics *(akhlāq)*, 27, 95, 147. *See also* virtues
etiquette: courtly, 39; scholarly, violation of, 116, 118
European: books, 76; libraries, 2; manuscript codices, 23, 45; perspective, 168
explanatory re-writing (*majāz*), 42–43, 52–53, 55, 58, 74
explication (*maʿānī*, sing. *maʿnā*), 42; part of title, 42, 53, 59, 63
extracts *(intizāʿāt)*, 158. *See also* Arabic book: abridgment

fable, 8, 26, 163; decoding of, 159. *See also* parable
faḥl (pl. *fuḥūl*). *See* great poet
fahm. *See* understanding
fantasy stories (*khurāfāt*, sing. *khurāfa*), 63
fascicles (*ajzā'*, sing. *juz'*), 43, 131, 135, 142
fay'. *See* taxes and dues
fiction, fictionality, fictional, 22, 29–30, 60; character, 157, 160; verisimilitude in, 32, 162
fihrist. *See* Arabic book: list. *See also* Index of Names and Works: Ibn al-Nadīm

Middle Persian (Pahlavi), 5, 62, 156–159, 161; books, 148–149; book redaction, 150, 157, 159; *See also* translation
mise-en-page. *See* Arabic book: layout
mobility, 113, 192n146
modern, modernism. *See* Arabic poetry: modern style of
motif. *See* Arabic poetry
muʿāriḍ mustaʾjar. *See* collator
mūbadh al-mūbadhān. *See* Zoroastrian: high priest
muḥaddithūn. *See* traditionists
muḥarrir. *See* copyist: clean-copyist
mujallid. *See* bookbinder
mukhaḍram. *See* Arabic poet: straddling the period of Islam
muṣannaf. *See* Arabic book: compilation
music, poetry put to, 82, 90, 163
Muslim campaigns *(maghāzī)*, 13, 116, 146
mustamlī. *See* dictation: assistant
muwallad. *See* Arabic language: hybrid

nāqiṭ, *naqqāṭ*. *See* copyist's assistant
nāsikh. *See* copyist
naẓara fī. *See* studying
nisba. *See* epithet of provenance, profession
note *(ruqʿa)*, 80
notebook(s) (*daftar*, pl. *dafātir*), 82–83, 140; accounts *(akhbār)* in, 29, 32; before paper, 4; as compilation *(taṣnīf)*, 27; copying of, 142; as evidence of plagiarism, 34, 84–89, 100, 165; in form of fascicles *(ajzāʾ)*, 131; as mnemonic aid, 27, 88, 96–97; poems in, 83, 131; of poets, 96–97, 121, 158; of stationers, 129; in teaching process, 10; of wisdom sayings, 158
notes, written, 83, 88–89, 97, 113–114
note-taking, 80, 114. *See also* dictation

Pahlavi. *See* Middle Persian
paper, paper *(kāghad, kāghid)*, 60, 82, 97, 105, 132, 153, 168; early books on, 15; early fragments, 62–63, 153; introduction of, 3, 11–12, 103–104; Jaʿfarī type, 104; prices of, 23, 60, 132, 143; production, 4–5, 12, 23, 60, 72, 76, 165–166; purchase of, 132; Samarqand type, 143; Sulaymānī type, 59; types of, 104, 143; word origin, 106; as writing material, 31, 103
papermaker *(kāghadī, kaghghād)*, 105–106, 108, 110–112. *See also* Arabic stationer
papyrus *(qirṭās)*, 1, 5, 23, 31, 59, 82; Arabic books, notebooks on, 14–15, 21–22, 83; cost of, 132; dependence on, 12; scrap of, 82; scroll, 3, 12; sealed *(ṭūmār makhtūm)*, 151; sown sheets, 4; writing on, 81
parables (*amthāl*, sing. *mathal*), 156–158, 161–162. *See also* fable; proverbs
parasang (marching mile), 101
parchment *(jild, riqq)*, 60; and inkwell *(jild wa-dawāt)*, 82; scroll, 82, 150
particle (in grammar) (*ḥarf*, pl. *ḥurūf*), 25
patron(s), patronage, 23, 38, 97, 102, 146, 155; authorship without, 76; in Baghdad, 6; Barmakid, 130, 150; book dedication to, 62, 131; panegyric of, 91; of poets, 78, 81, 95, 130–131, 146; satire of, 78–79, 81, 95, 145. *See also* sponsorship
performance, 164; oral, 11, 40–41, 74, 118; of scholars, 49–51, 77
Persian: advice literature, 148; books, 101, 146–147; converts, 146; literature, 81; loan word, 4, 41; speakers of, 10; statecraft, 8, 39. *See also* Iranian; Manichaean; Middle Persian; translation; Zoroastrian
Persians, 3, 6, 79, 91; lore of, 152
philosophy, 26, 143
picaresque tales (*maqāmāt*, sing. *maqāma*), 29, 153
piece of writing *(kitāb)*, 25, 89, 193n17
pithy saying (*kalima*, pl. *kalimāt*), 67, 145
plagiarism, 33–34, 61; accusation of, 85, 88–92, 96, 165. *See also* Arabic poetry: borrowing; theft
poetry. *See* Arabic poetry; Jewish poets
preface. *See* Arabic book